# A.U.A. Language Center
# Thai Course

## Book 1

*Prepared by*

J. Marvin Brown

Published by

Cornell University Southeast Asia Program

Ithaca, N.Y.

1991

Cornell Southeast Asia Program Publications
640 Stewart Avenue, Ithaca, NY 14850-3857



Originally published by the American University Alumni Association Language Center, Bangkok, Thailand. Reprinted with permission by the Cornell Southeast Asia Program 1991, 1995, 1998, 2000, and 2004.



Printed in the United States of America

ISBN 0-87727-506-8

For a master set of A.U.A. tapes, institutions should order directly from A.U.A. Language Center, 179 Rajadamri Road, Bangkok 10330, Thailand.

# PREFACE

The AUA Language Center Thai Course has developed slowly over a period of years. In 1962 it consisted of a set of dialogs and drills prepared by Churee Indaniyom under the direction of Gordon F. Schmader. Over the years many things have been added and many things changed, but most of the dialogs are still basically those of Khun Churee. The present edition is a major revision of the preceding edition which was tested over a period of fifteen months. Both teachers (especially Matana Chutrakul, Niphapharn Chutrakul, Nitaya Amaraket, Saengthong Beokhaimook, Srim Nolrajsuwaj, Khomsan Hathaidharm, and Preecha Ratanodom) and students (especially Robert S. Campbell and John Ratliff) who used that edition made many valuable suggestions, and the author is deeply indebted to them for most of the improvements, though he alone is responsible for the actual contents. The revision was read by the above named teachers and three colleagues (Peter J. Bee, Jimmy Harris, and Daniel Hantman), and thanks is due to all of them for their helpful suggestions.

Especially valuable over the years been the constant assistance of Preecha Ratanodom. Almost all of the ideas that arose during the development of the course were immediately checked with him: the poorer ones were thus rejected and the better ones thus refined.

J. M. B.

Bangkok, Thailand
October 1967

# CONTENTS

# INTRODUCTION

A language class typically consists of four components (students, a teacher, a language, and a book) participating in a process (learning). The *student learns* the *language* with the help of a *teacher* and a *book*.

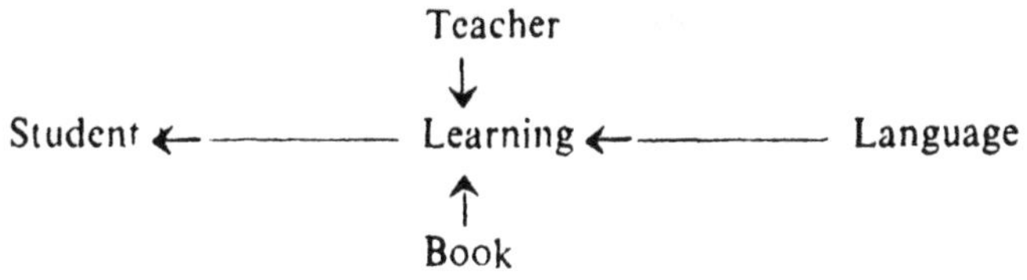

The class that this book is designed to play a part in assumes: cooperative, adult, English-speaking students; the standard language of Thailand; the focus-practice method of learning; and a teacher who is a native speaker of Thai and who has been trained in the focus-practice method. The five parts of the above diagram are discussed below in detail.

**1. The Language.**

There are four main Thai languages spoken in Thailand: Northern Thai, Northeastern Thai, Central Thai, and Southern Thai. They are almost as different from each other as are Spanish, Italian, and Portuguese. The language taught in this book is Central Thai.

There are different regional dialects of Central Thai. These include, for example, the dialects of Uttaradit, Supan Buri, and Bangkok. Standard Thai is the language taught in the schools throughout the country and corresponds to no one regional dialect. It can best be described as having vowels common to all central dialects, the consonants of Supan Buri, and the tones of Bangkok.

Even if a person intends to use Thai exclusively in the Bangkok area, he is advised to learn to *speak* Standard Thai. But he must also learn to *understand* Bangkok Thai. The principal differences are shown below.

| Standard Thai | Bangkok | Standard Thai | Bangkok |
|---|---|---|---|
| khl | kh | kl | k |
| khr | kh | kr | k |
| khw | f | kw | f |
| phl | ph | pl | p |
| phr | ph | pr | p |
| r | l | tr | k |

Stated as a historic development, it is easy to remember: *r* has changed to *l* and all double consonants have reduced to single ones.

## 2. Language Learning.

There are two quite different kinds of learning: the acquiring of knowledge and the acquiring of habits. The former takes place in the brain only. The latter involves muscles as well. Knowledge and habits are best taught and learned in quite different ways as shown below.

| | Acquiring knowledge (mental learning) | Acquiring habits (physical learning) |
|---|---|---|
| **Examples** | History<br>Mathematics<br>Philosophy | Dancing<br>Playing the piano<br>Playing tennis |
| **Taught mainly by** | Explaining (telling) | Modelling (showing) |
| **Learned mainly by** | Memorizing | Practicing |

Consider, now, where learning to speak a language belongs. Is it a case of knowledge or habits? It has traditionally been treated as knowledge and hence taught by explaining and learned by memorizing. But when it is compared with the above examples, it immediately becomes clear that it is an instance of habits, since muscles are obviously involved. Explanations and memory should play only the slightest part in language learning. Over 90 percent of classtime activity should consist of modelling (sounds, patterns, sentences) by the teacher and practicing by the student.

This general approach to language learning (as opposed to the traditional one) has been referred to as the aural-oral or audio-lingual approach in order to point up the emphasis on listening and speaking. Its use in the classroom made big gains during World War II when it was used by the U.S. Army. But many changes in techniques and emphasis have been made since the war, and the approach used in this course is sufficiently different from the 'Army Method' to require a new name. The important emphasis here is *directed* listening (noticing or focusing on the things that matter) and oral *practice* (practicing correct performances instead of correcting wrong ones). The approach might, therefore, be called focus-practice. The emphasis on practice should be clear from the following comparison of the three methods.

| **Traditional** | **Army** | **Focus-practice** |
|---|---|---|
| Explain.<br>Test.<br>If right,<br>stop and go on.<br>If wrong,<br>explain again. | Model.<br>Test.<br>If right,<br>stop and go on.<br>If wrong,<br>model again. | Model.<br>Test.<br>If right,<br>do again.<br>If wrong,<br>stop and go back. |

But the emphasis on focus requires more discussion.

When we look at or listen to anything, we notice less than one percent of what is there. We have learned to ignore the millions of things that are of no importance to us. If we want to learn a new dance, the model-practice combination alone might be useless. The model will be making slight movements with her eyes, lips, head, shoulders, hands, hips, feet, etc., and the possible combinations of these are infinite. Our preconceptions might lead us to notice only the feet. Though we are aware that the hands are moving, we might think these movements are part of the dancer's whims or personality - not part of the dance. But if, in fact, the hand movements are basic to the dance and the foot movements only incidental, we will fail to learn the dance. Or we might observe an expert billiard player for years until we think we have noticed every last detail, and then find that we cannot answer a question as basic as 'Was the point of his chin in front of or behind the point of his leading foot?' Obviously our attention must somehow be directed to the things that count.

A comparison of English and Thai syllables will illustrate how important 'ear focus' can be in language learning. There are 105 different possible centers in Thai syllables (21 vowels and vowel combinations with 5 tones) as against only 8 or 9 in English. And between the end of a vowel and the beginning of the next syllable, there are only 9 different possible sounds in Thai as against hundreds in English. Obviously the Thai speaker must pay more attention to the center of a syllable than to its end, and the English speaker must do just the opposite. If, in the stream of speech, we mark syllable centers with dots and the mid point between syllables with vertical lines, the dots show the points of focus of the Thai ear, and the lines those of the English ear.

· | · | · | ·

The Thai ear is almost completely closed to the space between syllables. When it hears an English expression like *finds out*, it 'filters out' or covers up some of the sounds in much the same way that a piece of paper with holes cut in it covers up some of the symbols.

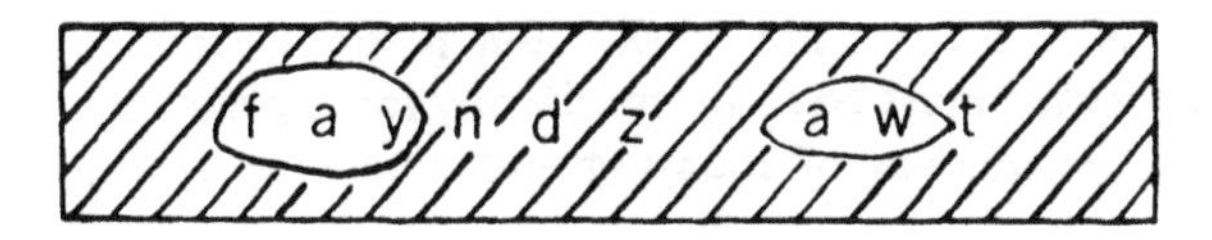


Similarly, when the English ear hears a Thai expression like *khâaw phàt*, some of the sounds are covered up.

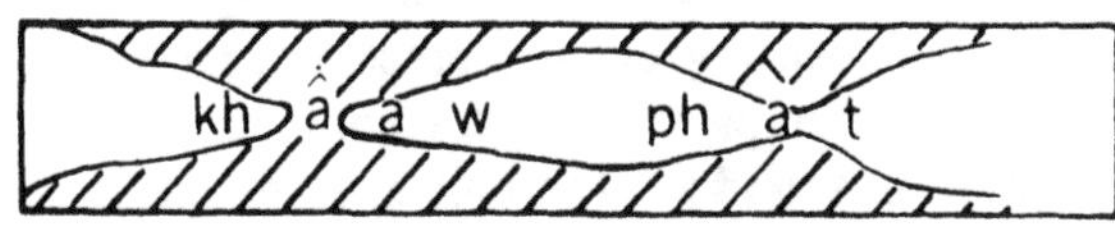


(A more accurate comparison would be a photograph of the symbols with the covered-up parts out of focus, hence blurred.)

From the above examples of learning to dance, play billiards, speak English, and speak Thai, we see that providing the student with a correct model is not enough by itself. We also have to tell him what to notice. (The main devices used to direct his attention to *sounds* are contrast drills, symbols, drawings, and exaggerations. The main device for getting his attention on *patterns* is the substitution drill. It is hardly ever necessary to focus on *words*. For the beginning student of a language, words are the least important part of all.) Once the student has got the proper parts in focus, hearing the previously ignored sounds is no more difficult than seeing the dancer's hands. Noticing the right parts (focus), the student is in a position to imitate. When he can imitate correctly, he is in a position to build the habit (practice). The term aural-oral labels an approach based on listening and speaking. But to be really effective this approach must use a certain kind of listening (directed) and a certain kind of speaking (repeated when correct). Not all aural-oral language classes do this. In fact, until quite recently very few did. Those that do can be distinguished from those that do not by the term focus-practice. But this term, too, needs modification now.

Through the principle of natural selection (successful changes propagate themselves while unsuccessful ones die without offspring) the various factors that *affect* a language become, over a period of time, the forces that *build* it. The three most important forces that build languages are efficiency of communication, ease of use, and ease of learning. The latter concerns us here.

Obviously, if a language is to survive more than one generation, it must be learned by the next generation. And this learning takes place almost exclusively in the minds of children. All living languages have been constantly passing through the sieve of child-learnability for thousands of years. Whenever one of the other forces produces something that cannot pass through this sieve, it doesn't survive (or it becomes part of the adjuncts that adults add to language, and these are of little importance). A perfect fit of the learnability of language to the child's mind is thus always ensured. In language learning the child reigns supreme; languages were built to be learned by him, not us. Language learning is literally (and necessarly must be) child's play.

We can now review the historical development of classroom language learning. At first the method was explanation-comprehension. This did not work. It was replaced by the aural-oral method. This sometimes did work. But it soon became apparent that to be really effective the aural-oral method must be more specifically focus-practice. And now it is suggested that the most successful techniques of focusing and practicing are childish ones.

Some of the drills and techniques of this book are indeed childish. (The main childish technique used is the substitution drill, which focuses on and practices a *pattern*. Most children's games and songs, and even their private mutterings take the form of substitution drills. For a childish example of focusing on and practicing *sounds*, note the following dialog: 'Dad blew Grandpa's horn.' 'Grandpa blew Dad's horn, too.' In Thai, all the words of this dialog begin with the problem sound *p*.) The only apology offered, though, is not that they are childish, but that they are not more so. The reason for conservatism in this respect is that most teachers and (though much less so) students are probably not yet ready for a more extreme approach. Later revisions will surely be in the direction of children's games.

**3. The Student.**

The main reason that children learn languages more easily than adults was mentioned above. Another reason is that adults already have a language, and the presence of this language interferes with the learning of another one. Different languages interfere in different ways. The native speaker of English and the native speaker of a Chinese language will have quite different problems in learning Thai. Ideally, a different book should be used for teaching Thai to speakers of each different language. This book was written primarily for native speakers of English, and the pronunciation drills are geared primarily to the English speakers' problems. It can, however, be used to teach Thai to speakers of any language if they know a little English as well.

By far the biggest problem that Thai presents to the speaker of English (and all non-tonal languages) is its tones. This book tries to meet the problem with extensive practice in identifying, producing, and manipulating tones. Students who already speak a tonal language lose nothing from this emphasis on tones, of course, since they can merely cut down on the time devoted to them. And consonants are drilled in such a way that speakers of most languages will get the practice they need. So only the vowels are slighted for non-native speakers of English. Appropriate drills can be added by the teacher when needed (the e–ɛ contrast, for example, for speakers of most Chinese languages).

It was mentioned earlier that this book was intended for cooperative, adult, English-speaking students. Children don't need it; they can learn faster by playing games with Thai speakers (preferably Thai children). And it can be adapted for speakers of other languages. But the 'cooperative' qualification needs discussion. Non-cooperative students can ruin a class, even though the teacher and book may be first rate. Cooperation refers primarily to going along with the childish focus-practice approach to language learning. The four main guides for being a cooperative student are discussed below.

1. Be prepared and willing to go through the awkward stage. You can't learn to water-ski without falling (and most likely being laughed at). If a person finds that it is not worth the sacrifice of his dignity to make the inevitable mistakes and be laughed at, then water-skiing and learning Thai are not for him. He should quit.

2. Don't ask questions. Students' questions are the main enemy of the focus-practice approach. Ninety percent of them don't have answers, and it takes time for the teacher to politely dodge meaningless questions. And it is not only the time of the asking and dodging that is wasted, for completely unrelated discussions often result as well. Remember that language is one of the things that is better learned by practice than by explanation. If less than ninety percent of class time is being spent on practice, something is wrong.

3. Don't ask for special vocabulary. Each student has different words that he thinks he needs. Valuable time is wasted in supplying these words and discussions often start. The book supplies vocabulary at the rate that it can be properly assimilated by the average student. If a student must have a certain word, he should at least ask for it outside of class so that the other students' time won't be wasted.

4. Don't tell the teacher how to teach. Again, the main reason is that practice time will be wasted; for discussions on the teacher's and various students' theories of language learning invariably start. A student might indeed have some very good suggestions for improving a class, but such suggestions should be directed to the teacher's supervisor.

### 4. The Teacher.

This book contains no sounds. By itself it is useless for learning Thai. The sounds must be supplied by either a teacher or recordings. Learning from recordings alone, however, is dangerous–especially with Book 1; for the recordings can't correct the student's mistakes, and the student can't trust his own ears. Ideally the student should have both a native-speaking teacher and the tapes that accompany the book. After the teacher has got the student performing each section perfectly, the student can then get additional practice by using the tapes.

The book programs the course into lessons and sections. The teacher's function is not only to provide the sounds but also to program each section (that is, to lead the student through certain steps). Instructions for programming the different types of sections are given the first time each type appears (mostly in lesson 1). More general advice to the teacher is given here.

The effective teacher, through skillful use of all the teaching tools of the trade, painlessly leads the student up a stairway of gradual steps to a level of fast, natural speech. As the student moves up these steps, he rarely makes a mistake. Whenever he does, the teacher immediately realizes that the step is too high and selects the appropriate tools to improvise an in-between step. A safe guide for the teacher is this: the average, cooperative, regularly-attending student should never encounter serious trouble. If he does, something is wrong with either the programming of the book or the demands of the teacher. But, at the same time, the teacher should never stop short of fast natural speech. Perfect renditions of slow, artificial speech (the kind found in most language classrooms throughout the world) should not be interpreted as success. It is, in fact a sure sign of inferior teaching.

The experienced teacher doesn't necessarily follow the programming of the book or the ordered steps for each section. Instead, he judges from the performance of the class just what tool is needed. A guide for judging what is needed (the remedy) by observing performance (the symptoms) is given below.

| SYMPTOMS | REMEDIES |
|---|---|
| 1. Student can't hear a distinction at normal speed. | Use listen and identify steps of the appropriate contrast drill. The goal is for the student to be able to identify each item after hearing a single, fast, natural repetition of it. Work towards this from two directions:<br>1) slow exaggerated to fast normal, and<br>2) many fast repetitions down to one. |
| 2. Student can hear a distinction easily but cannot pronounce the problem sound. | No general solution can be offered. Different techniques and tricks may be found for each specific problem. A technique for teaching the initial ŋ sound, for example, is given on page 43. This is the only point at which the teacher might sometimes have to give up. All other problems have solutions. |
| 3. Student can pronounce the problem sound, but only with difficulty. | Over a period of days or weeks, push for slight increases of speed in 'tongue-twister' drills. These can be in the form of simple sentences, substitution drills, or response drills. To be effective, such tongue-twisters should be only moderately difficult. |

| | |
|---|---|
| 4. Sentences of dialogs, substitution drills, or response drills contain no problem sounds, but the student cannot say them at normal speed. | Lead the student through expansions of the sentence with increasing speed. Find the speed that is just the slightest bit too fast for the student to repeat from a single hearing and let him hear it three or four times before repeating. Expansions should be built up structurally instead of linearally. But when possible, move from the end of the sentence to the beginning. |
| 5. Student can say all sentences of dialogs, substitution drills or response drills perfectly. | Practice both repeat and participate steps without books many times, constantly pushing for slightly greater speed. This is the pay-off. This is the step that builds the habit. |

**5. The Book**

Each book of the AUA Thai Course is designed for a term of 75 hours. If both a teacher and a laboratory are available, daily classes of one hour followed by a half-hour lab session has proved to be a practical schedule (50 days). Two such hour-and-a-half periods a day with a different teacher for each period and a half hour break in between is equally (if not slightly more) effective (25 days). Three such periods a day (the third coming after an hour or two break) can also be used, but the pace must be slowed down slightly. At least 18 days ( 81 hours) seems to be required. The above figures are intended as bare minimums, and then only with highly efficient teaching.

There are 20 lessons with 10 sections each. The center of each lesson is the dialog (section 3). Sections 1 and 2 give practice on the new words and patterns (respectively) that occur in the dialog, and section 7 contains grammar drills based on the dialog. Briefly, 1 and 2 lead up to 3, and 7 branches out from 3, as shown below.

| | | | |
|---|---|---|---|
| 1. Words. | | 7. a | |
| | | 7. b | Grammar |
| | 3. Dialog. | 7. c | |
| | | 7. d | Drills. |
| 2. Patterns. | | 7. e | |

These and the other six sections are described below.

**1. Vocabulary and expansions.** This section includes all new words used in the lesson. The focus is on sounds and meanings. The sounds are to be practiced to the point that all items can be said without the slightest hesitation, thus allowing the focus to shift elsewhere in the following sections. The meanings and uses are given by translations and explanations. This is the one place where explanations play a part.

**2. Patterns.** This section includes all new patterns used in the lesson. A pattern is a sentence or phrase with all of the content words removed. It consists of grammatical words and ordered slots held together by stress, rhythm, and (to some extent in Thai but especially in English) intonation: admittedly a difficult thing to focus on. Focus is achieved by *varying* the words in the slots (that is, giving several examples of the pattern filled with different words). Another way of bringing a pattern into focus is to fill the slots with nonsense words (as did Lewis Carroll in his 'Jabberwocky') or letters of the alphabet.

3. **Dialogs.** Just as the automobile manufacturer is concerned with the chassis and engine while the driver is concerned with the road, so the language learner must be concerned with sounds and patterns while the speaker is concerned with situations. The dialog section can be compared to the car builder taking his car out for a drive as soon as it has two wheels and a piston. The focus is supposedly on the road, but it must switch again and again to the inadequate parts as they break down. Users of the aural-oral approach vary all the way from strict avoidance of dialogs in the early stages to complete reliance on them as the only necessary and sufficient means of learning a language. The viewpoint in this course is closer to the former, and if the course were designed to be used outside of Thailand, the dialogs would either be omitted from Book 1 (thus allowing a more systematic presentation of grammar drills) or used for comprehension only. But for students in Thailand, psychological incentives demand dialogs, and the 'focus' part of focus-practice must be compromised. An attempt should be made to keep the focus on the situations, but it clearly must switch again and again to sounds and patterns.

4. **Tone identification and production.** From lesson 4 on, this section is divided into two parts: a) identification, and b) production. In part *a*, the student looks at the vowel and consonant symbols of a word as the teacher pronounces it. His only task is to name the tone. In this way, his whole attention is focused directly on the tone and nothing else. The teacher says the word once, then twice, then three times, and so on, until the student successfully identifies its tone. The student then notes down the number of repetitions it takes. This number presumably decreases for each tone as he proceeds through the book.

In part *b*, the student practices dialogs in which all words have the same tone. There are five dialogs (all following the same pattern and thus comprising a response drill) in each section: one for each tone. This tends to keep the attention on the tone and at the same time bring the pattern into focus. It is one of the two approaches used to fight the biggest battle the English speaker has: separating patterns and tones (see next section).

5. **Tone manipulation.** English uses the pitch of the voice to add secondary meanings (questioning, surprise, emphasis, etc.) to sentences. Notice the pitch of the two names in the following dialog.

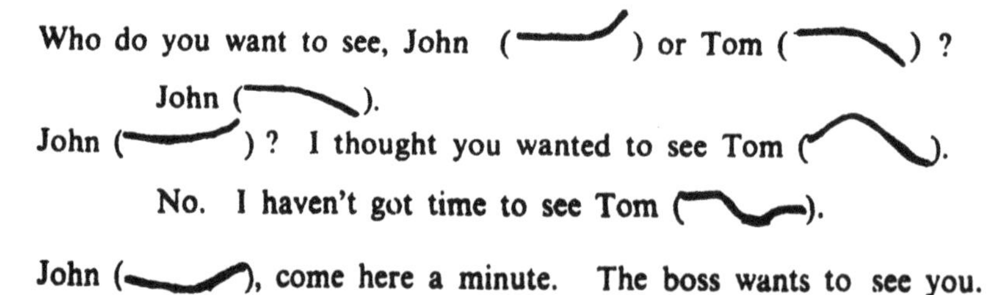


Thai uses the pitch of the voice like vowels and consonants. Each syllable is composed of a consonant at the beginning, a vowel in the middle, an optional consonant at the end, and a tone on top. (below, left).

T
C V C

t ɔ y

t ɔ y

If a name has a falling tone, for example, it must always be pronounced with a falling tone, no matter where it fits into a sentence or what secondary meaning is given. Two Thai names are shown above. Try substituting the first name (tɔ̂y) in place of John in the above dialog, and the second (tɔ̌y) in place of Tom, and notice the tensions that develop. The English intonations are pulling one way and the Thai tones another. If you follow the English intonations, the dialog becomes nonsense. If you keep the Thai tones, you feel that you aren't conveying your meaning. This illustrates the biggest problem of all that confronts the English speaker in learning Thai. Learning to identify and produce the Thai tones is relatively easy, but *keeping* these tones as they enter meaningful patterns is another matter. If, for example, you have five servants named *dɛɛŋ* (mid tone), *nɔ̀y* (low tone), *nɔ́ɔy* (high tône), *tɔ̂y* (falling tone), and *tɔ̌y* (rising tone), you may easily learn to *pronounce* their names correctly, but without special help you may never be able to *call* them correctly (you will want to use a 'calling' intonation). Section 5 of each lesson offers that special help.

The term 'tone manipulation' is used to suggest using or handling the tones in patterns. The typical tone manipulation drill runs five different tones through the same slot of the same pattern. The focus is on the *tone* of the *word* entering the *slot*. English habits demand that the slot determine the tone; Thai habits demand that the word determine it. The point is to keep the tone frozen to its word and uninfluenced by anything else as the drill picks up speed. At high speed, the word-tone association is forced from conscious control to automatic, where it belongs.

It is suggested that each class period begin with a review of section 5 from earlier lessons. This serves as a warming up exercise for the all-important laryngeal muscles. Even fluent non-native speakers of Thai can benefit from periodic review at high speed of the tone manipulation sections of all books.

At this point the following question might occur to the student. 'If Thai doesn't use intonations to show secondary meanings, just how does it show them?' It uses sentence particles: short syllables tacked on to the end of the sentence. Compare, for example, the English and Thai ways of questioning something.

English puts the questioning sound on top of the sentence; Thai puts it at the end.

**6. Vowel and consonant drills.** This is the section that deals with (non-tonal) problem sounds (see the first three suggestions in the teacher's guide on page xvii). Contrast drills are used to teach the distinction between two sounds that at first sound alike to the student. Alternation drills and speed drills are used to increase the facility of producing problem sounds. And substitution and response drills are used to practice problem sounds as the focus shifts to patterns and meaning. As with all 'tongue-twisters' (for example, Peter Piper picked a peck of pickled peppers) the meaning is rarely brilliant or even useful. In fact almost all sentences in this section are downright silly. This hardly ever bothers the student, but some teachers react against such childishness. If these teachers keep in mind the purpose of such drills (practicing sounds, not learning useful words and sentences) together with the advantages of childishness (see page xv), they should be able to take advantage of this very valuable practice.

**7. Grammar drills.** Most of the sentences we use every day are sentences we have never used (or even heard) before: the number of possible sentences in a language is infinite. The language learner must obviously be able to make up sentences that do not occur in his textbook. The traditional method of language learning accomplished this by having the student memorize words and grammar rules. The focus-practice method does it by having him practice sentences and variation drills. The sentences are practiced in section 3; the variations, in section 7. Section 7 is the most important part of each lesson. It teaches the language; all other sections (except the one on writing) merely prepare the student to drill it more effectively. *But, teachers please take note:* the grammar drills do not necessarily teach the language unless they are worked up to a moderately fast speed without books.

**8. Numbers.** The Thai number system is quite simple. It can be learned in less than an hour. But to be able to use numbers quickly takes months of practice. Most of the practice on section 8 can be done by the student outside of class if he can trust his tones. He merely notes the time it takes him to read an exercise and then keeps trying to reduce the time.

**9. Conversation.** If the use of dialogs in a beginning book is like driving a car on two wheels and a piston, the use of conversation is like trying to do tricks with it. Any attempt at free conversation is a complete waste of time. But with rigid controls (that is, restrictions on the freedom the student has in responding to a given situation), conversation can be useful. If, in response to a situation, there is only one thing the student can say and only one way he can say it, and if that particular response is one that the student can give fluently, then the conversation is only one step beyond a response drill: the focus has merely shifted from the pattern to the situation. In the example below, the focus is on the pattern. This is an item of a response drill, and all other items would follow the same pattern.

Is A bigger than B?
No. B is bigger than A.

But in the next example, the focus must shift to the meaning.

Is a chicken bigger than a cow?
No. A cow is bigger than a chicken.

Is a horse bigger than a dog?
Yes. A horse is bigger than a dog.

This is an example of one of the three types of conversations that appear in section 9. The controls are complete.

An example of another type from section 9 is given below.

(John went home.)
Who went home?
John.
Where did John go?
Home.
What did John do?
He went home.

Again, the controls are complete.

In the third type, the student makes suggested departures from a memorized dialog. If, for example, the dialog is about a 10-baht taxi ride to the Erawan Hotel, the student participates in an otherwise identical dialog involving a 5-baht samlor ride to the American Embassy. The controls can be slightly relaxed by allowing the student to choose his own modifications.

Both teacher and students should make an effort to stay within the limitations. The teacher may be tempted from time to time to ask a slightly different question, knowing that the students have the vocabulary to answer it. But it may turn out that the answer requires an unfamiliar pattern and the student is thus left struggling with something beyond him. And the student is often tempted to give original answers (like 'Some dogs are bigger than some horses.') and again end up struggling with something he can't handle. Any hesitation of two seconds on the part of the student is a sure sign that something is wrong: either the limitations have been exceeded, or previous sections haven't been drilled sufficiently. *Class time should be spent practicing, not struggling.*

**10. Writing.** Since this section is not an integral part of the course (no other section depends on it), and since it is designed almost exclusively for home (not class) work, it can be either left out completely, studied only by interested students, or required by the teacher. The approach is such that it offers no interference to learning the sound system of the language: the sounds from the teacher come first; these are associated with symbols of the transcription; and these in turn are associated with letters of the Thai alphabet. Each section uses known words to introduce new symbols. Then, by changing one letter at a time, many new combinations are practiced. (This is comparable to learning grammar by starting with a dialog and practicing new combinations with substitution drills.) Most of the combinatons are not words known by the student, and some of them are not even words at all. Whenever a word that is known to the student occurs in an exercise, however, it is marked with an asterisk to call the student's attention to it as a word with meaning. The student covers the transcription column with a card and practices reading the Thai writing—uncovering the transcription to confirm his reading as he proceeds. Then he covers the Thai writing and practices writing each word — again confirming immediately by uncovering the Thai writing. About the only thing that is required in class is for the teacher to demonstrate how to write new symbols as they are introduced and to check the students' handwriting occasionally to guard against forming wrong writing habits.

# TRANSCRIPTION

## Vowels

There are nine vowels in Thai. The symbols *a*, *e*, *i*, *o*, and *u* are used for five of these much as they are used in most European languages. (Notice, for example, the notes of the scale: do, re, mi, fa.) For the other four vowels, the following symbols are used.

| | |
|---|---|
| ɔ as in c*au*ght or c*ou*rt | ʉ like *u* with a smile |
| ɛ as in c*a*t | ə like *o* with a smile |

Examples of these vowels and combinations of them with each other and with the final consonants *y* and *w* are given below. Remember that these symbols stand for *Thai sounds.* To learn these sounds, you should listen to a Thai pronounce the examples. In many cases an English word which in some dialects of English is similar to the Thai example is given in parentheses. This is only to give you something to start with in learning how the symbols are used. Even if you happen to speak the dialect of English intended for a given example (for example, British for the example *sir*), the Thai sounds are not the same as the English but only similar. *Do not learn the Thai sounds by using the English words in the parentheses.* Learn them by imitating a Thai pronouncing the Thai examples.

| | | | | | | | |
|---|---|---|---|---|---|---|---|
| i | sìp | ten | (sip) | ii | thîi | at | (tea) |
| e | phèt | hot | (pet) | ee | lêek | number | (lake) |
| ɛ | mɛ̀m | Ma'am | (Ma' am) | ɛɛ | khɛ̌ɛn | arm | (can) |
| ʉ | nʉ̀ŋ | one | | ʉʉ | mʉʉ | hand | |
| ə | ŋən | money | | əə | sə̂ə | stupid | (sir) |
| a | fan | teeth | (fun) | aa | phâa | cloth | (Pa) |
| u | lúk | rise | (look) | uu | hǔu | ear | (who) |
| o | khon | person | (cone) | oo | sôo | chain | (so) |
| ɔ | lɔ̀n | she | lawn) | ɔɔ | phɔ̂ɔ | father | (paw) |

| | | | | | | | |
|---|---|---|---|---|---|---|---|
| ia | bia | beer | (beer) | iaw | líaw | turn | (Leo) |
| ʉa | rʉa | boat | | ʉay | nʉ̀ay | tired | |
| ua | phǔa | husband | (poor) | uay | ruay | rich | (roué) |

| | | | | | | | |
|---|---|---|---|---|---|---|---|
| uy | khuy | chat | (gooey) | iw | hǐw | hungry | (hue) |
| ooy | dooy | with, by | (doughy) | ew | rew | fast | (ray-o) |
| əəy | nəəy | butter | | eew | leew | bad | (lay-o) |
| ɔy | thɔ̌y | back up | (toy) | ɛw | thɛ̌w | row | |
| ɔɔy | rɔ́ɔy | 100 | (Roy) | ɛɛw | mɛɛw | cat | |
| ay | mây | not | (my) | aw | khâw | enter | (cow) |
| aay | máay | wood | (my) | aaw | khâaw | rice | (cow) |

## Consonants

There are 21 consonants in Thai. Five of these are written with an *h*, which stands for a puff of air: *h*, *ph*, *th*, *ch*, *kh*. These are very similar to the English consonants *h*, *p*, *t*, *ch*, *k*. Corresponding to these are five similar consonants pronounced without a puff of air: *ʔ*, *p*, *t*, *c*, *k*. The last four of these are similar to the Spanish *p*, *t*, *ch*, *c/ qu*. The symbol *ʔ* stands for a closing of the throat as in the middle of *uh ʔuh* (the English grunt meaning 'no'). The symbol *ŋ* is similar to the English *ng* (its shape indicates the combination of *n* and *g*). The remaining ten consonants are similar to the English consonants and the same letters are used (*b*, *d*, *f*, *s*, *m*, *n*, *r*, *l*, *y*, *w*). Examples of the Thai consonants are given below. The English words in parentheses show the nearest English consonants. When two English words are given, the Thai sound is *in between* the two English sounds.

| | | | | | | | |
|---|---|---|---|---|---|---|---|
| h | hěn | see | (hen) | ʔ | ʔit | brick | (it) |
| ph | phìt | wrong | (pit) | p | pɛ̀ɛt | eight | (pat, bat) |
| th | thîi | at | (tea) | t | tûu | cupboard | (to, do) |
| ch | chìit | inject | (cheat) | c | cèt | seven | (Chet, jet) |
| kh | khít | think | (kit) | k | kàt | bite | (cut, gut) |
| | | | | | | | |
| b | bàat | baht | (baht) | f | fan | teeth | (fun) |
| d | duu | look at | (do) | s | sìi | four | (see) |
| m | mii | have | (me) | y | yùu | be at | (you) |
| n | nâw | rotten | (now) | w | wǐi | comb | (we) |
| ŋ | ŋuu | snake | | l | lɛ̂ɛk | exchange | (lack) |
| | | | | r | rɛ̂ɛk | first | (rack) |

## Tones

There are five tones in Thai. The shapes, names, symbols, and an example of each are shown below. The symbols placed between two lines are to be compared with the pitch shapes. The end of the first line tells you where to start. The rest tells you where to go. If there is only one line, you don't go anywhere, but stay at the level you start at.

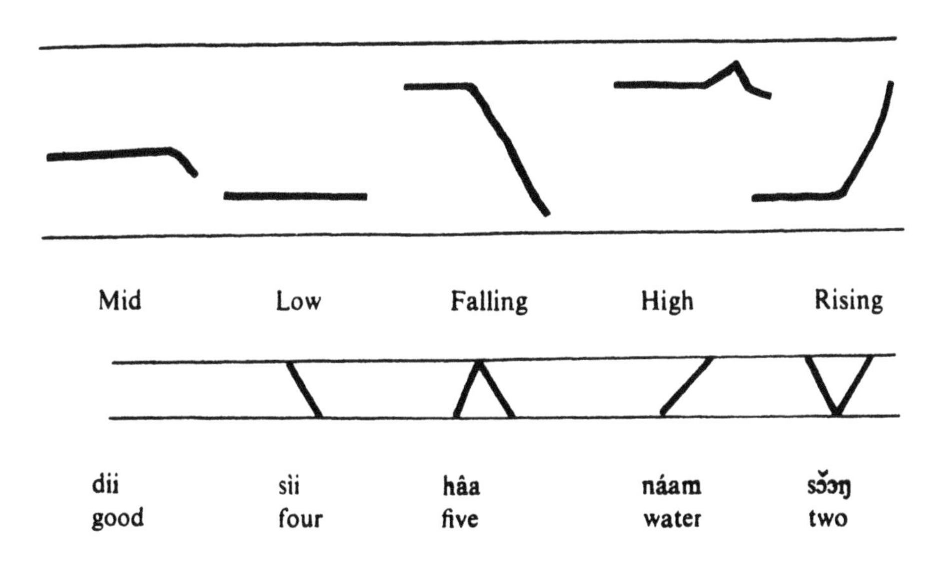

# LESSON 1

## 1.1 Vocabulary and expansions.

| | |
|---|---|
| wàt | |
| sawàt | Well-being, fortune (not used alone). |
| dii | To be good. |
| sawàtdii | A greeting used for either meeting or parting. Greetings! Hello! Goodbye! (The last syllable is simply an extention of the word *sawàt*. It is not the word for 'good.') |
| khráp<br>khâ<br>khą<br>câ<br>cá | Particles are short words that are used to convey feelings, not meaning. Their function is roughly comparable to that of intonations in English. The three words listed to the left (two of them have two variants) are polite particles. They are used at the end of sentences whenever extra politeness is called for. In such situations men use *khráp* when speaking to non-intimate equals or superiors and women use *khâ* (*khá* with questions). Both men and women use *câ* (*cá* with questions) when speaking to intimate equals, inferiors, or children. The use or non-use of a particle is a matter of formality and politeness. The choice between *khráp* or *khâ* on the one hand and *câ* on the other is a matter of relative status and social relationship, not politeness. Here are some examples to guide you in their use (and non-use). With your own servants, no particle; but with servants at the boss's house, *câ*. With your friends at the office or at school, no particle; but with their parents, *khráp* or *khâ*. With a taxi driver or salesman, no particle; but with with a stranger, *khráp* or *khâ*, and with his children, *câ*. A romance usually proceeds from *khráp* to *câ* to no particle (*câ* corresponding to 'sweet talk'). |
| ʔûan | To be fat. |
| phɔ̌ɔm | To be thin. |
| máy | One of several question particles (similar to a spoken question mark). This one is used to ask for an opinion or a decision. |
| mây | Not. |
| kháw | He, she, they (people only). |
| sɔ̌ɔŋ | Two. |
| sǎam | Three. |
| hâa | Five. |

Before leaving section 1 of each lesson, the student should be able to say all items correctly, fast, and without the slightest hesitation. Whenever the student is learning a new item, he needs to hear it several times before he tries to say it; and after he can say it perfectly, he needs to practice saying it many times. An example of how the teacher might handle this section is shown in the following formula where T means the teacher says an item and S means the student says it.

TTTT T S T S T S T S SSSS

Or the teacher might go through all items the first time like this: TTT S TTT S; and then like this: T S T S. If too complicated a procedure is used, the student might not always know what he is supposed to do. An effective compromise is simple triple repetition: TTT SSS.

### 1.2 Patterns.

| | |
|---|---|
| sawàtdii khráp. | Hello! (Man to superior or non-intimate equal.) |
| sawàtdii khâ. | Hello! (Woman to superior or non-intimate equal.) |
| sawàtdii câ. | Hello! (Man or woman to inferior or intimate.) |

The teacher should let the student hear the pattern (collection of similar items) several times and then have him repeat it with increasing speed. Substitution can also be used if desired (see section 1.5).

### 1.3 Dialog.

A. sawàtdii khráp. — Hello!
 B. sawàtdii khâ — Hello!

As with almost everything else in language learning, work on dialogs should proceed from more emphasis on hearing to more emphasis on practicing. Here is an example of how a dialog might be drilled. *T* means teacher gives the Thai item and *E* means he gives the English translation. *S* means student gives the Thai.

| | |
|---|---|
| 1st step. | TTT S TTT S with all sentences (or parts of sentences). |
| 2nd step. | TTT SSS TTT SSS with all sentences. |
| 3rd step. | (Without books from here on.) TS TS TS TS TS ES ES ES ES. |
| 4th step. | TS TS ES ES ES. |
| 5th step. | ES ES ES. |

If the teacher prefers not to use the English translation, the instruction 'again' can be used instead. The next steps use participation where the teacher (shown with capitals) takes one part and the student (shown with small letters) takes the other.

| | |
|---|---|
| 6th step. | A b BBB A b BB A b B A b A b A b A b with each A–B interchange. |
| 7th step. | A b straight through dialog many times. |

### 1.4 Tone identification and production.

| | | |
|---|---|---|
| naa | Rice field, | Mid tone. |
| nâa | Face. | Falling tone. |
| nǎa | Thick. | Rising tone. |

The teacher should write the above drill on the blackboard and go through the following. steps.

1. Listen. The teacher lets the students hear each word many times; at first several times each, and then alternately.

| | | |
|---|---|---|
| naa naa naa naa | nâa nâa nâa nâa | nǎa nǎa nǎa nǎa |
| naa naa | nâa nâa | nǎa nǎa |
| naa | nâa | nǎa |

It is especially important that the teacher always points at the word as he says it so that the student will always be sure when he is saying which one.

2. Identify. Without pointing, the teacher should pronounce one of the words chosen randomly (several times if necessary) and the student should identify it by naming its tone.

| | |
|---|---|
| Teacher: | naa. |
| Student: | Falling. |
| Teacher: | No. naa naa naa naa. |
| Student: | Mid. |

This should be done many times with just enough repetitions of each word so that the student feels sure of his answer. The point of this type of drilling is to force the student's attention to the tone.

3. Repeat. The student should practice saying the words after the teacher.

4. Alternate. As a final step, the student should practice alternations like the following.

| | |
|---|---|
| naa nâa naa nâa naa | nâa naa nâa naa nâa |
| naa năa naa năa naa | năa naa năa naa năa |
| nâa năa nâa năa nâa | năa nâa năa nâa năa |

These four steps should be used in all contrast drills. (These appear, among other types of drills, in sections 4 and 6 of each lesson.)

**1.5 Tone manipulation.**

**a. Substitution drill.**

| | | |
|---|---|---|
| dii máy. | (ʔûan) | Good? Do you think it's good? How is it? (fat) |
| ʔûan máy. | (phɔ̌ɔm) | Fat? Do you think she's fat? (thin) |
| phɔ̌ɔm máy | (dii) | Thin? Do you think he's thin? (good) |

Translations can never be completely accurate. Sometimes they are used to suggest the Thai structure (Good?); sometimes they are used to point up nuances of meaning or implications contained in the Thai meaning (Do you think it's good? where 'do you think' suggests that *máy* is asking for an opinion); and sometimes they give the English that would normally be used in the same situation even though it doesn't conform to the Thai wording (How is it?). And in some cases English grammar requires filling a slot that can be empty in Thai (Is *he* good? Is *she* good? Is *it* good? Are *they* good?). The student should refer back to the vocabulary section for literal meanings and explanations, and he should try to get from the translations accompanying dialogs and drills whatever kind of help is intended. He should not expect anything like one-to-one correspondences.

The following steps should be used with **substitution** drills. (These appear, among other types of drills, in sections 5 and 7 of **each** lesson.)

1. Listen. The teacher simply reads the items of the drill for the student to listen to (several times through with short drills like the one above). The pattern stays the same while the words change. In this step the student gets the pattern ringing in his ears.

| | | | |
|---|---|---|---|
| Teacher: | dii máy. | ʔûan máy. | phɔ̌ɔm máy. |
| | dii máy. | ʔûan máy. | phɔ̌ɔm máy. |
| | dii máy. | ʔûan máy. | phɔ̌ɔm máy. |

2. Repeat. The student simply repeats each item after the teacher several times through. With the pattern ringing in his ears, he now acquires the necessary muscular facility needed for the succeeding steps.

3. Substitute. The teacher reads an item of the pattern and then a parenthesized word. The student puts the parenthesized word into the pattern, and the teacher confirms (repeats the new item that the student has formed). The student is now exercising the pattern itself, not just individual examples of it.

| | | | | |
|---|---|---|---|---|
| Teacher: | dii máy. | (ʔûan) | Student: | ʔûan máy. |
| | ʔûan máy. | (phɔ̌ɔm) | | phɔ̌ɔm máy. |
| | phɔ̌ɔm máy. | (dii) | | dii máy. |
| | Etc. | | | |

4. Substitute without books. Step 2 might have built nothing more than a pathway from ear to mouth. And step 3 might have built only a pathway from eye to mouth. The real practice on the pattern itself comes in this step and the next.

5. Substitute without books or confirmation. The confirmation was necessary to let the student know how well he did. After he is able to do the substitutions consistently perfect and fast, he no longer needs the confirmation. He is now in a position to burn the pattern into the brain by going through the drill (random order of items now) many times with increasing speed.

| | | | | |
|---|---|---|---|---|
| Teacher: | dii máy. | (phɔ̌ɔm) | Student: | phɔ̌ɔm máy. |
| | (ʔûan) | | | ʔûan máy. |
| | (phɔ̌ɔm) | | | phɔ̌ɔm máy. |

Etc., pushing to the maximum speed that the student can do with good pronunciation, but not beyond.

In steps 3 through 5, the English parenthesized words might be used from time to time instead of the Thai words, as a means of getting the student's attention on the meaning, but this technique isn't necessary and in some cases (when translations are awkward) isn't advisable.

**b. Substitution drill.**

| | | | | |
|---|---|---|---|---|
| mây dii. | (ʔûan) | Not good. | It isn't good. | (fat) |
| mây ʔûan. | (phɔ̌ɔm) | Not fat. | She isn't fat. | (thin) |
| mây phɔ̌ɔm. | (dii) | Not thin. | He isn't thin. | (nice) |

**c. Response drill.**

| | |
|---|---|
| dii máy. | Do you think it's good? |
| mây dii. | No, I don't. |
| ʔûan máy. | Do you think she's fat? |
| mây ʔûan. | No, I don't. |
| phɔ̌ɔm máy. | Do you think he's thin? |
| mây phɔ̌ɔm. | No, I don't. |

The same steps are used with response drills as with substitution drills. Simply replace the instruction 'substitute' with 'respond' Whenever a response is not good (wrong, badly pronounced, or too slow), the teacher should use multiple confirmations ('corrections' is a better description in this case).

| Teacher | Student | |
|---|---|---|
| dii máy. | mây dii. | (poorly) |
| mây dii. mây dii. mây dii. | | |
| dii máy. | mây dii. | (a little better) |
| mây dii. mây dii. | | |
| dii máy. | mây dii. | (good) |
| mây dii. | | |
| dii máy. | mây dii. | (perfect) |
| dii máy. | mây dii. | |
| dii máy. | mây dii. | |

## 1.6 Vowel and consonant drills.

**a. u-ʉ contrast drill.**

1. thǔŋ Sack.
2. thʉ̌ŋ Reach.

The sound *ʉ* has nearly the same tongue position as *u*. The main difference is that the lips are spread with *ʉ* and rounded with *u*. The symbol *ʉ* suggests trying to say a *u* with a stick (—) sideways in the mouth to keep the lips from rounding. Use the four steps described in section 1.4. In step 2, the word can be identified by giving its number or meaning.

**b. b-p contrast drill.**

1. bay Leaf.
2. pay Go.

**c. d-t contrast drill.**

1. dii Good.
2. tii Hit.

## 1.7 Grammar drills.

**a. Substitution drill.**

| | |
|---|---|
| sawàtdii khráp. (khâ) | Hello from man to superior. |
| sawàtdii khâ. (câ) | Hello from woman to superior. |
| sawàtdii câ. (khráp) | Hello to inferior or intimate. |

Use the 5 steps described in section 1.5. Students needn't worry about practicing the part of the opposite sex. No harm is done, and the pattern is drilled.

### 1.8 Numbers.

| | |
|---|---|
| sɔ̌ɔŋ | Two. |
| sǎam | Three. |
| hâa | Five. |

Practice reading the following numbers at home. (235 is to be read sɔ̌ɔŋ sǎam hâa.) Time yourself. Try to get the time under 10 seconds. Be especially careful with the tones.

235 352 532 253 325 523

### 1.9 Conversation.

**a.** The teacher states an attribute of *kháw* (he or she) and then asks the student about it.

| Teacher | | Student |
|---|---|---|
| (kháw phɔ̌ɔm) | kháw phɔ̌ɔm máy khá. | phɔ̌ɔm khráp. |
| (kháw mây dii) | kháw dii máy khá. | mây dii khráp. |

Etc.

The emphasis in this section is meaning. In other sections it is either sounds or patterns. The conversations should be primarily between teacher and student. Only when a conversation can be done with complete fluency should two students converse with each other. If a student ever has more than two seconds of hesitation, it means that he isn't ready for this section. Sections 3 and 5 need more work.

The student should always give the expected answer. He should never try to be original. Competition among students should not consist of coming up with more original answers, but of giving expected answers with greater speed and better pronunciation.

This section should always be done without books.

**b.** Exchange hellos all around.

### 1.10 Writing.

Thai writing is alphabetic like that of European languages, but unlike European languages there is an added complication with both vowels and consonants.

**Vowels.** Not only must the symbol be learned, but also its position. Some vowels appear after the initial consonant, some before it, some above it, some below it, some with combinations of these positions, and some with none of them (that is, with no symbol at all).

**Consonants.** Not only must the symbol be learned, but also its tone class. The initial consonant of *dii* without a tonal marker gives the syllable a mid tone; while that of *phɔ̌ɔm* gives a rising tone.

| ดี | ผอม |
|---|---|
| dii | phɔ̌ɔm´ |
| Good. | Thin. |

| | | | |
|---|---|---|---|
| ดี | *dii | ผี | phǐi |
| ดอ | dɔɔ | ผีม | phǐim |
| ดอม | dɔɔm | ดีม | diim |
| ผอม | *phɔ̌ɔm | ดี | *dii |
| ผอ | phɔ̌ɔ | ผี | phǐi |

The asterisk marks words known by the student. Whenever you see an asterisk, recall the meaning of the word.

Practice reading the Thai writing with the transcription column covered with a card. After reading each word, slide the card down uncovering the transcription to confirm or correct your reading. Then practice writing each word with the Thai writing covered. Slide the card down to check yourself after each attempt.

Lesson 1 appears again on the following pages without the clutter of instructions to acquaint teacher and students with the normal format of the lessons. Use it now for review.

From here on the regular text will appear on the right-hand pages only. On the pages facing from the left, all Thai words and sentences of the text will be printed in normal Thai orthography. Most teachers will find it easier to use the left-hand pages while doing drills. Those students who have learned to read and write Thai but not to speak it will also find it easier to follow the left-hand pages. The normal student, however, is advised to follow only the right-hand pages. He will stand a much better chance of ending up with good pronunciation if he does so. After he finishes Book 2, though, he might want to review Book 1 by following the Thai writing. The repetitive nature of the substitution drills offers an excellent means of building speed of recognition.

# บทที่ ๑

## ๑.๑ คำศัพท์

หวัด
สวัสดิ์
ดี
สวัสดี
ครับ
ค่ะ
คะ
จ้ะ
จ๊ะ
อ้วน
ผอม
ไหม
ไม่
เขา
สอง
สาม
ห้า

## ๑.๒ โครงสร้างของประโยค

สวัสดีครับ
สวัสดีค่ะ
สวัสดีจ้ะ

## ๑.๓ บทสนทนา

ก. สวัสดีครับ
ข. สวัสดีค่ะ

## ๑.๔ แบบฝึกหัดการฟังและการออกเสียงสูงต่ำ

นา
หน้า
หนา

นา หน้า นา หน้า นา
นา หนา นา หนา นา
หน้า หนา หน้า หนา หน้า

หน้า นา หน้า นา หน้า
หนา นา หนา นา หนา
หนา หน้า หนา หน้า หนา

# LESSON 1

## 1.1 Vocabulary and expansions.

| | |
|---|---|
| wàt | |
| sawàt | Well-being, fortune (not used alone). |
| dii | To be good. |
| sawàtdii | A greeting used for either meeting or parting. Greetings! Aloha! Hello! Goodbye! |
| khráp<br>khâ<br>khá<br>câ<br>cá | Particles are short words that are used to convey feelings, not meaning. Their function is roughly comparable to that of intonations in English. The three words listed to the left (two of them have two variants) are polite particles. They are used at the end of sentences whenever extra politeness is called for. In such situations men use *khráp* when speaking to non-intimate equals or superiors and women use *khâ* (*khá* with questions). Both men and women use *câ* (*cá* with questions) when speaking to intimate equals, inferiors, or children. (See page 1.) |
| ʔûan | To be fat. |
| phɔ̌ɔm | To be thin. |
| máy | One of several question particles (similar to a spoken question mark). This one is used to ask for an opinion or a decision. |
| mây | Not. |
| kháw | He, she, they (people only). |
| sɔ̌ɔŋ | Two. |
| sǎam | Three. |
| hâa | Five. |

## 1.2 Patterns.

| | | |
|---|---|---|
| sawàtdii khráp. | Hello! | (Man to superior.) |
| sawàtdii khâ. | Hello! | (Woman to superior.) |
| sawàtdii câ. | Hello! | (Man or woman to inferior.) |

## 1.3 Dialog.

A. sawàtdii khráp. — Hello!

B. sawàtdii khâ. — Hello!

## 1.4 Tone identification and production.

| | | |
|---|---|---|
| naa | Rice field. | Mid tone. |
| nâa | Face. | Falling tone. |
| nǎa | Thick. | Rising tone. |

naa nâa naa nâa naa — nâa naa nâa naa nâa
naa nǎa naa nǎa naa — nǎa naa nǎa naa nǎa
nâa nǎa nâa nǎa nâa — nǎa nâa nǎa nâa nǎa

### ๑.๕ แบบฝึกหัดการสลับเสียงสูงต่ำ

ก.

ดีไหม (อ้วน)
อ้วนไหม (ผอม)
ผอมไหม (ดี)

ข.

ไม่ดี (อ้วน)
ไม่อ้วน (ผอม)
ไม่ผอม (ดี)

ค.

ดีไหม
ไม่ดี
อ้วนไหม
ไม่อ้วน
ผอมไหม
ไม่ผอม

### ๑.๖ แบบฝึกหัดการออกเสียงสระและพยัญชนะ

| | | |
|---|---|---|
| ก. | ๑. ถุง | ๒. ถึง |
| ข. | ๑. ใบ | ๒. ไป |
| ค. | ๑. ดี | ๒. ตี |

### ๑.๗ แบบฝึกหัดไวยากรณ์

สวัสดีครับ (ค่ะ)
สวัสดีค่ะ (จ้ะ)
สวัสดีจ้ะ (ครับ)

### ๑.๘ เลข

สอง สาม ห้า

๒๓๕ ๓๕๒ ๕๓๒ ๒๕๓ ๓๒๕ ๕๒๓

### 1.5 Tone manipulation.

**a. Substitution drill.**

| | |
|---|---|
| dii máy. (ʔûan) | Good? Do you think it's good? (fat) |
| ʔûan máy. (phɔ̆ɔm) | Fat? Do you think she's fat? (thin) |
| phɔ̆ɔm máy. (dii) | Thin? Do you think he's thin? (good) |

**b. Substitution drill.**

| | |
|---|---|
| mây dii. (ʔûan) | Not good. It isn't good. (fat) |
| mây ʔûan. (phɔ̆ɔm) | Not fat. She isn't fat. (thin) |
| mây phɔ̆ɔm. (dii) | Not thin. He isn't thin. (nice) |

**c. Response drill.**

| | |
|---|---|
| dii máy. | Do you think it's good? |
| mây dii. | No, I don't. |
| ʔûan máy. | Do you think she's fat? |
| mây ʔûan. | No, I don't. |
| phɔ̆ɔm máy. | Do you think he's thin? |
| mây phɔ̆ɔm. | No, I don't. |

### 1.6 Vowel and consonant drills.

**a. u-ɯ contrast drill.**

1. thǔŋ Sack. 2. thɯ̌ŋ Reach.

**b. b-p contrast drill.**

1. bay Leaf. 2. pay Go.

**c. d-t contrast drill.**

1. dii Good. 2. tii Hit.

### 1.7 Grammar drills.

**a. Substitution drill.**

| | |
|---|---|
| sawàtdii khráp. (khâ) | Hello from man to superior. |
| sawàtdii khâ. (câ) | Hello from woman to superior. |
| sawàtdii câ. (khráp) | Hello to inferior or intimate. |

### 1.8 Numbers.

| | |
|---|---|
| sɔ̆ɔŋ | Two. |
| sǎam | Three. |
| hâa | Five. |

Practice reading the following numbers at home. Time yourself. Try to get the time under 10 seconds. Be especially careful with the tones.

235 352 532 253 325 523

**๑.๙ การสนทนาโต้ตอบ**

ก.

| | | |
|---|---|---|
| (เขาผอม) | เขาผอมไหมคะ | ผอมครับ |
| (เขาไม่ดี ) | เขาดีไหมคะ | ไม่ดีครับ |

**๑.๑๐ การเขียน**

ดี ผอม

| | |
|---|---|
| ดี | ผี |
| ดอ | ผีม |
| ดอม | ดีม |
| ผอม | ดี |
| ผอ | ผี |

**1.9 Conversation.**

**a.** The teacher states an attribute of *kháw* and then asks the student about it.

| | | |
|---|---|---|
| (kháw phɔ̌ɔm) | kháw phɔ̌ɔm máy khá. | phɔ̌ɔm khráp. |
| (kháw mây dii) | kháw dii máy khá. | mây dii khráp. |

Etc.

**b.** Exchange hellos all around.

**1.10 Writing.**

| ดี | ผอม |
|---|---|
| dii | phɔ̌ɔm |
| Good. | Thin. |

| | | | |
|---|---|---|---|
| ดี | *dii | ผี | phǐi |
| ดอ | dɔɔ | ผีม | phǐim |
| ดอม | dɔɔm | ดีม | diim |
| ผอม | *phɔ̌ɔm | ดี | *dii |
| ผอ | phɔ̌ɔ | ผี | phǐi |

# บทที่ ๒

## ๒.๑ คำศัพท์

บาย
สบาย
สบายดี
หรือ

ขอ
โทษ
ขอโทษ

ไร
เป็น
เป็นไร
ไม่เป็นไร

ใหญ่
เล็ก
สูง
เตี้ย
ร้อน
เย็น
คน
นั้น
คนนั้น
หนึ่ง
สี่
หก

## ๒.๒ โครงสร้างของประโยค

ร้อนหรือ
เย็นหรือ
ใหญ่หรือ
สบายดีหรือ

เขาหรือ
คนนั้นหรือ

# LESSON 2

## 2.1 Vocabulary and expansions.

| | |
|---|---|
| baay | |
| sabaay | To be comfortable, feel nice. |
| sabaay dii | To be well. |
| lɔ̌ɔ | A question particle used to ask for a confirmation. The speaker makes a guess based on the way things seem to him and then asks if he is right. 'Am I right in assuming that . . . '. |
| khɔ̌ɔ | To ask for. |
| thôot | Punishment. |
| khɔ̌ɔ thôot | Excuse me! I'm sorry! |
| ray | Shortened form of *ʔaray* which means 'what' or 'something'. |
| pen | To be something or someone. |
| pen ray | |
| mây pen ray | It's nothing. Not at all. Don't mention it. |
| yày | To be big. |
| lék | To be little. |
| sǔuŋ | To be tall. |
| tîa | To be short (in height). |
| rɔ́ɔn | To be hot. |
| yen | To be cold. |
| khon | Person, people. |
| nán | That (adjective). |
| khon nán | That person. |
| nùŋ | One. |
| sìi | Four. |
| hòk | Six. |

## 2.2 Patterns.

| | |
|---|---|
| rɔ́ɔn lɔ̌ɔ. | (You act as if it's hot, so I assume that) it's hot. Am I right? |
| yen lɔ̌ɔ. | I assume it's cold. Am I right? |
| yày lɔ̌ɔ. | It's big, is it? |
| sabaay dii lɔ̌ɔ. | You appear to be feeling well. Are you? |
| kháw lɔ̌ɔ. | Him? You mean him? |
| khon nán lɔ̌ɔ. | That person? |

### ๒.๓ บทสนทนา

ก. สวัสดีค่ะ

ข. สวัสดีครับ

ก. สบายดีหรือคะ

ข. สบายดีครับ

ก. ขอโทษค่ะ

ข. ไม่เป็นไรครับ

### ๒.๔ แบบฝึกหัดการฟังและการออกเสียงสูงต่ำ

หล่ม

ลม

ล้ม

ลม หล่ม ลม หล่ม ลม
ลม ล้ม ลม ล้ม ลม
หล่ม ล้ม หล่ม ล้ม หล่ม

หล่ม ลม หล่ม ลม หล่ม
ล้ม ลม ล้ม ลม ล้ม
ล้ม หล่ม ล้ม หล่ม ล้ม

### ๒.๕ แบบฝึกหัดการสลับเสียงสูงต่ำ

**ก.**

| | | | |
|---|---|---|---|
| ดีไหม | (ใหญ่) | เย็นไหม | (ร้อน) |
| ใหญ่ไหม | (เล็ก) | ร้อนไหม | (สูง) |
| เล็กไหม | (ผอม) | สูงไหม | (เตี้ย) |
| ผอมไหม | (อ้วน) | เตี้ยไหม | |
| อ้วนไหม | (เย็น) | | |

**2.3 Dialogs.**

**a. A greeting.**

| | |
|---|---|
| A. sawàtdii khâ. | Hello! |
| B. sawàtdii khráp. | Hello! |
| A. sabaay dii lɔ̌ɔ khá. | How are you? |
| B. sabaay dii khráp. | I'm fine. |

**b. An apology.**

| | |
|---|---|
| A. khɔ̌ɔ thôot khâ. | Excuse me. |
| B. mây pen ray khráp. | That's all right. |

**2.4 Tone identification and production.**

| | | |
|---|---|---|
| lòm | A muddy place. | Low. |
| lom | Wind. | Mid. |
| lóm | To fall over. | High. |

| | |
|---|---|
| lom lòm lom lòm lom | lòm lom lòm lom lòm |
| lom lóm lom lóm lom | lóm lom lóm lom lóm |
| lòm lóm lòm lóm lòm | lóm lòm lóm lòm lóm |

**2.5 Tone manipulation.**

**a. Substitution drill.**

| | | | |
|---|---|---|---|
| dii máy. | (yày) | Do you think it's good? | (big) |
| yày máy. | (lék) | Do you think it's big? | (little) |
| lék máy. | (phɔ̌ɔm) | Do you think it's little? | (thin) |
| phɔ̌ɔm máy. | (ʔûan) | Do you think he's thin? | (fat) |
| ʔûan máy. | (yen) | Do you think he's fat? | (cold) |
| yen máy. | (rɔ́ɔn) | Do you think it's cold? | (hot) |
| rɔ́ɔn máy. | (sǔuŋ) | Do you think it's hot? | (tall) |
| sǔuŋ máy. | (tîa) | Do you think he's tall? | (short in height) |
| tîa máy. | | Do you think he's short? | |

ข.

| | |
|---|---|
| ไม่ผอม | (สูง) |
| ไม่สูง | (ดี) |
| ไม่ดี | (เตี้ย) |
| ไม่เตี้ย | (ใหญ่) |
| ไม่ใหญ่ | (อ้วน) |
| ไม่อ้วน | (เล็ก) |
| ไม่เล็ก | (ร้อน) |
| ไม่ร้อน | (เย็น) |
| ไม่เย็น | |

ค.

ผอมไหม
ไม่ผอม

เล็กไหม
ไม่เล็ก

ดีไหม
ไม่ดี

ร้อนไหม
ไม่ร้อน

สูงไหม
ไม่สูง

เย็นไหม
ไม่เย็น

เตี้ยไหม
ไม่เตี้ย

ใหญ่ไหม
ไม่ใหญ่

อ้วนไหม
ไม่อ้วน

**๒.๖ แบบฝึกหัดการออกเสียงสระและพยัญชนะ**

ก.

๑. ทำ ๒. เทอม

**b. Substitution drill.**

| | | | |
|---|---|---|---|
| mây phɔ̌ɔm. | (sǔuŋ) | He isn't thin. | (tall) |
| mây sǔuŋ. | (dii) | He isn't tall. | (nice) |
| mây dii. | (tîa) | He isn't nice. | (short in height) |
| mây tîa. | (yày) | He isn't short. | (big) |
| mây yày. | (ʔûan) | He isn't big. | (fat) |
| mây ʔûan. | (lék) | He isn't fat. | (little) |
| mây lék. | (rɔ́ɔn) | He isn't little. | (hot) |
| mây rɔ́ɔn. | (yen) | It isn't hot. | (cold) |
| mây yen. | | It isn't cold. | |

**c. Response drill.**

| | |
|---|---|
| phɔ̌ɔm máy. | Do you think he's thin? |
| mây phɔ̌ɔm. | No, I don't. |
| lék máy. | Do you think it's little? |
| mây lék. | No, I don't. |
| dii máy. | Do you think it's good? |
| mây dii. | No, I don't. |
| rɔ́ɔn máy. | Do you think it's hot? |
| mây rɔ́ɔn. | No, I don't. |
| sǔuŋ máy. | Do you think he's tall? |
| mây sǔuŋ. | No, I don't. |
| yen máy. | Do you think it's cold? |
| mây yen. | No, I don't. |
| tîa máy. | Do you think he's short in height? |
| mây tîa. | No, I don't. |
| yày máy. | Do you think it's big? |
| mây yày. | No, I don't. |
| ʔûan máy. | Do you think he's fat? |
| mây ʔûan. | No, I don't. |

**2.6 Vowel and consonant drills.**

**a. a-əə contrast drill.**

Try saying the English world *term* without the *r* (as in British English). Then listen to the Thai word *thəəm*.

1. tham  To do.  2. thəəm  Term.

The sound *ə* has nearly the same tongue position as *o*. The main difference is that the lips are spread with *ə* and rounded with *o*. The symbol *ə* (something like *e*) suggests trying to say an *o* with a stick sideways in the mouth to keep the lips from rounding.

ข.

๑. บ่า ๒. ป่า ๓. ผ่า

บ่า ป่า บ่า ป่า บ่า ป่า บ่า ป่า บ่า ป่า
ผ่า ป่า ผ่า ป่า ผ่า ป่า ผ่า ป่า ผ่า ป่า

ค.

๑. ดี่ ๒. ตี่ ๓. ที่

ดี่ ตี่ ดี่ ตี่ ดี่ ตี่ ดี่ ตี่ ดี่ ตี่
ที่ ตี่ ที่ ตี่ ที่ ตี่ ที่ ตี่ ที่ ตี่

## ๒.๗ แบบฝึกหัดไวยากรณ์

ก.

สบายดีครับ (ค่ะ)
สบายดีค่ะ (จ้ะ)
สบายดีจ้ะ (ครับ)

ข.

สบายดีหรือครับ (คะ)
สบายดีหรือคะ (จ๊ะ)
สบายดีหรือจ๊ะ (ครับ)

ค.

อ้วนหรือ (ใหญ่)
ใหญ่หรือ (ผอม)
ผอมหรือ (ดี)
ดีหรือ (เล็ก)
เล็กหรือ (เตี้ย)
เตี้ยหรือ (สูง)
สูงหรือ (สบายดี)
สบายดีหรือ

## ๒.๘ เลข

๑ ๒ ๓ ๔ ๕ ๖
หนึ่ง สอง สาม สี่ ห้า หก

**๔๒๖ ๑๔๖ ๕๖๑ ๑๓๔ ๒๖๓ ๖๕๑ ๓๑๔ ๔๑๒ ๖๔๕**

**b. b-p-ph contrast drill.**

| 1. bàa Shoulder. | 2. pàa Jungle. | 3. phàa To split. |
|---|---|---|
| bàa pàa bàa pàa bàa | pàa bàa pàa bàa pàa | |
| phàa pàa phàa pàa phàa | pàa phàa pàa phàa pàa | |

**c. d-t-th contrast drill.**

| 1. dii Good. | 2. tii To hit. | 3. thii A time. |
|---|---|---|
| dii tii dii tii dii | tii dii tii dii tii | |
| thii tii thii tii thii | tii thii tii thii tii | |

## 2.7 Grammar drills.

**a. Substitution drill.**

| | | |
|---|---|---|
| sabaay dii khráp. | (khâ) | I'm fine. |
| sabaay dii khâ. | (câ) | I'm fine. |
| sabaay dii câ. | (khráp) | I'm fine. |

**b. Substitution drill.**

| | | |
|---|---|---|
| sabaay dii lɔ̌ə khráp. | (khá) | You're well? |
| sabaay dii lɔ̌ə khá. | (cá) | You're well? |
| sabaay dii lɔ̌ə cá. | (khráp) | You're well? |

**c. Substitution drill.**

| | | | |
|---|---|---|---|
| ʔûan lɔ̌ə. | (yày) | He's fat? | (big) |
| yày lɔ̌ə. | (phɔ̌ɔm) | He's big? | (thin) |
| phɔ̌ɔm lɔ̌ə. | (dii) | He's thin? | (nice) |
| dii lɔ̌ə. | (lék) | He's nice? | (little) |
| lék lɔ̌ə. | (tîa) | He's little? | (short in height) |
| tîa lɔ̌ə. | (sǔuŋ) | He's short? | (tall) |
| sǔuŋ lɔ̌ə. | (sabaay dii) | He's tall? | (well) |
| sabaay dii lɔ̌ə. | | He's well? | |

## 2.8 Numbers.

| 1 | 2 | 3 | 4 | 5 | 6 |
|---|---|---|---|---|---|
| nùŋ | sɔ̌ɔŋ | sǎam | sìi | hâa | hòk |

Practice reading the following numbers at home. Try to get the time under 15 seconds. Be especially careful with the tones.

426 146 561 134 263 651 314 412 645

## ๒.๙ การสนทนาโต้ตอบ

ก.

| | | |
|---|---|---|
| (คนนั้นใหญ่) | คนนั้นใหญ่ไหมคะ | ใหญ่ครับ |
| (คนนั้นไม่อ้วน) | คนนั้นอ้วนไหมคะ | ไม่อ้วนครับ |

## ๒.๑๐ การเขียน

สอง สาม

| | | |
|---|---|---|
| สอง | สา | คอ |
| สาง | ดา | ผอ |
| ดาง | ผา | ผอม |
| ผาง | ผี | สอม |
| ผาม | ดี | คอม |
| ดาม | สี | ดอง |
| สาม | สอ | ผอง |

**2.9 Conversation.**

**a.** Teacher states an attribute of *khon nán* and then asks about it.

| | | |
|---|---|---|
| (khon nán yày) | khon nán yày máy khá. | yày khráp. |
| (khon nán mây ʔûan) | khon nán ʔûan máy khá. | mây ʔûan khráp. |

Etc.

**b.** Exchange greetings (section 2.3a) all around.

**c.** Everyone apologize (and be excused) for something: coming late, interrupting, bumping another's chair, etc.

**2.10 Writing.**

| สอง | สาม |
|---|---|
| sɔ̌ɔŋ | sǎam |
| Two. | Three. |

| | | | | | |
|---|---|---|---|---|---|
| สอง | *sɔ̌ɔŋ | สา | sǎa | ดอ | dɔɔ |
| สาง | sǎaŋ | ดา | daa | ผอ | phɔ̌ɔ |
| ดาง | daaŋ | ผา | phǎa | ผอม | *phɔ̌ɔm |
| ผาง | phǎaŋ | ผี | phǐi | สอม | sɔ̌ɔm |
| ผาม | phǎam | ดี | *dii | ดอม | dɔɔm |
| ดาม | daam | สี | sǐi | ดอง | dɔɔŋ |
| สาม | *sǎam | สอ | sɔ̌ɔ | ผอง | phɔ̌ɔŋ |

# บทที่ ๓

### ๓.๑ คำศัพท์

อาหาร
ร้าน
ร้านอาหาร
ร้านอาหารนิค

ตัด

ผม

ตัดผม
ร้านตัดผม

ห้อง
ห้องอาหาร

ที่
ไหน
ที่ไหน

อยู่
อยู่ที่ไหน

นี่

โน่น

ขอบคุณ
มาก
ขอบคุณมาก

ยาว
สั้น

ครับ
ค่ะ
จ้ะ
ฮึ่ม

ดีหรือ
ครับ (ดี)

ไม่ดีหรือ
ครับ (ไม่ดี)

# LESSON 3

**3.1 Vocabulary and expansions.**

| | |
|---|---|
| ʔaahǎan | Food. |
| ráan | Shop, store. |
| ráan ʔaahǎan | Restaurant. |
| ráan ʔaahǎan ník | Nick's Restaurant. |
| | |
| tàt | To cut. |
| phǒm | Hair (head only). |
| tàt phǒm | To cut the hair. |
| ráan tàt phǒm | Barber shop. |
| | |
| hɔ̂ŋ | Room. |
| hɔ̂ŋ ʔaahǎan | Dining room. |
| | |
| thîi | At. |
| nǎy | Which, where. |
| thîi nǎy | Where at. |
| yùu | To be some place. |
| yùu thîi nǎy | Where is it? |
| nîi | Here, this (noun). |
| nôon | Over there, that (noun). |
| | |
| khɔ̀ɔpkhun | Thanks. |
| mâak | Very, a lot. |
| khɔ̀ɔpkhun mâak | Thanks a lot. |
| | |
| yaaw | To be long. |
| sân | To be short (in length). |

khráp

khâ

câ

hm̂m

The polite particles are used alone to confirm *lɔ̌ɔ* questions. They are often translated in this use by *yes*, but this is misleading. They are *confirmatives; yes* is an *affirmative*. A confirmative comments on a person's conjecture; an affirmative comments on the truth or occurrence of the verb. The choice of confirmatives parallels that of polite particles. In situations where no polite particle would be used, *hm̂m* can be used as a confirmative. (The actual sound cannot be written accurately in the transcription or in Thai writing. The teacher should make the actual sound and not try to follow the writing used to suggest it.) But one should be freer in using *khráp*, *khâ* and *câ* as confirmatives than as particles. That is, there are in-between situations where the polite particles would be used as confirmatives. though not as particles.

| | | |
|---|---|---|
| dii lɔ̌ɔ. | It is good. Am I right? | It's good, isn't it? |
| khráp (dii). | You are right (it is good). | Yes. |
| | | |
| mây dii lɔ̌ɔ. | It isn't good. Am I right? | It isn't good. is it? |
| khráp (mây dii). | You are right (it isn't good). | No. |

### ๓.๒ โครงสร้างของประโยค

| | |
|---|---|
| อยู่ที่ไหน | ห้องอาหาร |
| อยู่ที่นี่ | ร้านอาหาร |
| อยู่ที่โน่น | ร้านตัดผม |

| | |
|---|---|
| ห้องอยู่ที่ไหน | ร้อนมาก |
| ร้านอยู่ที่ไหน | ดีมาก |
| อาหารอยู่ที่ไหน | ใหญ่มาก |
| | สูงมาก |
| ห้องอยู่ที่โน่น | อ้วนมาก |
| ร้านอยู่ที่โน่น | |
| อาหารอยู่ที่โน่น | |

### ๓.๓ บทสนทนา

ก. ขอโทษ
ร้านอาหารอยู่ที่ไหน

ข. อยู่ที่โน่น

ก. ขอบคุณมาก

ข. ไม่เป็นไร

### ๓.๔ แบบฝึกหัดการฟังและการออกเสียงสูงต่ำ

ใหม่ ไหม้ ไหม

ใหม่ ไหม้ ใหม่ ไหม้ ใหม่ ไหม้ ใหม่ ไหม้ ใหม่ ไหม้

ใหม่ ไหม ใหม่ ไหม ใหม่ ไหม ใหม่ ไหม ใหม่ ไหม

ไหมใหม่ไหม้ไหม

ไหมใหม่ไม่ไหม้

### 3.2 Patterns.

| | |
|---|---|
| yùu thîi nǎy. | Where is it? |
| yùu thîi nîi. | It's here. |
| yùu thîi nôon. | It's over there. |
| hɔ̂ŋ yùu thîi nǎy. | Where's the room? |
| ráan yùu thîi nǎy. | Where's the shop? |
| ʔaahǎan yùu thîi nǎy. | Where's the food? |
| hɔ̂ŋ yùu thîi nôon. | The room is over there. |
| ráan yùu thîi nôon. | The shop is over there. |
| ʔaahǎan yùu thîi nôon. | The food is over there. |
| hɔ̂ŋ ʔaahǎan | Dining room (food room). |
| ráan ʔaahǎan | Restaurant (food shop). |
| ráan tàt phǒm | Barber shop (cut hair shop). |
| rɔ́ɔn mâak | Very hot, |
| dii mâak | Very good. |
| yày mâak | Very big. |
| sǔuŋ mâak | Very tall. |
| ʔûan mâak | Very fat. |

### 3.3 Dialog.

A. khɔ̌ɔ thôot. — Excuse me.
ráan ʔaahǎan yùu thîi nǎy. — Where is there a restaurant?

B. yùu thîi nôon. — There's one over there.

A. khɔ̀ɔpkhun mâak. — Thanks a lot.

B. mây pen ray. — Not at all.

### 3.4 Tone identification and production.

| | | |
|---|---|---|
| mày | New. | Low. |
| mây | To burn. | Falling. |
| mǎy | Silk. | Rising. |

mày mây mày mây mày — mây mày mây mày mây
mày mǎy mày mǎy mày — mǎy mày mǎy mày mǎy

mǎy mày mây máy. — Does new silk burn?
mǎy mày mây mây. — New silk doesn't burn.

## ๓.๕ แบบฝึกหัดการสลับเสียงสูงต่ำ

ก.

ยาวมาก (สูง)
สูงมาก (ใหญ่)
ใหญ่มาก (ร้อน)
ร้อนมาก (สั้น)
สั้นมาก (อ้วน)
อ้วนมาก (เตี้ย)
เตี้ยมาก (ยาว)

ข.

ยาวหรือ
ฮื่ม, ยาวมาก

ร้อนหรือ
ฮื่ม, ร้อนมาก

ใหญ่หรือ
ฮื่ม, ใหญ่มาก

สูงหรือ
ฮื่ม, สูงมาก

เล็กหรือ
ฮื่ม, เล็กมาก

เย็นหรือ
ฮื่ม, เย็นมาก

ผอมหรือ
ฮื่ม, ผอมมาก

ดีหรือ
ฮื่ม, ดีมาก

สั้นหรือ
ฮื่ม, สั้นมาก

อ้วนหรือ
ฮื่ม, อ้วนมาก

เตี้ยหรือ
ฮื่ม, เตี้ยมาก

## ๓.๖ แบบฝึกหัดการออกเสียงสระและพยัญชนะ

ก.

๑. ลาลาว
๒. แลแลว

ข.

๑. ปา ตา จา กา
๒. พา ทา ชา คา

### 3.5 Tone manipulation.

**a. Substitution drill.**

| | | | |
|---|---|---|---|
| yaaw mâak. | (sǔuŋ) | It's very long. | (tall) |
| sǔuŋ mâak. | (yày) | It's very tall. | (big) |
| yày mâak. | (rɔ́ɔn) | It's very big. | (hot) |
| rɔ́ɔn mâak. | (sân) | It's very hot. | (short in length) |
| sân mâak. | (ʔûan) | It's very short. | (fat) |
| ʔûan mâak. | (tîa) | It's very fat. | (short in height) |
| tîa mâak. | (yaaw) | It's very short. | (long) |

**b. Response drill.**

| | |
|---|---|
| yaaw lɔ̌ə. | It's long? |
| hm̂m. yaaw mâak. | Yes. It's very long. |
| rɔ́ɔn lɔ̌ə. | It's hot? |
| hm̂m. rɔ́ɔn mâak. | Yes. It's very hot. |
| yày lɔ̌ə. | It's big? |
| hm̂m. yày mâak. | Yes. It's very big. |
| sǔuŋ lɔ̌ə. | It's tall? |
| hm̂m. sǔuŋ mâak. | Yes. It's very tall. |
| lék lɔ̌ə. | It's little? |
| hm̂m. lék mâak. | Yes. It's very little. |
| yen lɔ̌ə. | It's cold? |
| hm̂m. yen mâak. | Yes. It's very cold. |
| phɔ̌ɔm lɔ̌ə. | It's thin? |
| hm̂m. phɔ̌ɔm mâak. | Yes. It's very thin. |
| dii lɔ̌ə. | It's good? |
| hm̂m. dii mâak. | Yes. It's very good. |
| sân lɔ̌ə. | It's short in length? |
| hm̂m. sân mâak. | Yes. It's very short. |
| ʔûan lɔ̌ə. | It's fat? |
| hm̂m. ʔûan mâak. | Yes. It's very fat |
| tîa lɔ̌ə. | It's short in height? |
| hm̂m. tîa mâak. | Yes. It's very short. |

### 3.6 Vowel and consonant drills.

**a. aaw-ɛɛw contrast drill.**

1. laalaaw
2. lɛɛlɛɛw

**b. p t c k-ph th ch kh contrast drill.**

1. paa taa caa kaa
2. phaa thaa chaa khaa

### ๓.๗ แบบฝึกหัดไวยากรณ์

ก.

ร้านอยู่ที่ไหน (ร้านอาหาร)
ร้านอาหารอยู่ที่ไหน (ห้อง)
ห้องอยู่ที่ไหน (ร้านอาหารนิค)
ร้านอาหารนิคอยู่ที่ไหน (เขา)
เขาอยู่ที่ไหน (ร้านตัดผม)
ร้านตัดผมอยู่ที่ไหน (อาหาร)
อาหารอยู่ที่ไหน (คนนั้น)
คนนั้นอยู่ที่ไหน (ห้องอาหาร)
ห้องอาหารอยู่ที่ไหน

ข.

อยู่ที่นี่ (ร้านอาหาร)
อยู่ที่ร้านอาหาร (โน่น)
อยู่ที่โน่น (ร้านตัดผม)
อยู่ที่ร้านตัดผม (ห้อง)
อยู่ที่ห้อง (ร้านอาหารนิค)
อยู่ที่ร้านอาหารนิค (เขา)
อยู่ที่เขา (ห้องอาหาร)
อยู่ที่ห้องอาหาร (คนนั้น)
อยู่ที่คนนั้น

ค.

ร้านอยู่ที่ไหน
ร้านอยู่ที่โน่น

อาหารอยู่ที่ไหน
อาหารอยู่ที่โน่น

เขาอยู่ที่ไหน
เขาอยู่ที่โน่น

ร้านอาหารนิคอยู่ที่ไหน
ร้านอาหารนิคอยู่ที่โน่น

ร้านตัดผมอยู่ที่ไหน
ร้านตัดผมอยู่ที่โน่น

ห้องอาหารอยู่ที่ไหน
ห้องอาหารอยู่ที่โน่น

### ๓.๘ เลข

| ๗ | ๘ | ๙ | ๑๐ |
|---|---|---|---|
| เจ็ด | แปด | เก้า | สิบ |

๗๔๙ ๙๘๖ ๑๗๓ ๘๙๗ ๗๙๖ ๙๗๘ ๒๙๑ ๔๘๗ ๘๕๔ ๘๑๗ ๙๖๘ ๕๙๕

### 3.7 Grammar drills.

**a. Substitution drill.**

| | |
|---|---|
| ráan yùu thîi nǎy. (ráan ʔaahǎan) | Where's the shop? (restaurant) |
| ráan ʔaahǎan yùu thîi nǎy. (hɔ̂ŋ) | Where's the restaurant? (room) |
| hɔ̂ŋ yùu thîi nǎy. (ráan ʔaahǎan ník) | Where's the room? (Nick's Restaurant) |
| ráan ʔaahǎan ník yùu thîi nǎy. (kháw) | Where's Nick's Restaurant? (he) |
| kháw yùu thîi nǎy. (ráan tàt phǒm) | Where's he? (barber shop) |
| ráan tàt phǒm yùu thîi nǎy. (ʔaahǎan) | Where's the barber shop? (food) |
| ʔaahǎan yùu thîi nǎy. (khon nán) | Where's the food? (that person) |
| khon nán yùu thîi nǎy. (hɔ̂ŋ ʔaahǎan) | Where's that person? (dining room) |
| hɔ̂ŋ ʔaahǎan yùu thîi nǎy. | Where's the dining room? |

**b. Substitution drill.**

| | |
|---|---|
| yùu thîi nîi. (ráan ʔaahǎan) | It's here. (restaurant) |
| yùu thîi ráan ʔaahǎan. (nôon) | It's at the restaurant. (there) |
| yùu thîi nôon. (ráan tàt phǒm) | It's there. (barber shop) |
| yùu thîi ráan tàt phǒm. (hɔ̂ŋ) | It's at the barber shop. (room) |
| yùu thîi hɔ̂ŋ. (ráan ʔaahǎan ník) | It's in the room. (Nick's Restaurant) |
| yùu thîi ráan ʔaahǎan ník. (kháw) | It's at Nick's Restaurant. (he) |
| yùu thîi kháw. (hɔ̂ŋ ʔaahǎan) | He has it. (dining room) |
| yùu thîi hɔ̂ŋ ʔaahǎan. (khon nán) | It's in the dining room. (that person) |
| yùu thîi khon nán. | That person has it. |

**c. Response drill.**

| | |
|---|---|
| ráan yùu thîi nǎy. | Where's the shop? |
| ráan yùu thîi nôon. | The shop's over there. |
| ʔaahǎan yùu thîi nǎy. | Where's the food? |
| ʔaahǎan yùu thîi nôon. | The food's over there. |
| kháw yùu thîi nǎy. | Where's he? |
| kháw yùu thîi nôon. | He's over there. |
| ráan ʔaahǎan ník yùu thîi nǎy. | Where's Nick's Restaurant? |
| ráan ʔaahǎan ník yùu thîi nôon. | Nick's Restaurant's over there. |
| ráan tàt phǒm yùu thîi nǎy. | Where's the barber shop? |
| ráan tàt phǒm yùu thîi nôon. | The barber shop's over there. |
| hɔ̂ŋ ʔaahǎan yùu thîi nǎy. | Where's the dining room? |
| hɔ̂ŋ ʔaahǎan yùu thîi nôon. | The dining room's over there. |

### 3.8 Numbers.

| 7 | 8 | 9 | 10 |
|---|---|---|---|
| cèt | pɛ̀ɛt | kâaw | sìp |

Practice reading the following numbers at home. Try to get the time under 25 seconds. Be especially careful with the tones.

749 986 173 897 796 978 291 487 854 817 968 595

**๓.๕ การสนทนาโต้ตอบ**

ก.

| | |
|---|---|
| ผอมไหมคะ | ผอมครับ |
| อ้วนไหมคะ | ไม่อ้วนครับ, ผอม |
| อ้วนไหมคะ | อ้วนครับ |
| ผอมไหมคะ | ไม่ผอมครับ, อ้วน |
| ใหญ่ไหมคะ | ใหญ่ครับ |
| เล็กไหมคะ | ไม่เล็กครับ, ใหญ่ |
| เล็กไหมคะ | เล็กครับ |
| ใหญ่ไหมคะ | ไม่ใหญ่ครับ, เล็ก |
| สูงไหมคะ | สูงครับ |
| เตี้ยไหมคะ | ไม่เตี้ยครับ, สูง |
| เตี้ยไหมคะ | เตี้ยครับ |
| สูงไหมคะ | ไม่สูงครับ, เตี้ย |
| ร้อนไหมคะ | ร้อนครับ |
| เย็นไหมคะ | ไม่เย็นครับ, ร้อน |
| เย็นไหมคะ | เย็นครับ |
| ร้อนไหมคะ | ไม่ร้อนครับ, เย็น |
| ยาวไหมคะ | ยาวครับ |
| สั้นไหมคะ | ไม่สั้นครับ, ยาว |
| สั้นไหมคะ | สั้นครับ |
| ยาวไหมคะ | ไม่ยาวครับ, สั้น |

**ข.**

| | |
|---|---|
| **ขอโทษค่ะ** | **ขอบคุณมากค่ะ** |
| **....................อยู่ที่ไหนคะ** | **ไม่เป็นไรครับ** |

**อยู่ที่....................ครับ**

**3.9 Conversation.**

a. The teacher should draw pictures like those below on the blackboard and ask the following questions as she points at them.

| | |
|---|---|
| phɔ̌ɔm máy khá.<br>ʔûan máy khá. | phɔ̌ɔm khráp.<br>mây ʔûan khráp. phɔ̌ɔm. |
| ʔûan máy khá.<br>phɔ̌ɔm máy khá. | ʔûan khráp.<br>mây phɔ̌ɔm khráp. ʔûan. |
| yày máy khá.<br>lék máy khá. | yày khráp.<br>mây lék khráp. yày. |
| lék máy khá.<br>yày máy khá. | lék khráp.<br>mây yày khráp. lék. |
| sǔuŋ máy khá.<br>tîa máy khá. | sǔuŋ khráp.<br>mây tîa khráp. sǔuŋ. |
| tîa máy khá.<br>sǔuŋ máy khá. | tîa khráp.<br>mây sǔuŋ khráp. tîa. |
| rɔ́ɔn máy khá.<br>yen máy khá. | rɔ́ɔn khráp.<br>mây yen khráp. rɔ́ɔn. |
| yen máy khá.<br>rɔ́ɔn máy khá. | yen khráp.<br>mây rɔ́ɔn khráp. yen. |
| yaaw máy khá.<br>sân máy khá. | yaaw khráp.<br>mây sân khráp. yaaw. |
| sân máy khá.<br>yaaw máy khá. | sân khráp.<br>mây yaaw khráp. sân. |

b. Practice the conversation suggested below. First the teacher should ask each student where the suggested places are, then the students should ask the teacher.

khɔ̌ɔ thôot khâ.
...............yùu thîi nǎy khá.

| | |
|---|---|
| the shop | the barber shop |
| the room | Nick's Restaurant |
| the food | the dining room |
| he | the restaurant |

yùu thîi............khráp.

here
over there

khɔ̀ɔpkhun mâak khâ.

mây pen ray khráp.

Don't go beyond these limitations even if you happen to know the names of articles in the room. The temptation to introduce or ask for new vocabulary in this section should always be resisted. Simply play the game as skillfully (that is, sounding as much like the teacher) as possible. Conformity, not originality, is the key to language learning. Above all, avoid trying to express reality of the situation through tone of voice.

### ๓.๑๐ การเขียน

ผม　　　　คน

| | | |
|---|---|---|
| คน | ดง | คอง |
| ผน | สง | คอม |
| ดน | คง | คาม |
| สน | ผง | สาม |
| สม | ผอง | สาน |
| คม | ผอม | ดาน |
| ผม | ผอน | คาน |
| ดม | คอน | ผาน |

### 3.10 Writing.

| ผม | คน |
|---|---|
| phǒm | khon |
| Hair. | People. |

| | | | | | |
|---|---|---|---|---|---|
| คน | *khon | ดง | doŋ | คอง | khɔɔŋ |
| ผน | phǒn | สง | sǒŋ | คอม | khɔɔm |
| ดน | don | คง | khoŋ | คาม | khaam |
| สน | sǒn | ผง | phǒŋ | สาม | *sǎam |
| สม | sǒm | ผอง | phɔ̌ɔŋ | สาน | sǎan |
| คม | khom | ผอม | *phɔ̌ɔm | ดาน | daan |
| ผม | *phǒm | ผอน | phɔ̌ɔn | คาน | khaan |
| ดม | dom | คอน | khɔɔn | ผาน | phǎan |

# บทที่ ๔

## ๔.๑ คำศัพท์

คุณ

คุณสวัสดิ์

คุณยัง

หนู

ตลาด

ทาง

ซ้าย

ทางซ้าย

ขวา

ทางขวา

แล้ว

ล่ะ

โรง

แรม

โรงแรม

ข้าง

หน้า

ข้างหน้า

หลัง

ข้างหลัง

ไป

ตรง

ตรงไป

ตรงไปข้างหน้า

เลย

ไม่. . . .เลย

เอ็ด

## ๔.๒ โครงสร้างของประโยค

ทางไหน

ทางขวา

ทางซ้าย

ข้างขวา

ข้างซ้าย

ข้างหน้า

ข้างหลัง

# LESSON 4

**4.1 Vocabulary and expansions.**

| | |
|---|---|
| khun | A respectful title (Mr., Mrs., Miss) used with a person's first name. (With foreigners, it is used with either the first or last name.) As with similar titles in most European languages (but not English), it is used without a name to call a stranger. |
| khun sawàt | Khun Sawat. |
| khun yaŋ | Mr. Young. |
| nǔu | Mouse. This word is used to call children. Like *khun*, it can be used with or without the first name. |
| talàat | Market. |
| thaaŋ | Way, path |
| sáay | Left. |
| thaaŋ sáay | To the left. |
| khwǎa | Right. |
| thaaŋ khwǎa | To the right. |
| lέεw | And then, subsequently. |
| lâ | A question particle used to ask the same thing (as a previous question) about something else. 'And what about...?' |
| rooŋ | |
| rεεm | |
| rooŋrεεm | Hotel. |
| khâaŋ | Side. |
| nâa | Face, front. |
| khâŋ nâa | The front side, ahead, in front of. |
| lǎŋ | Back. |
| khâŋ lǎŋ | The back side of, in back of, behind. |
| pay | To go. |
| troŋ | To be straight. |
| troŋ pay | To go straight. |
| troŋ pay khâŋ nâa | To go straight ahead. |
| lɔɔy | |
| mây ... lɔɔy | Not ... at all. |
| ʔèt | One (used in combinations like 21, 31). |

**4.2 Patterns.**

| | |
|---|---|
| thaaŋ nǎy | Which way? |
| thaaŋ khwǎa | To the right. |
| thaaŋ sáay | To the left. |
| khâŋ khwǎa | On the right side. |
| khâŋ sáay | On the left side. |
| khâŋ nâa | In front. |
| khâŋ lǎŋ | In back. |

(More.)

คุณครับ
คุณคะ
หนูจ๊ะ

อยู่ทางซ้าย
อยู่ทางขวา
อยู่ตรงไปข้างหน้า

แล้วเขาล่ะ
แล้วคนนั้นล่ะ
แล้วตลาดล่ะ
แล้วโรงแรมล่ะ

ไม่ดีเลย
ไม่ใหญ่เลย
ไม่ร้อนเลย
ไม่อ้วนเลย

## ๔.๓ บทสนทนา

ก. คุณครับ
ตลาดอยู่ที่ไหน

ข. อยู่ทางซ้าย

ก. แล้วโรงแรมล่ะ
อยู่ที่ไหน

ข. โรงแรมอยู่ตรงไปข้างหน้า

## ๔.๔ แบบฝึกหัดการฟังและการออกเสียงสูงต่ำ

**ก.**

ปลา ไก่ หมู กุ้ง เนื้อ

| | |
|---|---|
| khun khráp. | Excuse me, Mister. Excuse me, Lady. (Man speaking.) |
| khun khá. | Excuse me, Mister. Excuse me, Lady. (Woman speaking.) |
| nǔu cá. | Hey, little one. Hey, Sonny. |
| yùu thaaŋ sáay. | It's to the left. |
| yùu thaaŋ khwǎa. | It's to the right. |
| yùu troŋ pay khâŋ nâa. | It's straight ahead. |
| léɛw kháw lâ. | And what about him? |
| léɛw khon nán lâ. | And what about that person? |
| léɛw talàat lâ. | And what about the market? |
| léɛw rooŋrɛɛm lâ | And what about the hotel? |
| mây dii ləəy. | It isn't good at all. |
| mây yày ləəy. | It isn't big at all. |
| mây rɔ́ɔn ləəy. | It isn't hot at all. |
| mây ?ûan ləəy. | It isn't fat at all. |

**4.3 Dialog.**

A. khun khráp. — Excuse me, Mister.
talàat yùu thîi nǎy. — Where's the market?

B. yùu thaaŋ sáay. — It's to the left.

A. **léɛw rooŋrɛɛm lâ.** — And how about the hotel?
yùu thîi nǎy. — Where is it?

B. rooŋrɛɛm yùu troŋ pay (khâŋ nâa). — The hotel is straight ahead.

**4.4 Tone identification and production.**

**a.** Five words are listed below without the tones written in. (The asterisk means that the tone isn't written and it is thus not necessarily a mid tone. Whenever an actual symbol for mid tone is needed, a horizontal line can be used. For example, the tone on the toneless **dii* can be written thus: *dīī*.)

| | | |
|---|---|---|
| Fish | *plaa | ............ |
| Chicken | *kay | ............ |
| Pork | *muu | ............ |
| Shrimps | *kuŋ | ............ |
| Beef | *nɯa | ............ |

The teacher should say each word once, allowing time for the student to write in the tone if he can identify it. Then the teacher should say each word twice, and then three times, and so on until the student has identified all of the tones. The student should wait until he is perfectly sure of the tone before writing it: he should never guess. After identifying a tone correctly, he should write after the word the number of repetitions it took. If he is still unsure after ten repetitions, he should mark it wrong. This exercise is continued throughout the book. The student can keep track of his progress in identifying each tone by comparing the number of repetitions it takes him to identify it as he proceeds through the book. Needless to say, the exercise is ruined if the student prepares in advance by looking ahead to find a word's tone. And if the student happens to already know the word, he should disregard it as a measure of his progress.

ข.

น้ำ
หน้า
หนา

น้ำ หน้า น้ำ หน้า น้ำ    หน้า น้ำ หน้า น้ำ หน้า
น้ำ หนา น้ำ หนา น้ำ    หนา น้ำ หนา น้ำ หนา

## ๔.๕ แบบฝึกหัดการสลับเสียงสูงต่ำ

ก.

ไม่ร้อนเลย (สูง)
ไม่สูงเลย (ใหญ่)
ไม่ใหญ่เลย (อ้วน)
ไม่อ้วนเลย (ยาว)
ไม่ยาวเลย (ร้อน)

ข.

ไม่สั้นหรือ
ฮึ่ม, ไม่สั้นเลย

ไม่เย็นหรือ
ฮึ่ม, ไม่เย็นเลย

ไม่ผอมหรือ
ฮึ่ม, ไม่ผอมเลย

ไม่ร้อนหรือ
ฮึ่ม, ไม่ร้อนเลย

ไม่ใหญ่หรือ
ฮึ่ม, ไม่ใหญ่เลย

ไม่ดีหรือ
ฮึ่ม, ไม่ดีเลย

ไม่เตี้ยหรือ
ฮึ่ม, ไม่เตี้ยเลย

ไม่สูงหรือ
ฮึ่ม, ไม่สูงเลย

ไม่ยาวหรือ
ฮึ่ม, ไม่ยาวเลย

ไม่เล็กหรือ
ฮึ่ม, ไม่เล็กเลย

ไม่อ้วนหรือ
ฮึ่ม, ไม่อ้วนเลย

**b. Tone contrast drill.**

| | | |
|---|---|---|
| náa | Mother's younger brother or sister (aunt, uncle). | High. |
| nâa | Face. | Failing. |
| nǎa | Thick. | Rising. |

náa nâa náa nâa náa      nâa náa nâa náa nâa
náa nǎa náa nǎa náa      nǎa náa nǎa náa nǎa

**4.5 Tone manipulation.**

**a. Substitution drill.** (First practice saying: ləələələy ləələy ləələy.)

| | |
|---|---|
| mây rɔ́ɔn ləəy. (sǔuŋ) | It isn't hot at all. (tall) |
| mây sǔuŋ ləəy. (yày) | It isn't tall at all. (big) |
| mây yày ləəy. (ʔûan) | It isn't big at all. (fat) |
| mây ʔûan ləəy. (yaaw) | It isn't fat at all. (long) |
| mây yaaw ləəy. (rɔ́ɔn) | It isn't long at all. (hot) |

**b. Response drill.**

| | |
|---|---|
| mây sân lɔ̌ə. | Am I right in assuming that it isn't short in length? |
| hm̂m. mây sân ləəy. | You are right. It isn't short at all. |
| mây yen lɔ̌ə. | Isn't it cold? |
| hm̂m. mây yen ləəy. | No. It isn't cold at all. |
| mây phɔ̌ɔm lɔ̌ə. | Isn't it thin? |
| hm̂m. mây phɔ̌ɔm ləəy. | No. It isn't thin at all. |
| mây rɔ́ɔn lɔ̌ə. | Isn't it hot? |
| hm̂m. mây rɔ́ɔn ləəy. | No. It isn't hot at all. |
| mây yày lɔ̌ə. | Isn't it big? |
| hm̂m. mây yày ləəy. | No. It isn't big at all. |
| mây dii lɔ̌ə. | Isn't it good? |
| hm̂m. mây dii ləəy. | No. It isn't good at all. |
| mây tîa lɔ̌ə. | Isn't it short in height? |
| hm̂m. mây tîa ləəy. | No. It isn't short at all. |
| mây sǔuŋ lɔ̌ə. | Isn't it tall? |
| hm̂m. mây sǔuŋ ləəy. | No. It isn't tall at all. |
| mây yaaw lɔ̌ə. | Isn't it long? |
| hm̂m. mây yaaw ləəy. | No. It isn't long at all. |
| mây lék lɔ̌ə. | Isn't it little? |
| hm̂m. mây lék ləəy. | No. It isn't little at all. |
| mây ʔûan lɔ̌ə. | Isn't it fat? |
| hm̂m. mây ʔûan ləəy. | No. It isn't fat at all. |

## ๔.๖ แบบฝึกหัดการออกเสียงสระและพยัญชนะ

ก.

เอ–เออ–เอ–เออ–เอ–เออ–เอ–เออ–เอ
โอ–เออ–โอ–เออ–โอ–เออ–โอ–เออ–โอ
เอ–เออ–โอ–เออ–เอ–เออ–โอ–เออ–เอ
โอ–เออ–เอ–เออ–โอ–เออ–เอ–เออ–โอ

## ๔.๗ แบบฝึกหัดไวยากรณ์

ก.

| | |
|---|---|
| คุณครับ | (คะ) |
| คุณคะ | (หนู) |
| หนูจ๊ะ | (ครับ) |
| คุณครับ | (หนู) |
| หนูจ๊ะ | (คะ) |
| คุณคะ | (ครับ) |

ข.

| | |
|---|---|
| อยู่ทางซ้าย | (ทางขวา) |
| อยู่ทางขวา | (ตรงไป) |
| อยู่ตรงไป | (ข้างหน้า) |
| อยู่ข้างหน้า | (ข้างหลัง) |
| อยู่ข้างหลัง | (ข้างขวา) |
| อยู่ข้างขวา | (ข้างซ้าย) |
| อยู่ข้างซ้าย | (ตรงไปข้างหน้า) |
| อยู่ตรงไปข้างหน้า | (ทางไหน) |
| อยู่ทางไหน | (ข้างไหน) |
| อยู่ข้างไหน | |

**4.6 Vowel and consonant drills.**

**a. əə compared with ee and oo.**

Practice the following alternations, noting that the lips do not move.

ee–əə–ee–əə–ee–əə–ee–əə–ee

Now practice the following, noting that the tongue doesn't move.

oo–əə–oo–əə–oo–əə–oo–əə–oo

Practice the following alternations many times with increasing speed.

ee–əə–oo–əə–ee–əə–oo–əə–ee

oo–əə–ee–əə–oo–əə–ee–əə–oo

**b. The initial consonant ŋ.**

Practice emphasizing, prolonging, and shifting the English sound *ng* as suggested below. Then compare this with the Thai word that follows.

coming on
coming–ng–ng–ng–on
coming--------ngon
coming ngon
come ngon
tham ŋaan

**4.7 Grammar drills.**

**a. Substitution drill.** (Don't worry about the 'translations'.)

| | |
|---|---|
| khun khráp. (khá) | I say there! |
| khun khá. (nǔu) | Excuse me! |
| nǔu cá. (khráp) | Hey, Sonny! |
| khun khráp. (nǔu) | Sir? Lady? |
| nǔu cá. (khá) | Hey, Kid! |
| khun khá. (khráp) | Mister? Ma'am? |

**b. Substitution drill.**

| | |
|---|---|
| yùu thaaŋ sáay. (thaaŋ khwǎa) | It's to the left. (to the right) |
| yùu thaaŋ khwǎa. (troŋ pay) | It's to the right. (straight on) |
| yùu troŋ pay. (khâŋ nâa) | It's straight on. (in front) |
| yùu khâŋ nâa. (khâŋ lǎŋ) | It's in front. (in back) |
| yùu khâŋ lǎŋ. (khâŋ khwǎa) | It's in back. (on the right) |
| yùu khâŋ khwǎa. (khâŋ sáay) | It's on the right. (on the left) |
| yùu khâŋ sáay. (troŋ pay khâŋ nâa) | It's on the left. (straight ahead) |
| yùu troŋ pay khâŋ nâa. (thaaŋ nǎy) | It's straight ahead. (which way) |
| yùu thaaŋ nǎy. (khâŋ nǎy) | Which way is it? (which side) |
| yùu khâŋ nǎy. | Which side is it on? |

ค.

แล้วโรงแรมล่ะ (ตลาด)
แล้วตลาดล่ะ (ร้านตัดผม)
แล้วร้านตัดผมล่ะ (ห้อง)
แล้วห้องล่ะ (คุณสวัสดิ์)
แล้วคุณสวัสดิ์ล่ะ (เขา)
แล้วเขาล่ะ (คุณยัง)
แล้วคุณยังล่ะ

ง.

ตลาดอยู่ทางขวา (ซ้าย)
ตลาดอยู่ทางซ้าย (ตรงไป)
ตลาดอยู่ตรงไป (โรงแรม)
โรงแรมอยู่ตรงไป (ซ้าย)
โรงแรมอยู่ทางซ้าย (ขวา)
โรงแรมอยู่ทางขวา (ร้าน)
ร้านอยู่ทางขวา (ตรงไป)
ร้านอยู่ตรงไป (ซ้าย)
ร้านอยู่ทางซ้าย (ห้องอาหาร)
ห้องอาหารอยู่ทางซ้าย

จ.

ร้านอาหารอยู่ที่ไหน (ซ้าย)
ร้านอาหารอยู่ทางซ้าย

โรงแรมอยู่ที่ไหน (ขวา)
โรงแรมอยู่ทางขวา

ตลาดอยู่ที่ไหน (ตรงไป)
ตลาดอยู่ตรงไป

ร้านตัดผมอยู่ที่ไหน (ซ้าย)
ร้านตัดผมอยู่ทางซ้าย

ห้องอาหารอยู่ที่ไหน (ขวา)
ห้องอาหารอยู่ทางขวา

ร้านอาหารนิคอยู่ที่ไหน (ตรงไป)
ร้านอาหารนิคอยู่ตรงไป

c. **Substitution drill.**

| | |
|---|---|
| léew rooŋreem lâ. (talàat) | And how about the hotel? (market) |
| léew talàat lâ. (ráan tàt phǒm) | And how about the market? (barber shop) |
| léew ráan tàt phǒm lâ. (hɔ̂ŋ) | And how about the barber shop? (room) |
| léew hɔ̂ŋ lâ. (khun sawàt) | And how about the room? (Khun Sawat) |
| léew khun sawàt lâ. (kháw) | And how about Khun Sawat? (him) |
| léew kháw lâ. (khun yaŋ) | And how about him? (Mr. Young) |
| léew khun yaŋ lâ. | And how about Mr. Young? |

d. **Substitution drill.**

| | |
|---|---|
| talàat yùu thaaŋ khwǎa. (sáay) | The market is to the right. (left) |
| talàat yùu thaaŋ sáay. (troŋ pay) | The market is to the left. (straight on) |
| talàat yùu troŋ pay. (rooŋreem) | The market is straight on. (hotel) |
| rooŋreem yùu troŋ pay. (sáay) | The hotel is straight on. (left) |
| rooŋreem yùu thaaŋ sáay. (khwǎa) | The hotel is to the left. (right) |
| rooŋreem yùu thaaŋ khwǎa. (ráan) | The hotel is to the right. (shop) |
| ráan yùu thaaŋ khwǎa. (troŋ pay) | The shop is to the right. (straight on) |
| ráan yùu troŋ pay. (sáay) | The shop is straight on. (left) |
| ráan yùu thaaŋ sáay. (hɔ̂ŋ ʔaahǎan) | The shop is to the left. (dining room) |
| hɔ̂ŋ ʔaahǎan yùu thaaŋ sáay. | The dining room is to the left. |

e. **Response drill.**

| | |
|---|---|
| ráan ʔaahǎan yùu thîi nǎy. (sáay) | Where's the restaurant? (left) |
| ráan ʔaahǎan yùu thaaŋ sáay. | The restaurant's to the left. |
| rooŋreem yùu thîi nǎy. (khwǎa) | Where's the hotel? (right) |
| rooŋreem yùu thaaŋ khwǎa. | The hotel is to the right. |
| talàat yùu thîi nǎy. (troŋ pay) | Where's the market? (straight on) |
| talàat yùu troŋ pay. | The market is straight on. |
| ráan tàt phǒm yùu thîi nǎy. (sáay) | Where's the barber shop? (left) |
| ráan tàt phǒm yùu thaaŋ sáay. | The barber shop's to the left. |
| hɔ̂ŋ ʔaahǎan yùu thîi nǎy. (khwǎa) | Where's the dining room? (right) |
| hɔ̂ŋ ʔaahǎan yùu thaaŋ khwǎa. | The dining room's to the right. |
| ráan ʔaahǎan ník yùu thîi nǎy. (troŋ pay) | Where's Nick's Restaurant? (straight on) |
| ráan ʔaahǎan ník yùu troŋ pay. | Nick's Restaurant is straight on. |

### ๔.๘ เลข

| | |
|---|---|
| สิบคน | สิบห้าคน |
| สิบเอ็ดคน | สิบหกคน |
| สิบสองคน | สิบเจ็ดคน |
| สิบสามคน | สิบแปดคน |
| สิบสี่คน | สิบเก้าคน |

| | | | | |
|---|---|---|---|---|
| ๑๕ คน | ๑๙ คน | ๑๖ คน | ๑๗ คน | ๑๒ คน |
| ๑๗ คน | ๑๔ คน | ๑๐ คน | ๑๖ คน | ๑๘ คน |
| ๑๑ คน | ๑๘ คน | ๑๕ คน | ๑๑ คน | ๑๓ คน |
| ๑๒ คน | ๑๓ คน | ๑๙ คน | ๑๔ คน | ๑๐ คน |

### ๔.๙ การสนทนาโต้ตอบ

ก.

| | | | |
|---|---|---|---|
| ผอมไหมคะ | ผอมครับ, ผอมมาก | เตี้ยไหมคะ | เตี้ยครับ, เตี้ยมาก |
| อ้วนไหมคะ | ไม่อ้วนครับ, ไม่อ้วนเลย | สูงไหมคะ | ไม่สูงครับ, ไม่สูงเลย |
| อ้วนไหมคะ | อ้วนครับ, อ้วนมาก | ร้อนไหมคะ | ร้อนครับ, ร้อนมาก |
| ผอมไหมคะ | ไม่ผอมครับ, ไม่ผอมเลย | เย็นไหมคะ | ไม่เย็นครับ, ไม่เย็นเลย |
| ใหญ่ไหมคะ | ใหญ่ครับ, ใหญ่มาก | เย็นไหมคะ | เย็นครับ, เย็นมาก |
| เล็กไหมคะ | ไม่เล็กครับ, ไม่เล็กเลย | ร้อนไหมครับ | ไม่ร้อนครับ, ไม่ร้อนเลย |
| เล็กไหมคะ | เล็กครับ, เล็กมาก | ยาวไหมคะ | ยาวครับ, ยาวมาก |
| ใหญ่ไหมคะ | ไม่ใหญ่ครับ, ไม่ใหญ่เลย | สั้นไหมคะ | ไม่สั้นครับ, ไม่สั้นเลย |
| สูงไหมคะ | สูงครับ, สูงมาก | สั้นไหมคะ | สั้นครับ, สั้นมาก |
| เตี้ยไหมคะ | ไม่เตี้ยครับ, ไม่เตี้ยเลย | ยาวไหมคะ | ไม่ยาวครับ, ไม่ยาวเลย |

### 4.8 Numbers.

Numbers are rarely used alone in Thai. They are usually accompanied by the units they are being used to count.

| | | | |
|---|---|---|---|
| sìp khon | 10 people. | sìp hâa khon | 15 people. |
| sìp ʔèt khon | 11 people. | sìp hòk khon | 16 people. |
| sìp sɔ̌ɔŋ khon | 12 people. | sìp cèt khon | 17 people. |
| sìp sǎam khon | 13 people. | sìp pɛ̀ɛt khon | 18 people. |
| sìp sìi khon | 14 people. | sìp kâaw khon | 19 people. |

Practice reading the following numbers of people at home. Try to get the time under 20 seconds. Be especially careful with the tones.

| | | | | |
|---|---|---|---|---|
| 15 khon | 19 khon | 16 khon | 17 khon | 12 khon |
| 17 khon | 14 khon | 10 khon | 16 khon | 18 khon |
| 11 khon | 18 khon | 15 khon | 11 khon | 13 khon |
| 12 khon | 13 khon | 19 khon | 14 khon | 10 khon |

### 4.9 Conversation.

**a.** The teacher should draw pictures like those below on the blackboard and ask the following questions as she points at them.

| | |
|---|---|
|  phɔ̌ɔm máy khá.<br>ʔûan máy khá. | phɔ̌ɔm khráp. phɔ̌ɔm mâak.<br>mây ʔûan khráp. mây ʔûan lɔɔy. |
|  ʔûan máy khá.<br>phɔ̌ɔm máy khá. | ʔûan khráp. ʔûan mâak.<br>mây phɔ̌ɔm khráp. mây phɔ̌ɔm lɔɔy. |
|  yày máy khá.<br>lék máy khá. | yày khráp. yày mâak.<br>mây lék khráp. mây lék lɔɔy. |
| lék máy khá.<br>yày máy khá. | lék khráp. lék mâak.<br>mây yày khráp. mây yày lɔɔy. |
|  sǔuŋ máy khá.<br>tîa máy khá. | sǔuŋ khráp. sǔuŋ mâak.<br>mây tîa khráp. mây tîa lɔɔy. |
|  tîa máy khá.<br>sǔuŋ máy khá. | tîa khráp. tîa mâak.<br>mây sǔuŋ khráp. mây sǔuŋ lɔɔy. |
|  rɔ́ɔn máy khá.<br>yen máy khá. | rɔ́ɔn khráp. rɔ́ɔn mâak.<br>mây yen khráp mây yen lɔɔy. |
|  yen máy khá.<br>rɔ́ɔn máy khá. | yen khráp. yen mâak.<br>mây rɔ́ɔn khráp. mây rɔ́ɔn lɔɔy. |
|  yaaw máy khá.<br>sân máy khá. | yaaw khráp. yaaw mâak.<br>mây sân khráp. mây sân lɔɔy. |
|  sân máy khá.<br>yaaw máy khá. | sân khráp. sân mâak.<br>mây yaaw khráp. mây yaaw lɔɔy. |

**ข.**

คุณคะ

..............................อยู่ที่ไหนคะ

อยู่........................ครับ

แล้ว........................ล่ะคะ
อยู่ที่ไหน

..........................อยู่........................ครับ

## ๔.๑๐ การเขียน

โรงแรม

| | | |
|---|---|---|
| โรง | ผาน | โผ |
| โดง | ผน | โร |
| แดง | คน | แร |
| แสง | คม | แรม |
| สอง | คึม | แผม |
| สอน | คี | ผม |
| สาน | ดี | ดม |
| คาน | ผี | ดอม |

**b.** Practice the conversation suggested below. Ask about any of the pairs of people or places and answer with either of the pairs of locations.

| | |
|---|---|
| khun khá. | Khun Sawat, Mr. Young. |
| ......................yùu thîi nǎy khá. | The restaurant, the hotel. |
| yùu......................khráp. | The barber shop, the market. |
| léɛw......................la khá. | Here, over there. |
| yùu thîi nǎy. | To the right, to the left. |
| ......................yùu..................khráp. | |

**4.10 Writing.**

# โรงแรม

rooŋ reɛm
Hotel.

| | | | | | |
|---|---|---|---|---|---|
| โรง | *rooŋ | ผาน | phǎan | โผ | phǒo |
| โดง | dooŋ | ผน | phǒn | โร | roo |
| แดง | dɛɛŋ | คน | *khon | แร | rɛɛ |
| แสง | sɛ̌ɛŋ | คม | khom | แรม | *rɛɛm |
| สอง | *sɔ̌ɔŋ | คืม | khɨɨm | แผม | phɛ̌ɛm |
| สอน | sɔ̌ɔn | คี | khii | ผม | *phǒm |
| สาน | sǎan | ดี | *dii | ดม | dom |
| คาน | khaan | ผี | phǐi | ดอม | dɔɔm |

# บทที่ ๕

**ข.**

คุณสวัสดิ์อ้วน เขาอยู่ที่โรงแรม "สบาย" คุณยังผอม เขาอยู่ที่โรงแรม "สวัสดี"

คุณสวัสดิ์ตัดผมที่ร้านตัดผม "ยัง" ร้านตัดผมยังอยู่ข้างหลังโรงแรมสบาย คุณยังตัดผมที่ร้านตัดผม "สวัสดิ์" ร้านตัดผมสวัสดิ์อยู่ข้างหลังโรงแรมสวัสดี

โรงแรมสวัสดีใหญ่ โรงแรมสบายเล็ก ร้านตัดผมยังดี ร้านตัดผมสวัสดิ์ไม่ดี

# LESSON 5

### (Review)

**a.** Every fifth lesson is a review lesson. Review lessons include a narrative and sometimes a dialog, but little time need be spent on them. They are intended for passive comprehension–not active use. Most of the time should be spent reviewing sections 3, 5, 7, and 9 of the four preceding lessons. If the students have properly learned these four lessons (that is, reached the point of near-perfect performance), they are now ready for the real pay-off. Without books they quickly go through the listen and repeat steps and then practice the final step (participating in dialogs, substituting in substitution drills, and responding in response drills, all without confirmation) over and over, as their perfect performance gains speed. Of course, if they haven't learned the four lessons properly, more review time must be spent on earlier steps.

**b. Narrative.**

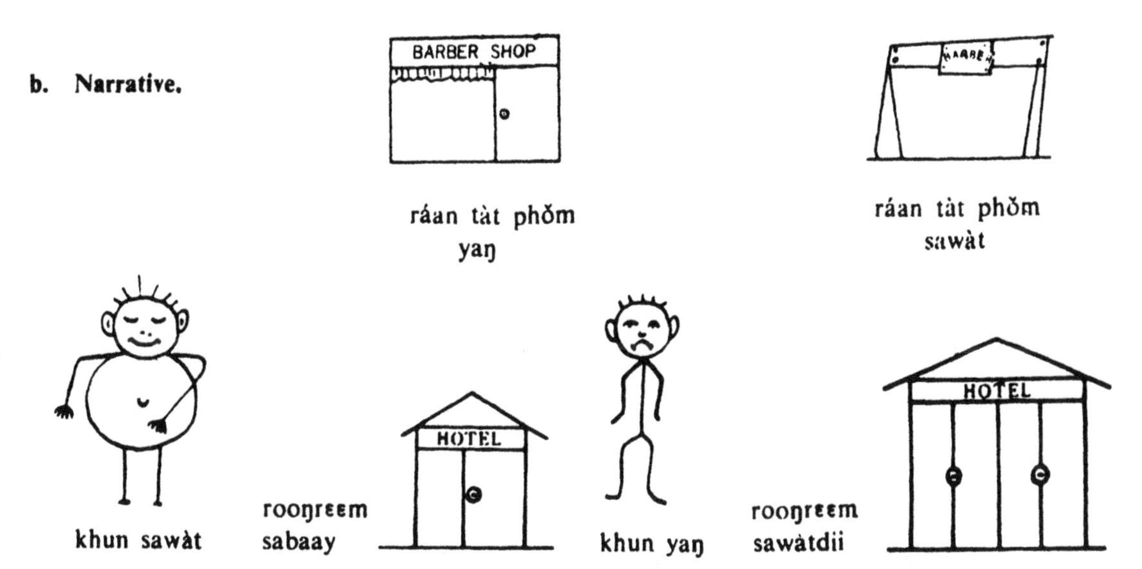


khun sawàt ʔûan. kháw yùu thîi rooŋrɛɛm 'sabaay'. khun yaŋ phɔ̌ɔm. kháw yùu thîi rooŋrɛɛm 'sawàtdii'.

khun sawàt tàt phǒm thîi ráan tàt phǒm 'yaŋ'. ráan tàt phǒm yaŋ yùu khâŋ lǎŋ rooŋrɛɛm sabaay. khun yaŋ tàt phǒm thîi ráan tàt phǒm 'sawàt'. ráan tàt phǒm sawàt yùu khâŋ lǎŋ rooŋrɛɛm sawàtdii.

rooŋrɛɛm sawàtdii yày. rooŋrɛɛm sabaay lék. ráan tàt phǒm yaŋ dii. ráan tàt phǒm sawàt mây dii.

The language student's ability to understand sentences, of course, grows much faster than his ability to produce them. You cannot be expected to produce all of the following sentences: some contain patterns of modification that you haven't had yet. But the chances are you will understand them. See how far you can get through the following four steps.

1. Read for comprehension.
2. Read the first sentence of each pair and produce the second one yourself.
3. Listen for comprehension.
4. Listen to the first sentence of each pair and produce the second one yourself.

คุณสวัสดิ์อยู่ที่โรงแรมเล็ก
คุณยังอยู่ที่โรงแรมใหญ่

คนอ้วนตัดผมที่ร้านตัดผมดี
คนผอมตัดผมที่ร้านตัดผมไม่ดี

โรงแรมเล็กอยู่ข้างหน้าร้านตัดผมดี
โรงแรมใหญ่อยู่ข้างหน้าร้านตัดผมไม่ดี

ร้านตัดผมยังอยู่ข้างหลังโรงแรมเล็ก
ร้านตัดผมสวัสดิ์อยู่ข้างหลังโรงแรมใหญ่

คนอ้วนอยู่ที่โรงแรมเล็ก
คนผอมอยู่ที่โรงแรมใหญ่

คุณสวัสดิ์ตัดผมที่ร้านตัดผมดี
คุณยังตัดผมที่ร้านตัดผมไม่ดี

ร้านตัดผมดีอยู่ข้างหลังโรงแรมสบาย
ร้านตัดผมไม่ดีอยู่ข้างหลังโรงแรมสวัสดี

โรงแรมเล็กอยู่ข้างหน้าร้านตัดผมยัง
โรงแรมใหญ่อยู่ข้างหน้าร้านตัดผมสวัสดิ์

คนอ้วนอยู่ที่โรงแรมสบาย
คนผอมอยู่ที่โรงแรมสวัสดี

ร้านตัดผมข้างหลังโรงแรมเล็กดี
ร้านตัดผมข้างหลังโรงแรมใหญ่ไม่ดี

โรงแรมสบายอยู่ข้างหน้าร้านตัดผมยัง
โรงแรมสวัสดีอยู่ข้างหน้าร้านตัดผมสวัสดิ์

คนอ้วนตัดผมที่ร้านตัดผมยัง
คนผอมตัดผมที่ร้านตัดผมสวัสดิ์

คุณสวัสดิ์อยู่ที่โรงแรมข้างหน้าร้านตัดผมดี
คุณยังอยู่ที่โรงแรมข้างหน้าร้านตัดผมไม่ดี

โรงแรมสบายอยู่ข้างหน้าร้านตัดผมดี
โรงแรมสวัสดีอยู่ข้างหน้าร้านตัดผมไม่ดี

ร้านตัดผมยังอยู่ข้างหลังโรงแรมสบาย
ร้านตัดผมสวัสดิ์อยู่ข้างหลังโรงแรมสวัสดี

คนอ้วนตัดผมที่ร้านตัดผมข้างหลังโรงแรมเล็ก
คนผอมตัดผมที่ร้านตัดผมข้างหลังโรงแรมใหญ่

คุณสวัสดิ์อยู่ที่โรงแรมข้างหน้าร้านตัดผมยัง
คุณยังอยู่ที่โรงแรมข้างหน้าร้านตัดผมสวัสดิ์

ร้านตัดผมข้างหลังโรงแรมสบายดี
ร้านตัดผมข้างหลังโรงแรมสวัสดีไม่ดี

โรงแรมข้างหน้าร้านตัดผมยังเล็ก
โรงแรมข้างหน้าร้านตัดผมสวัสดิ์ใหญ่

คุณสวัสดิ์ตัดผมที่ร้านตัดผมข้างหลังโรงแรมเล็ก
คุณยังตัดผมที่ร้านตัดผมข้างหลังโรงแรมใหญ่

คนอ้วนอยู่ที่โรงแรมข้างหน้าร้านตัดผมดี
คนผอมอยู่ที่โรงแรมข้างหน้าร้านตัดผมไม่ดี

โรงแรมข้างหน้าร้านตัดผมดีเล็ก
โรงแรมข้างหน้าร้านตัดผมไม่ดีใหญ่

khun sawàt yùu thîi rooŋrɛɛm lék.
  khun yaŋ yùu thîi rooŋrɛɛm yày.

khon ʔûan tàt phŏm thîi ráan tàt phŏm dii.
  khon phɔ̌ɔm tàt phŏm thîi ráan tàt phŏm mây dii.

rooŋrɛɛm lék yùu khâŋ nâa ráan tàt phŏm dii.
  rooŋrɛɛm yày yùu khâŋ nâa ráan tàt phŏm mây dii.

ráan tàt phŏm yaŋ yùu khâŋ lăŋ rooŋrɛɛm lék.
  ráan tàt phŏm sawàt yùu khâŋ lăŋ rooŋrɛɛm yày.

khon ʔûan yùu thîi rooŋrɛɛm lék.
  khon phɔ̌ɔm yùu thîi rooŋrɛɛm yày.

khun sawàt tàt phŏm thîi ráan tàt phŏm dii.
  khun yaŋ tàt phŏm thîi ráan tàt phŏm mây dii.

ráan tàt phŏm dii yùu khâŋ lăŋ rooŋrɛɛm sabaay.
  ráan tàt phŏm mây dii yùu khâŋ lăŋ rooŋrɛɛm sawàtdii.

rooŋrɛɛm lék yùu khâŋ nâa ráan tàt phŏm yaŋ.
  rooŋrɛɛm yày yùu khâŋ nâa ráan tàt phŏm sawàt.

khon ʔûan yùu thîi rooŋrɛɛm sabaay.
  khon phɔ̌ɔm yùu thîi rooŋrɛɛm sawàtdii.

ráan tàt phŏm khâŋ lăŋ rooŋrɛɛm lék dii.
  ráan tàt phŏm khâŋ lăŋ rooŋrɛɛm yày mây dii.

rooŋrɛɛm sabaay yùu khâŋ nâa ráan tàt phŏm yaŋ.
  rooŋrɛɛm sawàtdii yùu khâŋ nâa ráan tàt phŏm sawàt.

khon ʔûan tàt phŏm thîi ráan tàt phŏm yaŋ.
  khon phɔ̌ɔm tàt phŏm thîi ráan tàt phŏm sawàt.

khun sawàt yùu thîi rooŋrɛɛm khâŋ nâa ráan tàt phŏm dii.
  khun yaŋ yùu thîi rooŋrɛɛm khâŋ nâa ráan tàt phŏm mây dii.

rooŋrɛɛm sabaay yùu khâŋ nâa ráan tàt phŏm dii.
  rooŋrɛɛm sawàtdii yùu khâŋ nâa ráan tàt phŏm mây dii.

ráan tàt phŏm yaŋ yùu khâŋ lăŋ rooŋrɛɛm sabaay.
  ráan tàt phŏm sawàt yùu khâŋ lăŋ rooŋrɛɛm sawàtdii.

khon ʔûan tàt phŏm thîi ráan tàt phŏm khâŋ lăŋ rooŋrɛɛm lék.
  khon phɔ̌ɔm tàt phŏm thîi ráan tàt phŏm khâŋ lăŋ rooŋrɛɛm yày.

khun sawàt yùu thîi rooŋrɛɛm khâŋ nâa ráan tàt phŏm yaŋ.
  khun yaŋ yùu thîi rooŋrɛɛm khâŋ nâa ráan tàt phŏm sawàt.

ráan tàt phŏm khâŋ lăŋ rooŋrɛɛm sabaay dii.
  ráan tàt phŏm khâŋ lăŋ rooŋrɛɛm sawàtdii mây dii.

rooŋrɛɛm khâŋ nâa ráan tàt phŏm yaŋ lék.
  rooŋrɛɛm khâŋ nâa ráan tàt phŏm sawàt yày.

khun sawàt tàt phŏm thîi ráan tàt phŏm khâŋ lăŋ rooŋrɛɛm lék.
  khun yaŋ tàt phŏm thîi ráan tàt phŏm khâŋ lăŋ rooŋrɛɛm yày.

khon ʔûan yùu thîi rooŋrɛɛm khâŋ nâa ráan tàt phŏm dii.
  khon phɔ̌ɔm yùu thîi rooŋrɛɛm khâŋ nâa ráan tàt phŏm mây dii.

rooŋrɛɛm khâŋ nâa ráan tàt phŏm dii lék.
  rooŋrɛɛm khâŋ nâa ráan tàt phŏm mây dii yày.

**ค.**

ก. คุณครับ
ขอโทษ
ร้านตัดผมสวัสดิ์อยู่ที่ไหนครับ

ข. ร้านตัดผมสวัสดิ์หรือครับ
อยู่ที่โน่นครับ
ข้างหลังโรงแรมสวัสดี

ก. ดีไหมครับ

ข. ไม่ดีครับ
ไม่ดีเลย

ก. ร้านตัดผมที่ไหนดีครับ

ข. ร้านตัดผมยังดีครับ
ดีมาก

ก. อยู่ที่ไหนครับ

ข. อยู่ข้างหลังโรงแรมสบายครับ

ก. โรงแรมสบายอยู่ที่ไหนครับ

ข. อยู่ตรงไปข้างหน้าครับ

ก. ขอบคุณมากครับ

ข. ไม่เป็นไรครับ

c. **Dialog.**

A. khun khráp.
khɔ̌ɔ thôot.
ráan tàt phǒm sawàt yùu thîi nǎy khráp.

B. ráan tàt phǒm sawàt lɔ̌ə khráp.
yùu thîi nôon khráp.
khâŋ lǎŋ rooŋrɛɛm sawàtdii.

A. dii máy khráp.

B. mây dii khráp.
mây dii ləəy.

A. ráan tàt phǒm thîi nǎy dii khráp.

B. ráan tàt phǒm yaŋ dii khráp.
dii mâak.

A. yùu thîi nǎy khráp.

B. yùu khâŋ lǎŋ rooŋrɛɛm sabaay khráp.

A. rooŋrɛɛm sabaay yùu thîi nǎy khráp.

B. yùu troŋ pay khâŋ nâa khráp.

A. khɔ̀ɔpkhun mâak khráp.

B. mây pen ray khráp.

# บทที่ ๖

## ๖.๑ คำศัพท์

คุณ

หนู

รู้

จัก

รู้จัก

เอ

วัน

เอราวัณ

โรงแรมเอราวัณ

เดิน

นี้

ทางนี้

นั้น

โน้น

ทางโน้น

ถึง

แยก

สี่แยก

ถึงสี่แยก

เลี้ยว

แล้วเลี้ยว

แล้วเลี้ยวขวา

ควาย

วัว

กว่า

อะไร

กัน

ยี่

กับ

# LESSON 6

**6.1 Vocabulary and expansions.**

| | |
|---|---|
| khun<br>nǔu | The second person (you) in Thai presents a real problem for western learners. Titles, relationship terms, names, and combinations of these are used instead of pronouns. For example, when speaking to his brother named John, the speaker might use John, Brother, Mister, Mr. Brother, or Brother John in place of *you.* And the relationship terms are not restricted to one's relations. For example, when speaking to any woman a generation older than himself, the speaker might call her Auntie, or Mrs. Auntie. The term that is used depends on the social relationship, the situation, the speaker's mood, and many other things. The student is advised to start out using the most general title *khun* with strangers, *nǔu* with children, and the person's name with known inferiors (one's servants) and intimates. The rest will come later. Omit all pronouns and similar terms, however, when they are unnecessary to the meaning. For example, the parenthesized parts of the following sentences would rarely appear in Thai. 'Where (are you) going?' '(I'm) going home'. |
| rúu | |
| càk | |
| rúucàk | To know a person, place, or thing (that is, to be acquainted with). |
| ʔee | |
| wan | |
| ʔeerawan | Erawan. |
| rooŋrɛɛm ʔeerawan | The Erawan Hotel. |
| dəən | To walk. |
| níi | This (adjective). |
| thaaŋ níi | This way. |
| nán | That, the one mentioned (adjective). |
| nân | That, the one mentioned (noun). |
| nóon | That (farther away than *nán*). |
| thaaŋ nóon | That over there. |
| thǔŋ | To arrive at, reach. |
| yɛ̂ɛk | To fork, separate. |
| sìiyɛ̂ɛk | Intersection (four forks). |
| thǔŋ sìiyɛ̂ɛk | To arrive at the intersection. |
| líaw | To turn. |
| lɛ́ɛw líaw | Then turn. |
| lɛ́ɛw líaw khwǎa | Then turn right. |
| khwaay | Water buffalo. |
| wua | Cattle, cow, bull. |
| kwàa | More (than), -er (than). |
| ʔaray | What? |
| kan | The other, each other, mutually. |
| yîi | Two (used only for the twenties). |
| kàp, ka | With, and. |

### ๖.๒ โครงสร้างของประโยค

| | |
|---|---|
| รู้จักคุณสวัสดิ์ | ถึงสี่แยก |
| รู้จักคุณยัง | ถึงโรงแรม |
| รู้จักโรงแรมเอราวัณ | ถึงตลาด |
| ที่นี่ | แล้วเลี้ยวขวา |
| ที่นั่น | แล้วเลี้ยวซ้าย |
| ที่โน่น | แล้วตรงไป |
| ทางนี้ | ใหญ่กว่า |
| ทางนั้น | สูงกว่า |
| ทางโน้น | ร้อนกว่า |
| คนนี้ | ใหญ่กว่านี่ |
| คนนั้น | ใหญ่กว่านั่น |
| คนโน้น | ใหญ่กว่ากัน |

### ๖.๓ บทสนทนา

ก. คุณรู้จักโรงแรมเอราวัณไหม

ข. รู้จัก

ก. ไปทางไหน

ข. เดินตรงไปทางนี้ ถึงสี่แยกแล้วเลี้ยวขวา โรงแรมอยู่ทางซ้าย

ก. ขอบคุณมาก

ข. ไม่เป็นไร

### ๖.๔ แบบฝึกหัดการฟังและการออกเสียงสูงต่ำ

ก.

มี ชอบ เห็น ใส่ ซื้อ

**6.2 Patterns.**

| | |
|---|---|
| rúucàk khun sawàt | To know Khun Sawat. |
| rúucàk khun yaŋ | To know Mr. Young. |
| rúucàk rooŋrɛɛm ʔeerawan | To know the Erawan Hotel. |
| thîi nîi | Here. |
| thîi nân | There, at the stated place. |
| thîi nôon | Yonder. |
| thaaŋ níi | This way. |
| thaaŋ nán | That way, the aforesaid way. |
| thaaŋ nóon | That way over there. |
| khon níi | This person. |
| khon nán | That person, the aforesaid person. |
| khon nóon | That person over there. |
| thʉ̌ŋ siiyɛ̂ɛk | To get to the intersection. |
| thʉ̌ŋ rooŋrɛɛm | To get to the hotel. |
| thʉ̌ŋ talàat | To get to the market |
| lɛ́ɛw líaw khwǎa | Then turn right. |
| lɛ́ɛw líaw sáay | Then turn left. |
| lɛ́ɛw troŋ pay | Then go straight ahead. |
| yày kwàa | Bigger. |
| sǔuŋ kwàa | Taller. |
| rɔ́ɔn kwàa | Hotter. |
| yày kwàa nîi | Bigger than this. |
| yày kwàa nân | Bigger than that. |
| yày kwàa kan | Bigger than the other. |

**6.3. Dialog.**

| | | |
|---|---|---|
| A. | **khun rúucàk rooŋrɛɛm ʔeerawan máy.** | Do you know the Erawan Hotel? |
| B. | **rúucàk.** | Yes. |
| A. | **pay thaaŋ nǎy.** | Which way does one go? |
| B. | **dəən troŋ pay thaaŋ níi.**<br>thʉ̌ŋ siiyɛ̂ɛk lɛ́ɛw líaw khwǎa.<br>rooŋrɛɛm yùu thaaŋ sáay. | Walk straight along this way.<br>When you get to the corner, turn right.<br>The hotel is on the left. |
| A. | khɔ̀ɔpkhun mâak. | Thank you very much. |
| B. | mây pen ray. | Not at all. |

**6.4 Tone identification and production.**

**a.** Identify the tones and record the number of repetitions required.

| | | |
|---|---|---|
| To have , there is. | *mii | ........... |
| To like. | *chɔɔp | ........... |
| To see. | *hen | ........... |
| To put in or on. | *say | ........... |
| To buy. | *sʉʉ | ........... |

**ข.**

ไก่ ไก่ ไก่ ไก่ ไก่ ปลา ปลา ปลา ปลา ปลา เนื้อ เนื้อ เนื้อ เนื้อ เนื้อ

เห็น เห็น เห็น เห็น เห็น กุ้ง กุ้ง กุ้ง กุ้ง กุ้ง

## ๖.๕ แบบฝึกหัดการสลับเสียงสูงต่ำ

**ก.**

| | | | |
|---|---|---|---|
| ควายใหญ่กว่าวัว | (สูง) | วัวเล็กกว่าควาย | (ผอม) |
| ควายสูงกว่าวัว | (อ้วน) | วัวผอมกว่าควาย | (เตี้ย) |
| ควายอ้วนกว่าวัว | (เล็ก) | วัวเตี้ยกว่าควาย | (ใหญ่) |

**ข.**

อะไรใหญ่กว่ากัน
ควายใหญ่กว่าวัว

อะไรเล็กกว่ากัน
วัวเล็กกว่าควาย

อะไรอ้วนกว่ากัน
ควายอ้วนกว่าวัว

อะไรผอมกว่ากัน
วัวผอมกว่าควาย

อะไรสูงกว่ากัน
ควายสูงกว่าวัว

อะไรเตี้ยกว่ากัน
วัวเตี้ยกว่าควาย

## ๖.๖ แบบฝึกหัดการออกเสียงสระและพยัญชนะ

**ก.**

อี อือ อี อือ อี อือ อี อือ อี

อู อือ อู อือ อู อือ อู อือ อู

อี อือ อู อือ อี อือ อู อือ อี

อู อือ อี อือ อู อือ อี อือ อู

**ข.**

นาน นาน นาน นาง นาง นาง งาง งาง งาง งาน งาน งาน

**b. Tone speed drill.**

Practice saying the following with gradual increase in speed. The rising and falling tones will require the most practice.

kày kày kày kày kày  plaa plaa plaa plaa plaa  nɯ̀a nɯ̀a nɯ̀a nɯ̀a nɯ̀a
hěn hěn hěn hěn hěn  kûŋ kûŋ kûŋ kûŋ kûŋ

**6.5 Tone manipulation.**

**a. Substitution drill.**

| | | | |
|---|---|---|---|
| khwaay yày kwàa wua. | (sǔuŋ) | Buffalos are bigger than cows. | (tall) |
| khwaay sǔuŋ kwàa wua. | (ʔûan) | Buffalos are taller than cows. | (fat) |
| khwaay ʔûan kwàa wua. | (lék) | Buffalos are fatter than cows. | (small) |
| wua lék kwàa khwaay. | (phɔ̌ɔm) | Cows are smaller than buffalos. | (thin) |
| wua phɔ̌ɔm kwàa khwaay. | (tîa) | Cows are thinner than buffalos. | (short) |
| wua tîa kwàa khwaay. | (yày) | Cows are shorter than buffalos. | (big) |

**b. Response drill.**

ʔaray yày kwàa kan. — Which is bigger?
khwaay yày kwàa wua. — The buffalo is bigger than the cow.

ʔaray ʔûan kwàa kan. — Which is fatter?
khwaay ʔûan kwàa wua. — The buffalo is fatter than the cow.

ʔaray sǔuŋ kwàa kan. — Which is taller?
khwaay sǔuŋ kwàa wua. — The buffalo is taller than the cow.

ʔaray lék kwàa kan. — Which is smaller?
wua lék kwàa khwaay. — The cow is smaller than the buffalo.

ʔaray phɔ̌ɔm kwàa kan. — Which is thinner?
wua phɔ̌ɔm kwàa khwaay. — The cow is thinner than the buffalo.

ʔaray tîa kwàa kan. — Which is shorter?
wua tîa kwàa khwaay. — The cow is shorter than the buffalo.

**6.6 Vowel and consonant drills.**

**a. ɯɯ compared with ii and uu.**

Practice the following alternations, noting that the lips do not move.

ii-ɯɯ-ii-ɯɯ-ii-ɯɯ-ii-ɯɯ-ii

Now practice the following, noting that the tongue does not move.

uu-ɯɯ-uu-ɯɯ-uu-ɯɯ-uu-ɯɯ-uu

Practice the following alternations many times with increasing speed.

ii-ɯɯ-uu-ɯɯ-ii-ɯɯ-uu-ɯɯ-ii

uu-ɯɯ-ii-ɯɯ-uu-ɯɯ-ii-ɯɯ-uu

**b. ŋ speed drill.**

Practice saying the following with gradual increase in speed.

**naan naan naan  naaŋ naaŋ naaŋ  ŋaaŋ ŋaaŋ ŋaaŋ  ŋaan ŋaan ŋaan**

## ๖.๗ แบบฝึกหัดไวยากรณ์

**ก.**

| | |
|---|---|
| รู้จักโรงแรมเอราวัณไหม | (ร้านอาหารนิค) |
| รู้จักร้านอาหารนิคไหม | (คุณสวัสดิ์) |
| รู้จักคุณสวัสดิ์ไหม | (ร้านตัดผมสวัสดิ์) |
| รู้จักร้านตัดผมสวัสดิ์ไหม | (คุณยัง) |
| รู้จักคุณยังไหม | (โรงแรมเอราวัณ) |

**ข.**

| | |
|---|---|
| ถึงสี่แยกแล้วเลี้ยวซ้าย | (เลี้ยวขวา) |
| ถึงสี่แยกแล้วเลี้ยวขวา | (ตรงไป) |
| ถึงสี่แยกแล้วตรงไป | (ตลาด) |
| ถึงตลาดแล้วตรงไป | (เลี้ยวซ้าย) |
| ถึงตลาดแล้วเลี้ยวซ้าย | (โรงแรม) |
| ถึงโรงแรมแล้วเลี้ยวซ้าย | (เลี้ยวขวา) |
| ถึงโรงแรมแล้วเลี้ยวขวา | |

**ค.**

คนที่นี่

คนนี้

คนนี้

คนที่นี่

คนที่นั่น

คนนั้น

คนนั้น

คนที่นั่น

คนที่โน่น

คนโน้น

คนโน้น

คนที่โน่น

## 6.7 Grammar drills.

### a. Substitution drill.

| | |
|---|---|
| rúucàk rooŋrɛɛm ʔeerawan máy.<br>(ráan ʔaahǎan ník) | Do you know the Erawan Hotel?<br>(Nick's Restaurant) |
| rúucàk ráan ʔaahǎan ník máy.<br>(khun sawàt) | Do you know Nick's Restaurant?<br>(Khun Sawat) |
| rúucàk khun sawàt máy.<br>(ráan tàt phǒm sawàt) | Do you know Khun Sawat?<br>(Sawat's Barber Shop) |
| rúucàk ráan tàt phǒm sawàt máy.<br>(khun yaŋ) | Do you know Sawat's Barber Shop?<br>(Mr. Young) |
| rúucàk khun yaŋ máy.<br>(rooŋrɛɛm ʔeerawan) | Do you know Mr. Young?<br>(Erawan Hotel) |

### b. Substitution drill.

| | |
|---|---|
| thǔŋ sìiyɛ́ɛk lɛ́ɛw líaw sáay.<br>(líaw khwǎa) | Turn left when you get to the corner.<br>(turn right) |
| thǔŋ sìiyɛ̂ɛk lɛ́ɛw líaw khwǎa.<br>(troŋ pay) | Turn right when you get to the corner.<br>(go straight ahead) |
| thǔŋ sìiyɛ̂ɛk lɛ́ɛw troŋ pay.<br>(talàat) | Go straight on when you get to the corner.<br>(the market) |
| thǔŋ talàat lɛ́ɛw troŋ pay.<br>(líaw sáay) | Go straight on when you get to the market.<br>(turn left) |
| thǔŋ talàat lɛ́ɛw líaw sáay.<br>(rooŋrɛɛm) | Turn left when you get to the market.<br>(the hotel) |
| thǔŋ rooŋrɛɛm lɛ́ɛw líaw sáay.<br>(líaw khwǎa) | Turn left when you get to the hotel.<br>(turn right) |
| thǔŋ roonrɛɛm lɛ́ɛw líaw khwǎa. | Turn right when you get to the hotel. |

### c. Transformation drill. (To be drilled just like a response drill.)

| | |
|---|---|
| khon thîi nîi. | The person here. |
| khon níi. | This person. |
| khon thîi nân. | The person there. |
| khon nán. | That person. |
| khon thîi nôon. | The person over there. |
| khon nóon. | That person (yonder person). |
| khon níi. | This person. |
| khon thîi nîi. | The person here. |
| khon nán. | That person. |
| khon thîi nân. | The person there. |
| khon nóon. | That person (yonder person). |
| khon thîi nôon. | The person over there. |

ง.

ไปทางไหน (นี้)

ไปทางนี้

ไปทางไหน (ขวา)

ไปทางขวา

ไปทางไหน (โน้น)

ไปทางโน้น

ไปทางไหน (ซ้าย)

ไปทางซ้าย

## ๖.๘ เลข

| | | | |
|---|---|---|---|
| ยี่สิบคน | ยี่สิบห้าคน | สามสิบคน | สามสิบห้าคน |
| ยี่สิบเอ็ดคน | ยี่สิบหกคน | สามสิบเอ็ดคน | สามสิบหกคน |
| ยี่สิบสองคน | ยี่สิบเจ็ดคน | สามสิบสองคน | สามสิบเจ็ดคน |
| ยี่สิบสามคน | ยี่สิบแปดคน | สามสิบสามคน | สามสิบแปดคน |
| ยี่สิบสี่คน | ยี่สิบเก้าคน | สามสิบสี่คน | สามสิบเก้าคน |

| | | | | | |
|---|---|---|---|---|---|
| ๓๐ คน | ๓๖ คน | ๑๘ คน | ๑๗ คน | ๓๗ คน | ๓๔ คน |
| ๑๒ คน | ๒๐ คน | ๒๑ คน | ๓๑ คน | ๓๒ คน | ๒๘ คน |
| ๒๕ คน | ๓๙ คน | ๒๔ คน | ๓๕ คน | ๒๖ คน | ๓๘ คน |
| ๒๗ คน | ๒๒ คน | ๓๓ คน | ๒๙ คน | ๑๑ คน | ๑๔ คน |

## ๖.๙ การสนทนาโต้ตอบ

ก.

| | | | |
|---|---|---|---|
| วัวกับควายอะไรใหญ่กว่ากันคะ | ควายใหญ่กว่าวัวครับ | ควายกับวัวอะไรเล็กกว่ากันคะ | วัวเล็กกว่าควายครับ |
| แล้วอะไรเล็กกว่ากันคะ | วัวเล็กกว่าควายครับ | แล้วอะไรใหญ่กว่ากันคะ | ควายใหญ่กว่าวัวครับ |
| ควายกับวัวอะไรเตี้ยกว่ากันคะ | วัวเตี้ยกว่าควายครับ | วัวกับควายอะไรสูงกว่ากันคะ | ควายสูงกว่าวัวครับ |
| แล้วอะไรสูงกว่ากันคะ | ควายสูงกว่าวัวครับ | แล้วอะไรเตี้ยกว่ากันคะ | วัวเตี้ยกว่าควายครับ |
| วัวกับควายอะไรอ้วนกว่ากันคะ | ควายอ้วนกว่าวัวครับ | ควายกับวัวอะไรผอมกว่ากันคะ | วัวผอมกว่าควายครับ |
| แล้วอะไรผอมกว่ากันคะ | วัวผอมกว่าควายครับ | แล้วอะไรอ้วนกว่ากันคะ | ควายอ้วนกว่าวัวครับ |

**d. Response drill.**

| | |
|---|---|
| pay thaaŋ nǎy. (níi)<br>pay thaaŋ níi. | Which way shall I go? (this)<br>Go this way. |
| pay thaaŋ nǎy. (khwǎa)<br>pay thaaŋ khwǎa. | Which way shall I go? (right)<br>Go right. |
| pay thaaŋ nǎy. (nóon )<br>pay thaaŋ nóon. | Which that way shall I go? (that)<br>Go that way. |
| pay thaaŋ nǎy. (sáay)<br>pay thaaŋ sáay. | Which way shall I go? (left)<br>Go left. |

### 6.8 Numbers.

| | | | |
|---|---|---|---|
| yîi sìp khon | 20 people. | sǎam sìp khon | 30 people. |
| yîi sìp ʔèt khon | 21 people. | sǎam sìp ʔèt khon | 31 people. |
| yîi sìp sɔ̌ɔŋ khon | 22 people. | sǎam sìp sɔ̌ɔŋ khon | 32 people. |
| yîi sìp sǎam khon | 23 people. | sǎam sìp sǎam khon | 33 people. |
| yîi sìp sìi khon | 24 people. | sǎam sìp sìi khon | 34 people. |
| yîi sìp hâa khon | 25 people. | sǎam sìp hâa khon | 35 people. |
| yîi sìp hòk khon | 26 people. | sǎam sìp hòk khon | 36 people. |
| yîi sìp cèt khon | 27 people. | sǎam sìp cèt khon | 37 people. |
| yîi sìp pὲɛt khon | 28 people. | sǎam sìp pὲɛt khon | 38 people. |
| yîi sìp kâaw khon | 29 people. | sǎam sìp kâaw khon | 39 people. |

Practice reading the following numbers of people at home. Try to get the time under 35 seconds. Be especially careful with the tones.

| | | | | | |
|---|---|---|---|---|---|
| 30 khon | 36 khon | 18 khon | 17 khon | 37 khon | 34 khon |
| 12 khon | 20 khon | 21 khon | 31 khon | 32 khon | 28 khon |
| 25 khon | 39 khon | 24 khon | 35 khon | 26 khon | 38 khon |
| 27 khon | 22 khon | 33 khon | 29 khon | 11 khon | 14 khon |

### 6.9 Conversation.

a. Comparing buffalos and cows.

| | |
|---|---|
| wua kàp khwaay, ʔaray yày kwàa kan khá.<br>lέɛw ʔaray lék kwàa kan khá. | khwaay yày kwàa wua khráp.<br>wua lék kwàa khwaay khráp. |
| khwaay kàp wua, ʔaray tîa kwàa kan khá.<br>lέɛw ʔaray sǔuŋ kwàa kan khá. | wua tîa kwàa khwaay khráp.<br>khwaay sǔuŋ kwàa wua khráp. |
| wua kàp khwaay, ʔaray ʔûan kwàa kan khá.<br>lέɛw ʔaray phɔ̌ɔm kwàa kan khá. | khwaay ʔûan kwàa wua khráp.<br>wua phɔ̌ɔm kwàa khwaay khráp. |
| khwaay kàp wua, ʔaray lék kwàa kan khá.<br>lέɛw ʔaray yày kwàa kan khá. | wua lék kwàa khwaay khráp.<br>khwaay yày kwàa wua khráp. |
| wua kàp khwaay, ʔaray sǔuŋ kwàa kan khá.<br>lέɛw ʔaray tîa kwàa kan khá. | khwaay sǔuŋ kwàa wua khráp.<br>wua tîa kwàa khwaay khráp. |
| khwaay kàp wua, ʔaray phɔɔm kwàa kan khá.<br>lέɛw ʔaray ʔûan kwàa kan khá. | wua phɔ̌ɔm kwàa khwaay khráp.<br>khwaay ʔûan kwàa wua khráp. |

ข.

คุณรู้จัก..............................ไหมครับ

รู้จักค่ะ

ไปทางไหนครับ

เดินตรงไปทางนี้ค่ะ

ถึง ........................

แล้วเลี้ยว ........................

..........................อยู่ทาง.........................ค่ะ

ขอบคุณมากครับ

ไม่เป็นไรค่ะ

### ๖.๑๐ การเขียน

| ขอ | สูง | ทาง |
| --- | --- | --- |
| ขอ | ขา | ดน |
| คอ | คา | ดม |
| คู | โค | รม |
| ขู | โข | ราม |
| ขี | โขน | ทาม |
| คี | ขน | ทาง |
| แค | ทน | สาง |
| แข | ผน | สูง |

b. Practice the conversation suggested below.

| | |
|---|---|
| khun rúucàk.....................máy khráp. | The Erawan Hotel.<br>Nick's Restaurant.<br>Sawat's Barber Shop. |
| rúucàk khâ. | |
| pay thaaŋ nǎy khráp. | |
| dəən troŋ pay thaaŋ níi khâ. | |
| thǔŋ.................... | Intersection. Mark |
| lέεw líaw.................... . | Left. Right. |
| ...............yùu thaaŋ.....................khâ. | Right. Left |
| khɔ̀ɔpkhun mâak khráp. | |
| mây pen ray khâ | |

**6.10 Writing.**

| ขอ | สูง | ทาง |
|---|---|---|
| khɔ̌ɔ | sǔuŋ | thaaŋ |
| To ask for. | Tall. | Way. |

| | | | | | |
|---|---|---|---|---|---|
| ขอ | *khɔ̌ɔ | ขา | khǎa | ดน | don |
| คอ | khɔɔ | คา | khaa | ดม | dom |
| คู | khuu | โค | khoo | รม | rom |
| ขู | khǔu | โข | khǒo | ราม | raam |
| ขี | khǐi | โขน | khǒon | ทาม | thaam |
| คี | khii | ขน | khǒn | ทาง | *thaaŋ |
| แค | khεε | ทน | thon | สาง | sǎaŋ |
| แข | khε̌ε | ผน | phǒn | สูง | *sǔuŋ |

# บทที่ ๗

## ๗.๑ คำศัพท์

น้ำ
ห้องน้ำ

ส้วม
ห้องส้วม

สุขา
ห้องสุขา

นอน
ห้องนอน

ผู้
หญิง
ผู้หญิง

ชาย
ผู้ชาย

พ่อ

ลูก

เด็ก

ปลา

ไก่

เนื้อ

หมู

กุ้ง

มี

ใส่

ซื้อ

เห็น

ชอบ

บาท

ใคร

นะ

หรือ

# LESSON 7

**7.1 Vocabulary and expansions.**

| | |
|---|---|
| náam | Water, liquid, juice, fluid. |
| hɔ̂ŋ náam | Bathroom. |
| sûam | Toilet. |
| hɔ̂ŋ sûam | Water closet. As with *toilet* in English, this term is avoided when *hɔ̂ŋ náam* can be used unambiguously instead. But when the toilet is separate from the bathroom, it must be used to distinguish the two. |
| sùkhǎa | Toilet (the formal term). |
| hɔ̂ŋ sùkhǎa | Water closet. This is the usual word seen on signs, but it isn't common in speech. |
| nɔɔn | To lie down. |
| hɔ̂ŋ nɔɔn | Bedroom. |
| phûu | Person (rarely used alone). |
| yǐŋ | Female (people only). |
| phûu yǐŋ | Girl, woman. |
| chaay | Male (people only). |
| phûu chaay | Boy, man. |
| phɔ̂ɔ | Father. |
| lûuk | Child (the relationship term: son or daughter). |
| dèk | Child (the age term: boy or girl). |
| plaa | Fish. |
| kày | Chicken. |
| nʉ́a | Meat, beef. |
| mǔu | Pig, pork. |
| kûŋ | Shrimp. |
| mii | To have, there is. |
| sày | To put in or on. |
| sʉ́ʉ | To buy. |
| hěn | To see. |
| chɔ̂ɔp | To like. |
| bàat | Baht, tical (the Thai money unit, worth slightly less than five U. S. cents in 1967). |
| khray | Who? |
| ná | A question particle used to check to see whether a person is listening to or grasping what is being said.<br>'O.K.?' 'You see?' 'Got it?'<br>It regularly follows a piece of information. |
| rʉ́, rʉ̌ʉ | Or. |

### ๗.๒ โครงสร้างของประโยค

ห้องน้ำ
ห้องส้วม
ห้องนอน
ห้องอาหาร

ขวาหรือซ้าย
อ้วนหรือผอม
ที่นี่หรือที่โน่น
ผู้หญิงหรือผู้ชาย

ผู้หญิง
ผู้ชาย
ผู้ใหญ่

### ๗.๓ บทสนทนา

ก. ขอโทษ
ห้องน้ำอยู่ที่ไหน

ข. ห้องน้ำผู้หญิงอยู่ทางขวา
ห้องน้ำผู้ชายอยู่ทางซ้าย

ก. ขอบคุณมาก

ข. ไม่เป็นไร

### ๗.๔ แบบฝึกหัดการฟังและการออกเสียงสูงต่ำ

ก.

หวาน อบ แห้ง แพะ ทู

ข.

มีอะไร
มีปลา

ใส่อะไร
ใส่ไก่

ซื้ออะไร
ซื้อเนื้อ

เห็นอะไร
เห็นหมู

ชอบอะไร
ชอบกุ้ง

### 7.2 Patterns.

| | |
|---|---|
| hɔ̂ŋ náam | Bathroom. |
| hɔ̂ŋ sûam | Wather closet. |
| hɔ̂ŋ nɔɔn | Bedroom. |
| hɔ̂ŋ ʔaahǎan | Dining room. |
| phûu yǐŋ | Woman. |
| phûu chaay | Man. |
| phûu yày | Adult. |
| khwǎa rʉ́ sáay | Right or left? |
| ʔûan rʉ́ phɔ̌ɔm | Fat or thin? |
| thîi nîi rʉ́ thîi nôon | Here or there? |
| phûu yǐŋ rʉ́ phûu chaay | Woman or man? |

### 7.3 Dialog.

A. khɔ̌ɔ thôot. — Excuse me.
hɔ̂ŋ náam yùu thîi nǎy. — Where's the bathroom?

B. hɔ̂ŋ náam phûu yǐŋ yùu thaaŋ khwǎa. — The ladies' room is to the right.
hɔ̂ŋ náam phûu chaay yùu thaaŋ sáay. — The men's room is to the left.

A. khɔ̀ɔpkhun mâak. — Thanks a lot.

B. mây pen ray. — Not at all.

### 7.4 Tone identification and production.

**a.** Identify the tones and record the number of repetitions required.

| | | |
|---|---|---|
| To be sweet. | *waan | ......... |
| To roast. | *ʔop | ......... |
| To be dry. | *hɛɛŋ | ......... |
| Goat. | *phɛʔ | ......... |
| A kind of mackerel. | *thuu | ......... |

**b. Response drill.**

mii ʔaray. — What do you have?
mii plaa. — We have fish.

sày ʔaray. — What shall I put in it?
sày kày. — Put in some chicken.

sʉ́ʉ ʔaray. — What did you buy?
sʉ́ʉ nʉ́a. — I bought some beef.

hěn ʔaray. — What do you see?
hěn mǔu. — I see some pork.

chɔ̂ɔp ʔaray. — What do you like?
chɔ̂ɔp kûŋ. — I like shrimps.

### ๗.๕ แบบฝึกหัดการสลับเสียงสูงต่ำ

| ก. | ข. |
| --- | --- |
| พ่อใหญ่กว่าลูก<br>(สูง) | ใครใหญ่กว่ากัน<br>พ่อใหญ่กว่าลูก |
| พ่อสูงกว่าลูก<br>(อ้วน) | ใครอ้วนกว่ากัน<br>พ่ออ้วนกว่าลูก |
| พ่ออ้วนกว่าลูก<br>(เล็ก) | ใครสูงกว่ากัน<br>พ่อสูงกว่าลูก |
| ลูกเล็กกว่าพ่อ<br>(เตี้ย) | ใครเล็กกว่ากัน<br>ลูกเล็กกว่าพ่อ |
| ลูกเตี้ยกว่าพ่อ<br>(ผอม) | ใครผอมกว่ากัน<br>ลูกผอมกว่าพ่อ |
| ลูกผอมกว่าพ่อ<br>(ใหญ่) | ใครเตี้ยกว่ากัน<br>ลูกเตี้ยกว่าพ่อ |

### ๗.๖ แบบฝึกหัดการออกเสียงสระและพยัญชนะ

ก.

มี เมีย มี เมีย มี เมีย

มู มัว มู มัว มู มัว

มือ เมือ มือ เมือ มือ เมือ

ข.

นาน นาน งาน งาน นาน นาน
งาน งาน นาน นาน งาน งาน

ทั้ง งาน ทัน งาน ทำ งาน
ทั้ง งาน ทัน งาน ทำ งาน

## 7.5 Tone manipulation.

### a. Substitution drill.

phɔ̂ɔ yày kwàa lûuk. — The father is bigger than his son.
(sǔuŋ) — (tall)

phɔ̂ɔ sǔuŋ kwàa lûuk. — The father is taller than his son.
(ʔûan) — (fat)

phɔ̂ɔ ʔûan kwàa lûuk. — The father is fatter than his son.
(lék) — (small)

lûuk lék kwàa phɔ̂ɔ. — The son is smaller than his father.
(tîa) — (short)

lûuk tîa kwàa phɔ̂ɔ. — The son is shorter than his father.
(phɔ̌ɔm) — (thin)

lûuk phɔ̌ɔm kwàa phɔ̂ɔ. — The son is thinner than his father.
(yày) — (big)

### b. Response drill.

khray yày kwàa kan. — Who is bigger?
phɔ̂ɔ yày kwàa lûuk. — The father is bigger than the son.

khray ʔûan kwàa kan. — Who is fatter?
phɔ̂ɔ ʔûan kwàa lûuk. — The father is fatter than the son.

khray sǔuŋ kwàa kan. — Who is taller?
phɔ̂ɔ sǔuŋ kwàa lûuk. — The father is taller than the son.

khray lék kwàa kan. — Who is smaller?
lûuk lék kwàa phɔ̂ɔ. — The son is smaller than the father.

khray phɔ̌ɔm kwàa kan. — Who is thinner?
lûuk phɔ̌ɔm kwàa phɔ̂ɔ. — The son is thinner than the father.

khray tîa kwàa kan. — Who is shorter?
lûuk tîa kwàa phɔ̂ɔ. — The son is shorter than the father.

## 7.6 Vowel and consonant drills.

### a. ii-ia, uu-ua, and ʉʉ-ʉa alternation drills.

mii mia    mii mia    mii mia

muu mua    muu mua    muu mua

mʉʉ mʉa    mʉʉ mʉa    mʉʉ mʉa

### b. ŋ alternation drill.

naan naan    ŋaan ŋaan    naan naan    ŋaan ŋaan    naan naan    ŋaan ŋaan

thaŋ ŋaan    than ŋaan    tham ŋaan    thaŋ ŋaan    than ŋaan    tham ŋaan

๗.๗ แบบฝึกหัดไวยากรณ์

ก.

ผู้หญิง (ชาย)
ผู้ชาย (หญิง)

ข.

ห้องน้ำผู้ชาย (หญิง)
ห้องน้ำผู้หญิง (ชาย)

ค.

ห้องน้ำผู้หญิงอยู่ทางขวา
(ชาย)

ห้องน้ำผู้ชายอยู่ทางขวา
(หญิง)

ง.

ห้องน้ำผู้หญิงอยู่ทางขวา
(ซ้าย)

ห้องน้ำผู้หญิงอยู่ทางซ้าย
(ขวา)

จ.

ห้องน้ำผู้ชายอยู่ทางซ้าย
(หญิง)

ห้องน้ำผู้หญิงทางซ้าย
(ขวา)

ห้องน้ำผู้หญิงอยู่ทางขวา
(ชาย)

ห้องน้ำผู้ชายอยู่ทางขวา
(ซ้าย)

ฉ.

ห้องน้ำผู้ชายอยู่ที่ไหน
(ขวา)
ห้องน้ำผู้ชายอยู่ทางขวา
ห้องน้ำผู้หญิงอยู่ที่ไหน
(ซ้าย)
ห้องน้ำผู้หญิงอยู่ทางซ้าย

ห้องน้ำอยู่ที่ไหน
(ชาย – ซ้าย)
ห้องน้ำผู้ชายอยู่ทางซ้าย
(หญิง – ขวา)
ห้องน้ำผู้หญิงอยู่ทางขวา

ห้องน้ำอยู่ที่ไหน
(หญิง – ซ้าย, ชาย – ขวา)
ห้องน้ำผู้หญิงอยู่ทางซ้าย
ห้องน้ำผู้ชายอยู่ทางขวา

ห้องน้ำอยู่ที่ไหน
(ชาย – ซ้าย, หญิง – ขวา)
ห้องน้ำผู้ชายอยู่ทางซ้าย
ห้องน้ำผู้หญิงอยู่ทางขวา

7.7 **Grammar drills.**

a. **Substitution drill.**

| | |
|---|---|
| phûu yǐŋ. (chaay) | Girl. (male) |
| phûu chaay. (yǐŋ) | Man. (female) |

b. **Substitution drill.**

| | |
|---|---|
| hɔ̂ŋ náam phûu chaay. (yǐŋ) | Men's room. (female) |
| hɔ̂ŋ náam phûu yǐŋ. (chaay) | Ladies' room. (male) |

c. **Substitution drill.**

| | |
|---|---|
| hɔ̂ŋ náam phûu yǐŋ yùu thaaŋ khwǎa. (chaay) | The ladies' room is to the right. (men's) |
| hɔ̂ŋ náam phûu chaay yùu thaaŋ khwǎa. (yǐŋ) | The men's room is to the right. (ladies') |

d. **Substitution drill.**

| | |
|---|---|
| hɔ̂ŋ náam phûu yǐŋ yùu thaaŋ khwǎa. (sáay) | The ladies' room is to the right. (left) |
| hɔ̂ŋ náam phûu yǐŋ yùu thaaŋ sáay. (khwǎa) | The ladies' room is to the left. (right) |

e. **Substitution drill.**

| | |
|---|---|
| hɔ̂ŋ náam phûu chaay yùu thaaŋ sáay. (yǐŋ) | The men's room is to the left. (ladies') |
| hɔ̂ŋ náam phûu yǐŋ yùu thaaŋ sáay. (khwǎa) | The ladies' room is to the left. (right) |
| hɔ̂ŋ náam phûu yǐŋ yùu thaaŋ khwǎa. (chaay) | The ladies' room is to the right. (men's) |
| hɔ̂ŋ náam phûu chaay yùu thaaŋ khwǎa. (sáay) | The men's room is to the right. (left) |

f. **Response drill.**

| | |
|---|---|
| hɔ̂ŋ náam phûu chaay yùu thîi nǎy. | Where's the men's room? |
| (khwǎa) | (right) |
| hɔ̂ŋ náam phûu chaay yùu thaaŋ khwǎa. | The men's room is to the right. |
| hɔ̂ŋ náam phûu yǐŋ yùu thîi nǎy. | Where's the ladies' room? |
| (sáay) | (left.) |
| hɔ̂ŋ náam phûu yǐŋ yùu thaaŋ sáay. | The ladies' room is to the left. |
| hɔ̂ŋ náam yùu thîi nǎy. | Where are the bathrooms? |
| (chaay – sáay) | (men's – left) |
| hɔ̂ŋ náam phûu chaay yùu thaaŋ sáay. | The men's room is to the left. |
| (yǐŋ – khwǎa) | (ladies' – right) |
| hɔ̂ŋ náam phûu yǐŋ yùu thaaŋ khwǎa. | The ladies' room is to the right. |
| hɔ̂ŋ náam yùu thîi nǎy. | Where are the bathrooms? |
| (yǐŋ – sáay, chaay – khwǎa) | (ladies' – left, men's – right) |
| hɔ̂ŋ náam phûu yǐŋ yùu thaaŋ sáay. | The ladies'room is to the left. |
| hɔ̂ŋ náam phûu chaay yùu thaaŋ khwǎa. | The men's room is to the right. |
| hɔ̂ŋ náam yùu thîi nǎy. | Where are the bathrooms? |
| (chaay – sáay, yǐŋ – khwǎa) | (men's – left, ladies' – right) |
| hɔ̂ŋ náam phûu chaay yùu thaaŋ sáay. | The men's room is to the left. |
| hɔ̂ŋ náam phûu yǐŋ yùu thaaŋ khwǎa. | The ladies' room is to the right. |

## ๗.๘ เลข

| | | | | | |
|---|---|---|---|---|---|
| สี่สิบบาท | ๔๐ | ห้าสิบบาท | ๕๐ | หกสิบบาท | ๖๐ |
| สี่สิบเอ็ดบาท | ๔๑ | ห้าสิบเอ็ดบาท | ๕๑ | หกสิบเอ็ดบาท | ๖๑ |
| สี่สิบสองบาท | ๔๒ | ห้าสิบสองบาท | ๕๒ | หกสิบสองบาท | ๖๒ |
| สี่สิบสามบาท | ๔๓ | ห้าสิบสามบาท | ๕๓ | หกสิบสามบาท | ๖๓ |
| สี่สิบสี่บาท | ๔๔ | ห้าสิบสี่บาท | ๕๔ | หกสิบสี่บาท | ๖๔ |
| สี่สิบห้าบาท | ๔๕ | ห้าสิบห้าบาท | ๕๕ | หกสิบห้าบาท | ๖๕ |
| สี่สิบหกบาท | ๔๖ | ห้าสิบหกบาท | ๕๖ | หกสิบหกบาท | ๖๖ |
| สี่สิบเจ็ดบาท | ๔๗ | ห้าสิบเจ็ดบาท | ๕๗ | หกสิบเจ็ดบาท | ๖๗ |
| สี่สิบแปดบาท | ๔๘ | ห้าสิบแปดบาท | ๕๘ | หกสิบแปดบาท | ๖๘ |
| สี่สิบเก้าบาท | ๔๙ | ห้าสิบเก้าบาท | ๕๙ | หกสิบเก้าบาท | ๖๙ |

| | | | | | | |
|---|---|---|---|---|---|---|
| ๖๒ บาท | ๕๓ บาท | ๖๑ บาท | ๖๓ บาท | ๕๒ บาท | ๔๔ บาท | ๔๘ บาท |
| ๕๙ บาท | ๖๙ บาท | ๔๐ บาท | ๔๒ บาท | ๒๕ บาท | ๑๘ บาท | ๖๖ บาท |
| ๔๗ บาท | ๔๑ บาท | ๖๘ บาท | ๕๑ บาท | ๕๔ บาท | ๕๗ บาท | ๕๘ บาท |
| ๓๙ บาท | ๔๕ บาท | ๕๕บาท | ๔๙ บาท | ๖๕ บาท | ๖๐ บาท | ๕๖ บาท |

## ๗.๙ การสนทนาโต้ตอบ

### ก.

| | |
|---|---|
| พ่อกับลูกใครเล็กกว่ากันคะ | ลูกเล็กกว่าพ่อครับ |
| แล้วใครใหญ่กว่ากันคะ | พ่อใหญ่กว่าลูกครับ |
| ลูกกับพ่อใครสูงกว่ากันคะ | พ่อสูงกว่าลูกครับ |
| แล้วใครเตี้ยกว่ากันคะ | ลูกเตี้ยกว่าพ่อครับ |
| พ่อกับลูกใครผอมกว่ากันคะ | ลูกผอมกว่าพ่อครับ |
| แล้วใครอ้วนกว่ากันคะ | พ่ออ้วนกว่าลูกครับ |
| ลูกกับพ่อใครใหญ่กว่ากันคะ | พ่อใหญ่กว่าลูกครับ |
| แล้วใครเล็กกว่ากันคะ | ลูกเล็กกว่าพ่อครับ |
| พ่อกับลูกใครเตี้ยกว่ากันคะ | ลูกเตี้ยกว่าพ่อครับ |
| แล้วใครสูงกว่ากันคะ | พ่อสูงกว่าลูกครับ |
| ลูกกับพ่อใครอ้วนกว่ากันคะ | พ่ออ้วนกว่าลูกครับ |
| แล้วใครผอมกว่ากันคะ | ลูกผอมกว่าพ่อครับ |

### ข.

(ร้านอาหารสวัสดิ์อยู่ที่สี่แยก นะคะ)

| | |
|---|---|
| ร้านอาหารสวัสดิ์อยู่ที่ไหนคะ | อยู่ที่สี่แยกครับ |
| อะไรอยู่ที่สี่แยกคะ | ร้านอาหารสวัสดิ์ครับ |

(คุณยังอ้วนมากนะคะ)

| | |
|---|---|
| ใครอ้วนคะ | คุณยังครับ |
| คุณยังอ้วนหรือผอมคะ | อ้วนครับ |
| อ้วนมากไหมคะ | มากครับ |

(คุณสวัสดิ์รู้จักคุณยัง นะคะ)

| | |
|---|---|
| ใครรู้จักคุณยังคะ | คุณสวัสดิ์ครับ |
| คุณสวัสดิ์รู้จักใครคะ | คุณยังครับ |

7.8 **Numbers.**

| | | | | | |
|---|---|---|---|---|---|
| sìi sìp bàat | 40 | hâa sìp bàat | 50 | hòk sìp bàat | 60 |
| sìi sìp ʔèt bàat | 41 | hâa sìp ʔèt bàat | 51 | hòk sìp ʔèt bàat | 61 |
| sìi sìp sɔ̌ɔŋ bàat | 42 | hâa sìp sɔ̌ɔŋ bàat | 52 | hòk sìp sɔ̌ɔŋ bàat | 62 |
| sìi sìp sǎam bàat | 43 | hâa sìp sǎam bàat | 53 | hòk sìp sǎam bàat | 63 |
| sìi sìp sìi bàat | 44 | hâa sìp sìi bàat | 54 | hòk sìp sìi bàat | 64 |
| sìi sìp hâa bàat | 45 | hâa sìp hâa bàat | 55 | hòk sìp hâa bàat | 65 |
| sìi sìp hòk bàat | 46 | hâa sìp hòk bàat | 56 | hòk sìp hòk bàat | 66 |
| sìi sìp cèt bàat | 47 | hâa sìp cèt bàat | 57 | hòk sìp cèt bàat | 67 |
| sìi sìp pɛ̀ɛt bàat | 48 | hâa sìp pɛ̀ɛt bàat | 58 | hòk sìp pɛ̀ɛt bàat | 68 |
| sìi sìp kâaw bàat | 49 | hâa sìp kâaw bàat | 59 | hòk sìp kâaw bàat | 69 |

Practice reading the following amounts of money. Try to get the time under 45 seconds. Be especially careful with the tones.

| | | | | | | |
|---|---|---|---|---|---|---|
| 62 bàat | 53 bàat | 61 bàat | 63 bàat | 52 bàat | 44 bàat | 48 bàat |
| 59 bàat | 69 bàat | 40 bàat | 42 bàat | 25 bàat | 18 bàat | 66 bàat |
| 47 bàat | 41 bàat | 68 bàat | 51 bàat | 54 bàat | 57 bàat | 58 bàat |
| 39 bàat | 45 bàat | 55 bàat | 49 bàat | 65 bàat | 60 bàat | 56 bàat |

7.9 **Conversation.**

a. **Comparing father and son.** (The father is bigger, taller, and fatter.)

| | |
|---|---|
| phɔ̂ɔ kàp lûuk, khray lék kwàa kan khá. | lûuk lék kwàa phɔ̂ɔ khráp. |
| lɛ́ɛw khray yày kwàa kan khá. | phɔ̂ɔ yày kwàa lûuk khráp. |
| lûuk kàp phɔ̂ɔ, khray sǔuŋ kwàa kan khá. | phɔ̂ɔ sǔuŋ kwàa lûuk khráp. |
| lɛ́ɛw khray tîa kwàa kan khá. | lûuk tîa kwàa phɔ̂ɔ khráp. |
| phɔ̂ɔ kàp lûuk, khray phɔ̌ɔm kwàa kan khá. | lûuk phɔ̌ɔm kwàa phɔ̂ɔ khráp. |
| lɛ́ɛw khray ʔûan kwàa kan khá. | phɔ̂ɔ ʔûan kwàa lûuk khráp. |
| lûuk kàp phɔ̂ɔ, khray yày kwàa kan khá. | phɔ̂ɔ yày kwàa lûuk khráp. |
| lɛ́ɛw khray lék kwàa kan khá. | lûuk lék kwàa phɔ̂ɔ khráp. |
| phɔ̂ɔ kàp lûuk, khray tîa kwàa kan khá. | lûuk tîa kwàa phɔ̂ɔ khráp. |
| lɛ́ɛw khray sǔuŋ kwàa kan khá. | phɔ̂ɔ sǔuŋ kwàa lûuk khráp. |
| lûuk kàp phɔ̂ɔ, khray ʔûan kwàa kan khá. | phɔ̂ɔ ʔûan kwàa lûuk khráp. |
| lɛ́ɛw khray phɔ̌ɔm kwàa kan khá. | lûuk phɔ̌ɔm kwàa phɔ̂ɔ khráp. |

b. **Questioning information.**

(ráan ʔaahǎan sawàt yùu thîi sìiyɛ̂ɛk. ná khá.)

| | |
|---|---|
| ráan ʔaahǎan sawàt yùu thîi nǎy khá. | yùu thîi sìiyɛ̂ɛk khráp. |
| ʔaray yùu thîi sìiyɛ̂ɛk khá. | ráan ʔaahǎan sawàt khráp. |

(khun yaŋ ʔûan mâak. ná khá.)

| | |
|---|---|
| khray ʔûan khá. | khun yaŋ khráp. |
| khun yaŋ ʔûan rɯ́ phɔ̌ɔm khá. | ʔûan khráp. |
| ʔûan mâak máy khá. | mâak khráp. |

(khun sawàt rúucàk khun yaŋ. ná khá.)

| | |
|---|---|
| khray rúucàk khun yaŋ khá. | khun sawàt khráp. |
| khun sawàt rúucàk khray khá. | khun yaŋ khráp. |

(More.)

(คุณยังเลี้ยวขวาที่สี่แยกนะคะ)

| | |
|---|---|
| ใครเลี้ยวคะ | คุณยังครับ |
| เลี้ยวทางไหนคะ | เลี้ยวขวาครับ |
| เลี้ยวที่ไหนคะ | ที่สี่แยกครับ |

(ลูกสูงกว่าพ่อ นะคะ)

| | |
|---|---|
| ใครสูงกว่าคะ | ลูกสูงกว่าครับ |
| สูงกว่าใครคะ | สูงกว่าพ่อครับ |

**๗.๑๐ การเขียน**

| กัน | นอน | |
|---|---|---|
| กัน | สอน | นา |
| กน | สอ | นาง |
| ขน | ทอ | ราง |
| ขัน | ทู | รัง |
| คัน | ดู | กัง |
| คน | ผู | แกง |
| นน | ผี | โกง |
| นอน | นี | โขง |

(khun yaŋ líaw khwǎa thîi sìiyɛ̂ɛk. ná khá.)

| | |
|---|---|
| khray líaw khá. | khun yaŋ khráp. |
| líaw thaaŋ nǎy khá. | líaw khwǎa khráp. |
| líaw thîi nǎy khá. | thîi sìiyɛ̂ɛk khráp. |

(lûuk sǔuŋ kwàa phɔ̂ɔ. ná khá.)

| | |
|---|---|
| khray sǔuŋ kwàa khá. | lûuk sǔuŋ kwàa khráp. |
| sǔuŋ kwàa khray khá. | sǔuŋ kwàa phɔ̂ɔ khráp. |

## 7.10 Writing.

| กัน | นอน |
|---|---|
| kan | nɔɔn |
| Each other. | To lie down. |

| | | | | | |
|---|---|---|---|---|---|
| กัน | *kan | สอน | sɔ̌ɔn | นา | *naa |
| กน | kon | สอ | sɔ̌ɔ | นาง | naaŋ |
| ขน | khǒn | ทอ | thɔɔ | ราง | raaŋ |
| ขัน | khǎn | ทู | thuu | รัง | raŋ |
| คัน | khan | ดู | duu | กัง | kaŋ |
| คน | *khon | ผู | phǔu | แกง | kɛɛŋ |
| นน | non | ผี | phǐi | โกง | kooŋ |
| นอน | *nɔɔn | นี | nii | โขง | khǒoŋ |

# บทที่ ๘

## ๘.๑ คำศัพท์

ผม
ดิฉัน
ฉัน
หนู

เข้า
ใจ
เข้าใจ
ที
อีก
อีกที
พูด
พูดอีกที

ได้
บน
ข้างบน
ล่าง
ข้างล่าง

แล้ว
ไปแล้ว
ถึงแล้ว
มา
มาแล้ว
เข้าใจแล้ว

# LESSON 8

**8.1 Vocabulary and expansions.**

| | |
|---|---|
| phǒm<br>dichán<br>chán<br>nǔu | As with terms used for the second person, there are many different terms with which a person can refer to himself. The choice of term depends on the social relationship between the first and second person, the situation, the sex of the speaker, and many other things. In addition to several different pronouns, names and relationship terms can be used as well. The student is advised to use at least two different terms right from the start to get in the habit of having to make a choice. Men should use *chán* when speaking to children and obvious inferiors (like one's servants) and *phǒm* with everyone else. Women should use *dichán* with obvious superiors (like high officials and parents of friends) and *chán* with everyone else. Omit the pronoun, however, whenever possible. It might be added here that being forced by Thai pronouns to constantly keep social status in mind is not undemocratic, any more than English is immoral by constantly forcing the attention to sex (he, she). And calling your servant *khun* sounds just as foolish as referring to your mother as *he*. |
| khâw | |
| cay | |
| khâwcay | To understand. |
| thii | A time. |
| ʔiik | Another, one more, more. |
| ʔiik thii | Again. |
| phûut | To speak. |
| phûut ʔiik thii | To say again. |
| dây | Can, to be able. |
| bon | On, the upper part of. |
| khâŋ bon | Upstairs, on top of. |
| lâaŋ | Lower. |
| khâŋ lâaŋ | Downstairs, underneath. |
| lɛ́ɛw | When used at the end of a clause, *lɛ́ɛw* sometimes corresponds to the English 'already', sometimes to the perfect tense, and sometimes to 'now'. It marks a passing of time. The past, present, or imminent passing of the time of an action is relevant to the situation because of the *change* it brings about. |
| pay lɛ́ɛw | He has gone. The time of his leaving has passed, resulting in his not being here now. |
| thʉ̌ŋ lɛ́ɛw | Here we are. The time of our arriving is here, resulting in our finally being here. |
| maa | To come. |
| maa lɛ́ɛw | Here it comes now. We have been waiting for a bus and just now I catch sight of it in the distance. This is the most important change point in the waiting situation. The acutal arrival, though still in the future, is now a matter of course. |
| khâwcay lɛ́ɛw | Now I see. I didn't get it before, but your repetition (or explanation) has cleared it up for me. |

(More.)

ทู
ปลาทู

อบ
ไก่อบ

แห้ง
กุ้งแห้ง

แพะ
เนื้อแพะ

หวาน
หมูหวาน

**๘.๒ โครงสร้างของประโยค**

เขาอ้วน
ฉันอ้วน
คุณอ้วน

เขาไม่เข้าใจ
คุณไม่เข้าใจ
ฉันไม่เข้าใจ

เขารู้จักฉัน
คุณรู้จักเขา
ผมรู้จักคุณ

ฉันสูงกว่าเขา
เขาสูงกว่าคุณ
คุณสูงกว่าดิฉัน

เดินได้
เลี้ยวได้
อยู่ได้

เข้าใจแล้ว
รู้จักแล้ว
พูดได้แล้ว

**๘.๓ บทสนทนา**

ก. ขอโทษ
ฉันไม่เข้าใจ
พูดอีกทีได้ไหม

ข. ได้
ห้องน้ำผู้หญิงอยู่ข้างบน
ห้องน้ำผู้ชายอยู่ข้างล่าง
เข้าใจไหม

ก. เข้าใจแล้ว
ขอบคุณมาก

thuu
plaa thuu — A kind of mackerel. One of the commonest food fishes of central Thailand.

ʔòp — To roast.
kày ʔòp — Roast chicken.

hɛ̂ɛŋ — To be dry.
kûŋ hɛ̂ɛŋ — Dried shrimps.

phɛ́ʔ — Goat.
nʉ́a phɛ́ʔ — Goat meat.

wǎan — To be sweet.
mǔu wǎan — Sweet pork. A common Thai dish.

## 8.2 Patterns.

| | |
|---|---|
| kháw ʔûan. | He's fat. |
| chán ʔûan. | I'm fat. |
| khun ʔûan. | You're fat. |
| kháw mây khâwcay. | He doesn't understand. |
| khun mây khâwcay. | You don't understand. |
| chán mây khâwcay. | I don't understand. |
| kháw rúucàk chán. | He knows me. |
| khun rúucàk kháw. | You know him. |
| phǒm rúucàk khun. | I know you. |
| chán sǔuŋ kwàa kháw. | I'm taller than him. |
| kháw sǔuŋ kwàa khun. | He's taller than you. |
| khun sǔuŋ kwàa dichán. | You're taller than me. |
| dəən dây. | It's possible or permitted to walk. |
| líaw dây. | You can turn here. |
| yùu dây. | You can stay. |
| khâwcay lɛ́ɛw. | Now I get it. |
| rúucàk lɛ́ɛw. | I already know him. |
| phûut dây lɛ́ɛw. | He can already talk. |

## 8.3 Dialog.

| | | |
|---|---|---|
| A. | khɔ̌ɔ thôot. | Excuse me. |
| | chán mây khâwcay. | I don't understand. |
| | phûut ʔìik thii dây máy. | Could you say that again? |
| B. | dây. | Yes. |
| | hɔ̂ŋ náam phûu yǐŋ yùu khâŋ bon. | The ladies' room is upstairs. |
| | hɔ̂ŋ náam phûu chaay yùu khâŋ lâaŋ. | The men's room is downstairs. |
| | khâwcay máy. | Do you understand? |
| A. | khâwcay lɛ́ɛw. | Yes. Now I get it. |
| | khɔ̀ɔpkhun mâak. | Thanks a lot. |

### ๘.๔ แบบฝึกหัดการฟังและการออกเสียงสูงต่ำ

ก. พี่
น้อง
ปู่
ลุง
หลาน

**ข.**

ปลาอะไร
ปลาทู
ไก่อะไร
ไก่อบ
เนื้ออะไร
เนื้อแพะ

หมูอะไร
หมูหวาน
กุ้งอะไร
กุ้งแห้ง

### ๘.๕ แบบฝึกหัดการสลับเสียงสูงต่ำ

**ก.**

| | |
|---|---|
| มีไก่ไหม | (ปลา) |
| มีปลาไหม | (เนื้อ) |
| มีเนื้อไหม | (หมู) |
| มีหมูไหม | (กุ้ง) |
| มีกุ้งไหม | (ไก่) |

**ข.**

| | |
|---|---|
| ใส่ไก่ไหม | (ปลา) |
| ใส่ปลาไหม | (เนื้อ) |
| ใส่เนื้อไหม | (หมู) |
| ใส่หมูไหม | (กุ้ง) |
| ใส่กุ้งไหม | (ไก่) |

**ค.**

| | |
|---|---|
| ไม่มี, มีปลา | (ใส่) |
| ไม่ใส่, ใส่ปลา | (ไก่) |
| ไม่ใส่ ใส่ไก่ | (มี) |
| ไม่มี มีไก่ | (ปลา) |

### 8.4 Tone identification and production.

**a.** Identify the tones and record the number of repetitions required.

| | | |
|---|---|---|
| Older brother or sister. | *phii | ........... |
| Younger brother or sister. | *nɔɔŋ | ........... |
| Father's father. | *puu | ........... |
| Older brother of mother or father. | *luŋ | ........... |
| Nephew, niece, grandchild. | *laan | ........... |

**b. Response drill.**

| | |
|---|---|
| plaa ʔaray.<br>plaa thuu. | What kind of fish?<br>Mackerel. |
| kày ʔaray.<br>kày ʔòp. | What kind of chicken?<br>Roast chicken. |
| nʉ́a ʔaray.<br>nʉ́a phɛ́ʔ. | What kind of meat?<br>Goat meat. |
| mǔu ʔaray.<br>mǔu wǎan. | What kind of pork?<br>Sweet pork. |
| kûŋ ʔaray.<br>kûŋ hɛ̂ɛŋ. | What kind of shrimps?<br>Dried shrimps. |

### 8.5 Tone manipulation.

**a. Substitution drill.**

| | | | |
|---|---|---|---|
| mii kày máy. | (plaa) | Have you got any chicken? | (fish) |
| mii plaa máy. | (nʉ́a) | Have you got any fish? | (beef) |
| mii nʉ́a máy. | (mǔu) | Have you got any beef? | (pork) |
| mii mǔu máy. | (kûŋ) | Have you got any pork? | (shrimps) |
| mii kûŋ máy. | (kày) | Have you got any shrimps? | (chicken) |

**b. Substitution drill.**

| | | | |
|---|---|---|---|
| sày kày máy. | (plaa) | Shall I put some chicken in it? | (fish) |
| sày plaa máy. | (nʉ́a) | Shall I put some fish in it? | (beef) |
| sày nʉ́a máy. | (mǔu) | Shall I put some beef in it? | (pork) |
| sày mǔu máy. | (kûŋ) | Shall I put some pork in it? | (shrimps) |
| sày kûŋ máy. | (kày) | Shall I put some shrimps in it? | (chicken) |

**c. Substitution drill.**

| | | | | |
|---|---|---|---|---|
| mây mii. | mii plaa. | (sày) | No, we haven't. We have fish. | (put) |
| mây sày. | sày plaa. | (kày) | No, don't. Put in some fish. | (chicken) |
| mây sày. | sày kày. | (mii) | No, don't. Put in some chicken. | (have) |
| mây mii. | mii kày. | (plaa) | No, we haven't. We have chicken. | (fish) |

**๘.๖ แบบฝึกหัดการออกเสียงสระและพยัญชนะ**

ก.

มี มือ มู มือ มี มือ มู มือ มี

มีเมีย มือเมือ มูมัว มือเมือ มีเมีย

เมีย เมือ มัว เมือ เมีย เมือ มัว เมือ เมีย

ข.

ง่วงนอน

**๘.๗ แบบฝึกหัดไวยากรณ์**

ก.

ข้างขวา (ซ้าย)
ข้างซ้าย (หน้า)
ข้างหน้า (หลัง)
ข้างหลัง (บน)
ข้างบน (ล่าง)
ข้างล่าง (ขวา)

**ข.**

คุณรู้จักร้านอาหารนิคไหม
รู้จัก
แล้วร้านอาหารสวัสดิ์ล่ะ
รู้จักไหม
ไม่รู้จัก

โรงแรมเอราวัณดีไหม
ดี
แล้วโรงแรมนิคล่ะ
ดีไหม
ไม่ดี

คุณสวัสดิ์อยู่ไหม
อยู่
แล้วคุณยังล่ะ
อยู่ไหม
ไม่อยู่

เลี้ยวขวาได้ไหม
ได้
แล้วทางซ้ายล่ะ
เลี้ยวได้ไหม
ไม่ได้

อาหารที่ร้านนี้ดีไหม
ดี
แล้วอาหารที่ร้านโน้นล่ะ
ดีไหม
ไม่ดี

## 8.6 Vowel and consonant drills.

### a. ii-ʉʉ-uu and ia-ʉa-ua alternation drills.

mii mʉʉ muu mʉʉ mii   mʉʉ muu mʉʉ mii
mii mia   mʉʉ mʉa   muu mua   mʉʉ mʉa   mii mia
mia mʉa mua mʉa mia   mʉa mua mʉa mia

### b. ŋ speed drill.

ŋûaŋ nɔɔn   To be sleepy.

## 8.7 Grammar drills.

### a. Substitution drill.

| | |
|---|---|
| khâŋ khwǎa (sáay) | On the right side. (left) |
| khâŋ sáay (nâa) | On the left side. (front) |
| khâŋ nâa (lǎŋ) | In front. (back) |
| khâŋ lǎŋ (bon) | In back. (upper) |
| khâŋ bon (lâaŋ) | Upstairs. (lower) |
| khâŋ lâaŋ (khwǎa) | Downstairs. (right) |

### b. Response drill.

| | |
|---|---|
| khun rúucàk ráan ʔaahǎan nik máy. | Do you know Nick's Restaurant? |
| rúucàk. | Yes. |
| lɛ́ɛw ráan ʔaahǎan sawàt lâ. | And how about Sawat's Restaurant? |
| rúucàk máy. | Do you know it? |
| mây rúucàk. | No. |
| rooŋrɛɛm ʔeerawan dii máy. | Is the Erawan Hotel good? |
| dii. | Yes. |
| lɛ́ɛw rooŋrɛɛm ník lâ. | And how about Nick's Hotel? |
| dii máy. | Is it good? |
| mây dii. | No. |
| khun sawàt yùu máy. | Is Khun Sawat here? |
| yùu. | Yes. |
| lɛ́ɛw khun yaŋ lâ. | And how about Mr. Young? |
| yùu máy. | Is he here? |
| mây yùu. | No. |
| líaw khwǎa dây máy. | Can you turn right here? |
| dây. | Yes. |
| lɛ́ɛw thaaŋ sáay lâ. | And how about to the left? |
| líaw dây máy. | Can you turn? |
| mây dây. | No. |
| ʔaahǎan thîi ráan níi dii máy. | Is the food at this shop good? |
| dii. | Yes. |
| lɛ́ɛw ʔaahǎan thîi ráan nóon lâ. | And how about the food at that shop? |
| dii máy. | Is it good? |
| mây dii. | No. |

ค.

ห้องน้ำผู้ชายอยู่ที่ไหน
  ห้องน้ำผู้ชายหรือ
  อยู่ที่โน่น

โรงแรมเอราวัณอยู่ที่ไหน
  โรงแรมเอราวัณหรือ
  อยู่ที่โน่น

ร้านอาหารนิคอยู่ที่ไหน
  ร้านอาหารนิคหรือ
  อยู่ที่โน่น

ร้านตัดผมสวัสดิ์อยู่ที่ไหน
  ร้านตัดผมสวัสดิ์หรือ
  อยู่ที่โน่น

ห้องน้ำผู้หญิงอยู่ที่ไหน
  ห้องน้ำผู้หญิงหรือ
  อยู่ที่โน่น

## ๘.๘ เลข

| | | | | | |
|---|---|---|---|---|---|
| เจ็ดสิบบาท | ๗๐ | แปดสิบบาท | ๘๐ | เก้าสิบบาท | ๙๐ |
| เจ็ดสิบเอ็ดบาท | ๗๑ | แปดสิบเอ็ดบาท | ๘๑ | เก้าสิบเอ็ดบาท | ๙๑ |
| เจ็ดสิบสองบาท | ๗๒ | แปดสิบสองบาท | ๘๒ | เก้าสิบสองบาท | ๙๒ |
| เจ็ดสิบสามบาท | ๗๓ | แปดสิบสามบาท | ๘๓ | เก้าสิบสามบาท | ๙๓ |
| เจ็ดสิบสี่บาท | ๗๔ | แปดสิบสี่บาท | ๘๔ | เก้าสิบสี่บาท | ๙๔ |
| เจ็ดสิบห้าบาท | ๗๕ | แปดสิบห้าบาท | ๘๕ | เก้าสิบห้าบาท | ๙๕ |
| เจ็ดสิบหกบาท | ๗๖ | แปดสิบหกบาท | ๘๖ | เก้าสิบหกบาท | ๙๖ |
| เจ็ดสิบเจ็ดบาท | ๗๗ | แปดสิบเจ็ดบาท | ๘๗ | เก้าสิบเจ็ดบาท | ๙๗ |
| เจ็ดสิบแปดบาท | ๗๘ | แปดสิบแปดบาท | ๘๘ | เก้าสิบแปดบาท | ๙๘ |
| เจ็ดสิบเก้าบาท | ๗๙ | แปดสิบเก้าบาท | ๘๙ | เก้าสิบเก้าบาท | ๙๙ |

๗๕ บาท ๘๕ บาท ๙๘ บาท ๗๙ บาท ๙๔ บาท ๙๗ บาท ๗๘ บาท ๗๓ บาท
๙๐ บาท ๗๖ บาท ๙๕ บาท ๘๗ บาท ๗๑ บาท ๘๐ บาท ๘๓ บาท ๘๒ บาท
๘๔ บาท ๘๑ บาท ๗๒ บาท ๙๒ บาท ๘๙ บาท ๙๑ บาท ๖๗ บาท ๔๓ บาท
๙๙ บาท ๔๖ บาท ๘๘ บาท ๕๐ บาท ๗๔ บาท ๗๗ บาท ๙๖ บาท ๖๔ บาท

## ๘.๙ การสนทนาโต้ตอบ

ก.

| | |
|---|---|
| มีปลาไหมคะ | ไม่มีครับ, มีไก่ |
| ใส่ปลาไหมคะ | ไม่ใส่ครับ, ใส่ไก่ |
| มีไก่ไหมคะ | ไม่มีครับ, มีปลา |
| ใส่ไก่ไหมคะ | ไม่ใส่ครับ, ใส่ปลา |

c. **Response drill.**

| | |
|---|---|
| hɔ̂ŋ náam phûu chaay yùu thîi nǎy. | Where's the men's room? |
| hɔ̂ŋ náam phûu chaay lɔ̌ɔ. | The men's room? |
| yùu thîi nôon. | It's over there. |
| rooŋrɛɛm ʔeerawan yùu thîi nǎy. | Where's the Erawan Hotel? |
| rooŋrɛɛm ʔeerawan lɔ̌ɔ. | The Erawan Hotel? |
| yùu thîi nôon. | It's over there. |
| ráan ʔaahǎan ník yùu thîi nǎy. | Where's Nick's Restaurant? |
| ráan ʔaahǎan ník lɔ̌ɔ. | Nick's Restaurant? |
| yùu thîi nôon. | It's over there. |
| ráan tàt phǒm sawàt yùu thîi nǎy. | Where's Sawat's Barber Shop? |
| ráan tàt phǒm sawàt lɔ̌ɔ. | Sawat's Barber Shop? |
| yùu thîi nôon. | It's over there. |
| hɔ̂ŋ náam phûu yǐŋ yùu thîi nǎy. | Where's the ladies' room? |
| hɔ̂ŋ náam phûu yǐŋ lɔ̌ɔ. | The ladies' room? |
| yùu thîi nôon. | It's over there. |

**8.8 Numbers.**

| | | | | | |
|---|---|---|---|---|---|
| cèt sìp bàat | 70 | pɛ̀ɛt sìp bàat | 80 | kâaw sìp bàat | 90 |
| cèt sìp ʔèt bàat | 71 | pɛ̀ɛt sìp ʔèt bàat | 81 | kâaw sìp ʔèt bàat | 91 |
| cèt sìp sɔ̌ɔŋ bàat | 72 | pɛ̀ɛt sìp sɔ̌ɔŋ bàat | 82 | kâaw sìp sɔ̌ɔŋ bàat | 92 |
| cèt sìp sǎam bàat | 73 | pɛ̀ɛt sìp sǎam bàat | 83 | kâaw sìp sǎam bàat | 93 |
| cèt sìp sìi bàat | 74 | pɛ̀ɛt sìp sìi bàat | 84 | kâaw sìp sìi bàat | 94 |
| cèt sìp hâa bàat | 75 | pɛ̀ɛt sìp hâa bàat | 85 | kâaw sìp hâa bàat | 95 |
| cèt sìp hòk bàat | 76 | pɛ̀ɛt sìp hòk bàat | 86 | kâaw sìp hòk bàat | 96 |
| cèt sìp cèt bàat | 77 | pɛ̀ɛt sìp cèt bàat | 87 | kâaw sìp cèt bàat | 97 |
| cèt sìp pɛ̀ɛt bàat | 78 | pɛ̀ɛt sìp pɛ̀ɛt bàat | 88 | kâaw sìp pɛ̀ɛt bàat | 98 |
| cèt sìp kâaw bàat | 79 | pɛ̀ɛt sìp kâaw bàat | 89 | kâaw sìp kâaw bàat | 99 |

Practice reading the following amounts of money. Try to get the time under 45 seconds. Be especially careful with the tones.

| | | | | | | | |
|---|---|---|---|---|---|---|---|
| 75 bàat | 85 bàat | 98 bàat | 79 bàat | 94 bàat | 97 bàat | 78 bàat | 73 bàat |
| 90 bàat | 76 bàat | 95 bàat | 87 bàat | 71 bàat | 80 bàat | 83 bàat | 82 bàat |
| 84 bàat | 81 bàat | 72 bàat | 92 bàat | 89 bàat | 91 bàat | 67 bàat | 43 bàat |
| 99 bàat | 46 bàat | 88 bàat | 50 bàat | 74 bàat | 77 bàat | 96 bàat | 64 bàat |

**8.9 Conversation.**

a. **Chicken instead of fish, and vice versa.**

| | |
|---|---|
| mii plaa máy khá. | mây mii khráp. mii kày. |
| sày plaa máy khá. | mây sày khráp. sày kày. |
| mii kày máy khá. | mây mii khráp. mii plaa. |
| sày kày máy khá. | mây sày khráp. sày plaa. |

**b.** Practice the conversations of 4.9b and 6.9b again, but this time ask for (and get) repetitions from time to time.

**๘.๑๐ การเขียน**

ไป มี บน

| | | |
|---|---|---|
| ไป | มู | ผาม |
| ไส | มี | ผาง |
| ไม | บี | กาง |
| ไข | บอ | กัง |
| โข | สอ | กัน |
| โป | ทอ | บัน |
| แป | ทา | บน |
| ปู | ทาม | ขน |

## 8.10 Writing.

| ไป | มี | บน |
|---|---|---|
| pay | mii | bon |
| To go. | To have. | Upper. |

| | | | | | |
|---|---|---|---|---|---|
| ไป | *pay | มู | muu | ผาม | phǎam |
| ไส | sǎy | มี | *mii | ผาง | phǎaŋ |
| ไม | may | บี | bii | กาง | kaaŋ |
| ไข | khǎy | บอ | bɔɔ | กัง | kaŋ |
| โข | khǒo | สอ | sɔ̌ɔ | กัน | *kan |
| โป | poo | ทอ | thɔɔ | บัน | ban |
| แป | pɛɛ | ทา | thaa | บน | *bon |
| ปู | puu | ทาม | thaam | ขน | khǒn |

# บทที่ ๙

**๙.๑ คำศัพท์**

ทำ
งาน
ทำงาน

ถาน
สถาน
ทูต
สถานทูต

เม
กัน
อเมริกัน
สถานทูตอเมริกัน

อัง
กริด
อังกฤษ
สถานทูตอังกฤษ

วิท
ยุ
วิทยุ
ถนนวิทยุ

เพลิน
จิต
เพลินจิต
ถนนเพลินจิต

ใช่

**๙.๒ โครงสร้างของประโยค**

ไปโรงแรมเอราวัณ
ไปร้านอาหารนิค
ไปสถานทูตอเมริกัน
ไปห้องน้ำ
ไปตลาด

สถานทูตอเมริกัน
สถานทูตอังกฤษ
ถนนวิทยุ
ถนนเพลินจิต

ไปทำงาน
ไปตัดผม
ไปซื้อปลา

# LESSON 9

## 9.1 Vocabulary and expansions.

| | |
|---|---|
| tham | To do, make. |
| ŋaan | Work, party, ceremony. |
| tham ŋaan | To work. |
| thǎan | |
| sathǎan | |
| thûut | |
| sathǎanthûut | Embassy. |
| mee | |
| kan | |
| ʔameerikan | American. |
| sathǎanthûut ʔameerikan | American Embassy. |
| ʔaŋ | |
| krìt | |
| ʔaŋkrìt | England, English. |
| sathǎanthûut ʔaŋkrìt | British Embassy. |
| wít | |
| yúʔ | |
| wítthayúʔ | Radio, wireless. |
| thanǒn wítthayúʔ | Wireless Road. |
| phləən | |
| cìt | |
| phləəncìt | Ploenchit. |
| thanǒn phləəncìt | Ploenchit Road. |
| chây | To be the one meant, to be so, to be a fact. That's right. |

## 9.2 Patterns.

| | |
|---|---|
| pay rooŋrɛɛm ʔeerawan | To go to the Erawan Hotel. |
| pay ráan ʔaahǎan ník | To go to Nick's Restaurant. |
| pay sathǎanthûut ʔameerikan | To go to the American Embassy. |
| pay hɔ̂ŋ náam | To go to the bathroom. |
| pay talàat | To go to the market. |
| pay tham ŋaan | To go to work. |
| pay tàt phǒm | To go get a haircut. |
| pay sɨ́ɨ plaa | To go buy fish. |
| sathǎanthûut ʔameerikan | The American Embassy. |
| sathǎanthûut ʔaŋkrìt | The British Embassy. |
| thanǒn wítthayúʔ | Wireless Road. |
| thanǒn phləəncìt | Ploenchit Road. |

## ๕.๓ บทสนทนา

ก. ไปไหน

ข. ไปทำงาน

ก. คุณทำงานที่ไหน

ข. ที่สถานทูตอเมริกัน

ก. อยู่ที่ถนนวิทยุใช่ไหม

ข. ใช่

## ๕.๔ แบบฝึกหัดการฟังและการออกเสียงสูงต่ำ

**ก.**

ขาย กิน ทอด สั่ง พบ

**ข.**

มีอะไร
มีปลา
มีปลาอะไร
มีปลาทู

เห็นอะไร
เห็นหมู
เห็นหมูอะไร
เห็นหมูหวาน

ใส่อะไร
ใส่ไก่
ใส่ไก่อะไร
ใส่ไก่อบ

ชอบอะไร
ชอบกุ้ง
ชอบกุ้งอะไร
ชอบกุ้งแห้ง

ซื้ออะไร
ซื้อเนื้อ
ซื้อเนื้ออะไร
ซื้อเนื้อแพะ

### 9.3 Dialog.

| | |
|---|---|
| A. pay nǎy. | Where are you going? |
| B. pay tham ŋaan. | I'm going to work. |
| A. khun tham ŋaan thîi nǎy. | Where do you work? |
| B. thîi sathǎanthûut ʔameerikan. | At the American Embassy. |
| A. yùu thîi thanǒn wítthayú? chây máy. | It's on Wireless Road, isn't it? |
| B. chây. | That's right. |

### 9.4 Tone identification and production.

a. Identify the tones and record the number of repetitions required.

| | | |
|---|---|---|
| To sell. | *khaay | ........... |
| To eat. | *kin | ........... |
| To fry. | *thɔɔt | ........... |
| To order. | *saŋ | ........... |
| To meet or see. | *phop | ........... |

**b. Response drill.**

| | |
|---|---|
| mii ʔaray. | What do you have? |
| mii plaa. | I have fish. |
| mii plaa ʔaray. | What kind of fish do you have? |
| mii plaa thuu. | I have mackerel. |
| sày ʔaray. | What did you put in it? |
| sày kày. | I put chicken in it. |
| sày kày ʔaray. | What kind of chicken did you put in it? |
| sày kày ʔòp. | I put roast chicken in it. |
| sʉ́ʉ ʔaray. | What did you buy? |
| sʉ́ʉ nʉ́a. | I bought meat. |
| sʉ́ʉ nʉ́a ʔaray. | What kind of meat did you buy? |
| sʉ́ʉ nʉ́a phɛ́ʔ. | I bought goat meat. |
| hěn ʔaray. | What did you see? |
| hěn mǔu. | I saw pork. |
| hěn mǔu ʔaray. | What kind of pork did you see? |
| hěn mǔu wǎan. | I saw sweet pork. |
| chɔ̂ɔp ʔaray. | What do you like? |
| chɔ̂ɔp kûŋ. | I like shrimps. |
| chɔ̂ɔp kûŋ ʔaray. | What kind of shrimps do you like? |
| chɔ̂ɔp kûŋ hɛ̂ɛŋ. | I like dried shrimps. |

### ๕.๕ แบบฝึกหัดการสลับเสียงสูงต่ำ

**ก.**

ซื้อเนื้อไหม (ปลา)
ซื้อปลาไหม (ไก่)
ซื้อไก่ไหม (กุ้ง)
ซื้อกุ้งไหม (หมู)
ซื้อหมูไหม (เนื้อ)

**ข.**

เห็นเนื้อไหม (ปลา)
เห็นปลาไหม (ไก่)
เห็นไก่ไหม (กุ้ง)
เห็นกุ้งไหม (หมู)
เห็นหมูไหม (เนื้อ)

**ค.**

ไม่ซื้อ, ซื้อเนื้อ (เห็น)
ไม่เห็น, เห็นเนื้อ (หมู)

ไม่เห็น, เห็นหมู (ซื้อ)
ไม่ซื้อ, ซื้อหมู (เนื้อ)

### ๕.๖ แบบฝึกหัดการออกเสียงสระและพยัญชนะ

**ก.**

๑. (ผัก) กาด ๒. กัด ๓. เกิด

กาด กัด กาด กัด กาด
เกิด กัด เกิด กัด เกิด

กัด กาด กัด กาด กัด
กัด เกิด กัด เกิด กัด

**ข.**

ใครเป่าปี่
    ป๋าเป่าปี่
ป๋าเป่าปี่ใคร
    ป๋าเป่าปี่ปู่

ใครบีบบ่า
    เบิ้มบีบบ่า
เบิ้มบีบบ่าใคร
    เบิ้มบีบบ่าบิ๋ม

ใครพบผ้า
    พี่พบผ้า
พี่พบผ้าใคร
    พี่พบผ้าพ่อ

### 9.5 Tone manipulation.

**a. Substitution drill.**

| | |
|---|---|
| sʉ́ʉ nʉ́a máy. (plaa) | Do you want to buy some beef? (fish) |
| sʉ́ʉ plaa máy. (kày) | Do you want to buy some fish? (chicken) |
| sʉ́ʉ kày máy. (kûŋ) | Do you want to buy some chicken? (shrimps) |
| sʉ́ʉ kûŋ máy. (mǔu) | Do you want to buy some shrimps? (pork) |
| sʉ́ʉ mǔu máy. (nʉ́a) | Do you want to buy some pork? (beef) |

**b. Substitution drill.**

| | |
|---|---|
| hěn nʉ́a máy. (plaa) | Do you see the beef? (fish) |
| hěn plaa máy. (kày) | Do you see the fish? (chicken) |
| hěn kày máy. (kûŋ) | Do you see the chicken? (shrimps) |
| hěn kûŋ máy. (mǔu) | Do you see the shrimps? (pork) |
| hěn mǔu máy. (nʉ́a) | Do you see the pork? (beef) |

**c. Substitution drill.**

| | |
|---|---|
| mây sʉ́ʉ. sʉ́ʉ nʉ́a. (hěn) | No, I don't want to buy any.<br>I want to buy some beef. (see) |
| mây hěn. hěn nʉ́a. (mǔu) | No, I don't see any.<br>I see some beef. (pork) |
| mây hěn. hěn mǔu. (sʉ́ʉ) | No, I don't see any.<br>I see some pork. (buy) |
| mây sʉ́ʉ. sʉ́ʉ mǔu. (nʉ́a) | No, I don't want to buy any.<br>I want to buy some pork. (beef) |

### 9.6 Vowel and consonant drills.

**a. aa-a-əə contrast drill.**

1. (phàk) kàat Lettuce. 2. kàt To bite. 3. kə̀ət To be born.

kàat kàt kàat kàt kàat kàt kàat kàt kàat kàt
kə̀ət kàt kə̀ət kàt kə̀ət kàt kə̀ət kàt kə̀ət kàt

**b. Response drill.** (p, ph, and b).

| | |
|---|---|
| khray pàw pii. | Who played the horn? |
| pǎa pàw pii. | Papa played the horn. |
| pǎa pàw pii khray. | Whose horn did Papa play? |
| pǎa pàw pii pùu. | Papa played Grandpa's horn. |
| khray phóp phâa. | Who saw the cloth? |
| phîi phóp phâa. | Older One saw the cloth. |
| phîi phóp phâa khray. | Whose cloth did Older One see? |
| phîi phóp phâa phɔ̂ɔ. | Older One saw Father's cloth. |
| khray bìip bàa. | Who squeezed the shoulder? |
| bə̂m bìip bàa. | Berm squeezed the shoulder. |
| bə̂m bìip bàa khray. | Whose shoulder did Berm squeeze? |
| bə̂m bìip bàa bǐm. | Berm squeezed Bim's shoulder. |

## ๕.๗ แบบฝึกหัดไวยากรณ์

ก.

ห้องน้ำอยู่ข้างบน,
ใช่ไหม

ใช่, อยู่ข้างบน

ร้านอาหารนิคอยู่ที่โน่น,
ใช่ไหม

ใช่, อยู่ที่โน่น

โรงแรมเอราวัณอยู่ที่สี่แยก,
ใช่ไหม

ใช่, อยู่ที่สี่แยก

ห้องน้ำผู้หญิงอยู่ทางขวา,
ใช่ไหม

ใช่, อยู่ทางขวา

ห้องอาหารอยู่ข้างล่าง,
ใช่ไหม

ใช่, อยู่ข้างล่าง

สถานทูตอเมริกัน
อยู่ที่ถนนวิทยุ, ใช่ไหม

ใช่, อยู่ที่ถนนวิทยุ

ข.

ห้องน้ำอยู่ข้างล่าง,
ใช่ไหม

ไม่ใช่, อยู่ข้างบน

ห้องอาหารอยู่ข้างบน,
ใช่ไหม

ไม่ใช่, อยู่ข้างล่าง

ห้องนอนอยู่ข้างล่าง,
ใช่ไหม

ไม่ใช่, อยู่ข้างบน

วิทยุอยู่ข้างบน,
ใช่ไหม

ไม่ใช่, อยู่ข้างล่าง

สถานทูตอังกฤษอยู่ทางขวา
ใช่ไหม

ไม่ใช่, อยู่ทางซ้าย

คุณยังอ้วนใช่ไหม
ไม่ใช่, ผอม

คุณสวัสดิ์สูง, ใช่ไหม
ไม่ใช่, เตี้ย

### 9.7 Grammar drills.

**a. Response drill.**

| | |
|---|---|
| hɔ̂ŋ náam yùu khâŋ bon, chây máy.<br>chây. yùu khâŋ bon. | The bathroom is upstairs, isn't it?<br>Yes. It's upstairs. |
| ráan ʔaahǎan ník yùu thîi nôon, chây máy.<br>chây. yùu thîi nôon. | Nick's Restaurant is over there, isn't it?<br>Yes. It's over there. |
| rooŋrɛɛm ʔeerawan yùu thîi sìiyɛ̂ɛk, chây máy.<br>chây. yùu thîi sìiyɛ̂ɛk. | The Erawan Hotel is on the corner, isn't it?<br>Yes. It's on the corner. |
| hɔ̂ŋ náam phûu yǐŋ yùu thaaŋ khwǎa, chây máy.<br>chây. yùu thaaŋ khwǎa. | The ladies' room is to the right, isn't it?<br>Yes. It's to the right. |
| hɔ̂ŋ ʔaahǎan yùu khâŋ lâaŋ, chây máy.<br>chây. yùu khâŋ lâaŋ. | The dining room is downstairs, isn't it?<br>Yes. It's downstairs. |
| sathǎanthûut ʔameerikan yùu thîi thanǒn wítthayúʔ, chây máy.<br>chây. yùu thîi thanǒn wítthayúʔ. | The American Embassy is on Wireless Road, isn't it?<br>Yes. It's on Wireless Road. |

**b. Response drill.**

| | |
|---|---|
| hɔ̂ŋ náam yùu khâŋ lâaŋ, chây máy.<br>mây chây. yùu khâŋ bon. | The bathroom is downstairs, isn't it?<br>No. It's upstairs. |
| hɔ̂ŋ ʔaahǎan yùu khâŋ bon, chây máy.<br>mây chây. yùu khâŋ lâaŋ. | The dining room is upstairs, isn't it?<br>No. It's downstairs. |
| hɔ̂ŋ nɔɔn yùu khâŋ lâaŋ, chây máy.<br>mây chây. yùu khâŋ bon. | The bedroom is downstairs isn't it?<br>No. It's upstairs. |
| wítthayúʔ yùu khâŋ bon, chây máy.<br>mây chây. yùu khâŋ lâaŋ. | The radio is upstairs, isn't it?<br>No. It's downstairs. |
| sathǎanthûut ʔaŋkrìt yùu thaaŋ khwǎa, chây máy.<br>mây chây. yùu thaaŋ sáay. | The British Embassy is to the right, isn't it?<br>No. It's to the left. |
| khun yaŋ ʔûan, chây máy.<br>mây chây. phɔ̌ɔm. | Mr. Young is fat, isn't he?<br>No. He's thin. |
| khun sawàt sǔuŋ, chây máy.<br>mây chây. tîa. | Khun Sawat is tall, isn't he?<br>No. He's short. |

ค.

คุณยังไปทำงาน
(ตัดผม)

คุณยังไปตัดผม
(คุณสวัสดิ์)

คุณสวัสดิ์ไปตัดผม
(ตลาด)

คุณสวัสดิ์ไปตลาด
(โรงแรมเอราวัณ)

คุณสวัสดิ์ไปโรงแรมเอราวัณ
(คุณยัง)

คุณยังไปโรงแรมเอราวัณ
(สถานทูตอเมริกัน)

คุณยังไปสถานทูตอเมริกัน

**๙.๘ เลข**

๙๒ คน ๔๗ บาท ๗๕ คน ๓๔ บาท ๕๑ คน ๘๐ บาท
๗๓ บาท ๒๙ คน ๔๖ บาท ๗๐ คน ๗๒ บาท ๙๓ คน
๑๘ คน ๘๘ บาท ๖๓ คน ๑๒ บาท ๙๔ คน ๒๑ บาท
๒๖ บาท ๙๑ คน ๘๗ บาท ๙๕ คน ๑๕ บาท ๗๕ คน

๓๑ คน ๑๓ บาท ๕๙ คน ๒๘ บาท ๓๓ คน ๔๒ บาท
๕๕ บาท ๖๔ คน ๑๑ บาท ๔๓ คน ๒๗ บาท ๓๙ คน
๘๔ คน ๓๐ บาท ๒๒ คน ๘๙ บาท ๔๘ คน ๕๔ บาท
๖๐ บาท ๕๒ คน ๙๘ บาท ๖๖ คน ๖๙ บาท ๑๖ คน

**๙.๙ การสนทนาโต้ตอบ**

ก.

ซื้อหมูไหมคะ — ไม่ซื้อครับ, ซื้อเนื้อ
เห็นหมูไหมคะ — ไม่เห็นครับ, เห็นเนื้อ
มีหมูไหมคะ — ไม่มีครับ, มีเนื้อ
ใส่หมูไหมคะ — ไม่ใส่ครับ, ใส่เนื้อ
ซื้อเนื้อไหมคะ — ไม่ซื้อครับ, ซื้อหมู
มีเนื้อไหมคะ — ไม่มีครับ, มีหมู
เห็นเนื้อไม่คะ — ไม่เห็นครับ, เห็นหมู
ใส่เนื้อไหมคะ — ไม่ใส่ครับ, ใส่หมู

c. **Substitution drill.**

| | |
|---|---|
| khun yaŋ pay tham ŋaan.<br>(tàt phŏm) | Mr. Young went to work.<br>(cut hair) |
| khun yaŋ pay tàt phŏm.<br>(khun sawàt) | Mr. Young went to get a haircut.<br>(Khun Sawat) |
| khun sawàt pay tàt phŏm.<br>(talàat) | Khun Sawat went to get a haircut.<br>(market) |
| khun sawàt pay talàat.<br>(rooŋrεεm ʔeerawan) | Khun Sawat went to the market.<br>(Erawan Hotel) |
| khun sawàt pay rooŋrεεm ʔeerawan.<br>(khun yaŋ) | Khun Sawat went to the Erawan Hotel.<br>(Mr. Young) |
| khun yaŋ pay rooŋrεεm ʔeerawan.<br>(sathăanthûut ʔameerikan) | Mr. Young went to the Erawan Hotel.<br>(American Embassy) |
| khun yaŋ pay sathăanthûut ʔameerikan. | Mr. Young went to the American Embassy. |

## 9.8 Numbers.

Practice counting people and baht by tens up to ninety and by fives up to ninety-five.

Practice reading the following numbers of people and amounts of money. Try to get the time under 1 minute 25 seconds.

| | | | | | |
|---|---|---|---|---|---|
| 92 khon | 47 bàat | 75 khon | 34 bàat | 51 khon | 80 bàat |
| 73 bàat | 29 khon | 46 bàat | 70 khon | 72 bàat | 93 khon |
| 18 khon | 88 bàat | 63 khon | 12 bàat | 94 khon | 21 bàat |
| 26 bàat | 91 khon | 87 bàat | 95 khon | 15 bàat | 75 khon |
| | | | | | |
| 31 khon | 13 bàat | 59 khon | 28 bàat | 33 khon | 42 bàat |
| 55 bàat | 64 khon | 11 bàat | 43 khon | 27 bàat | 39 khon |
| 84 khon | 30 bàat | 22 khon | 89 bàat | 48 khon | 54 bàat |
| 60 bàat | 52 khon | 98 bàat | 66 khon | 69 bàat | 16 khon |

## 9.9 Conversation.

a. Answer 'beef' instead of 'pork', and vice versa.

| | |
|---|---|
| sɨ́ɨ mŭu máy khá. | mây sɨ́ɨ khráp. sɨ́ɨ nɨ́a. |
| hĕn mŭu máy khá. | mây hĕn khráp. hĕn nɨ́a. |
| mii mŭu máy khá. | mây mii khráp. mii nɨ́a. |
| sày mŭu máy khá. | mây sày khráp. sày nɨ́a. |
| sɨ́ɨ nɨ́a máy khá. | mây sɨ́ɨ khráp. sɨ́ɨ mŭu. |
| mii nɨ́a máy khá. | mây mii khráp. mii mŭu. |
| hĕn nɨ́a máy khá. | mây hĕn khráp. hĕn mŭu. |
| sày nɨ́a máy khá. | mây sày khráp. sày mŭu. |

ข.

ไปไหนคะ

ไป ................. ครับ

คุณ ................. ที่ไหนคะ

ที่ ................. ครับ

................. อยู่ที่ ................. ใช่ไหมคะ

................. ครับ

**๘.๑๐ การเขียน**

| งาน | ชาย | ยาว |
|---|---|---|
| งาน | ซอน | แผม |
| งาย | สอน | แคม |
| งาว | นอน | แขม |
| ยาว | นาน | โขม |
| ยาย | ผาน | โข |
| ขาย | ผาย | ไข |
| ชาย | ผาว | ได |
| ชอย | แผว | ไป |

**b.** Practice the conversations suggested below. Be sure to choose items that fit the meaning. Don't try to be original.

| | |
|---|---|
| pay nǎy khá. | |
| pay ................. khráp. | Work.<br>Get a haircut.<br>Buy some pork. |
| khun ................. thîi nǎy khá. | |
| thîi ................. khráp. | British Embassy.<br>American Embassy.<br>Sawat's Barber Shop.<br>The market.<br>The shop |
| ................. yùu thîi ................. chây máy khá. | Ploenchit Road.<br>Wireless Road.<br>The intersection. |
| ................. khráp. | Yes. No. |

**9.10 Writing.**

| งาน | ชาย | ยาว |
|---|---|---|
| ŋaan | chaay | yaaw |
| Work. | Male. | Long. |

| | | | | | |
|---|---|---|---|---|---|
| งาน | *ŋaan | ซอน | sɔɔn | แผม | phɛ̌ɛm |
| งาย | ŋaay | สอน | sɔ̌ɔn | แคม | khɛɛm |
| งาว | ŋaaw | นอน | *nɔɔn | แขม | khɛ̌ɛm |
| ยาว | *yaaw | นาน | naan | โขม | khǒom |
| ยาย | yaay | ผาน | phǎan | โข | khǒo |
| ขาย | khǎay | ผาย | phǎay | ไข | khǎy |
| ชาย | *chaay | ผาว | phǎaw | ได | day |
| ชอย | chɔɔy | แผว | phɛ̌ɛw | ไป | *pay |

# บทที่ ๑๐

**ข.**

คุณยังเป็นคนอังกฤษ บ้านเขาอยู่ที่ถนนวิทยุ เขาทำงานที่สถานทูตอังกฤษ สถานทูตอังกฤษอยู่ที่ถนนเพลินจิต

คุณสวัสดิ์เป็นคนไทย บ้านเขาอยู่ที่ถนนเพลินจิต เขาทำงานที่สถานทูตอเมริกัน สถานทูตอเมริกันอยู่ที่ถนนวิทยุ

บ้านคุณยังร้อน เขาไม่ชอบอยู่บ้าน เขาชอบไปทำงานมากกว่า บ้านคุณสวัสดิ์เย็น เขาชอบอยู่บ้าน เขาไม่ชอบไปทำงาน

อาหารที่บ้านคุณยังไม่ดี เขาไม่ชอบกินที่บ้าน เขาชอบไปกินที่ร้านอาหารนิคหรือที่โรงแรมเอราวัณ อาหารที่บ้านคุณสวัสดิ์ดี เขาชอบกินที่บ้าน เขาไม่ชอบกินที่ร้านอาหาร

คุณยังเป็นคนอเมริกันใช่ไหม
ไม่ใช่, เขาเป็นคนอังกฤษ

คุณสวัสดิ์ทำงานที่สถานทูตไทยใช่ไหม
ไม่ใช่, เขาทำงานที่สถานทูตอเมริกัน

คุณสวัสดิ์เป็นคนอังกฤษใช่ไหม
ไม่ใช่, เขาเป็นคนไทย

สถานทูตอังกฤษอยู่ที่ถนนวิทยุใช่ไหม
ไม่ใช่, สถานทูตอังกฤษอยู่ที่ถนนเพลินจิต

บ้านคุณยังอยู่ที่ถนนเพลินจิตใช่ไหม
ไม่ใช่, บ้านคุณยังอยู่ที่ถนนวิทยุ

สถานทูตอเมริกันอยู่ที่ถนนเพลินจิตใช่ไหม
ไม่ใช่, สถานทูตอเมริกันอยู่ที่ถนนวิทยุ

บ้านคุณสวัสดิ์อยู่ที่ถนนวิทยุใช่ไหม
ไม่ใช่,
บ้านคุณสวัสดิ์อยู่ที่ถนนเพลินจิต

บ้านคุณยังเย็นกว่าบ้านคุณสวัสดิ์ใช่ไหม
ไม่ใช่,
บ้านคุณสวัสดิ์เย็นกว่าบ้านคุณยัง

คุณยังทำงานที่สถานทูตอเมริกันใช่ไหม
ไม่ใช่
เขาทำงานที่สถานทูตอังกฤษ

บ้านคุณสวัสดิ์ร้อนกว่าบ้านคุณยังใช่ไหม
ไม่ใช่
บ้านคุณยังร้อนกว่าบ้านคุณสวัสดิ์

# LESSON 10

## (Review)

**a. Review sections 3, 5, 7, and 9 of lessons 6–9.**

**b. Narrative.** (For comprehension only.)

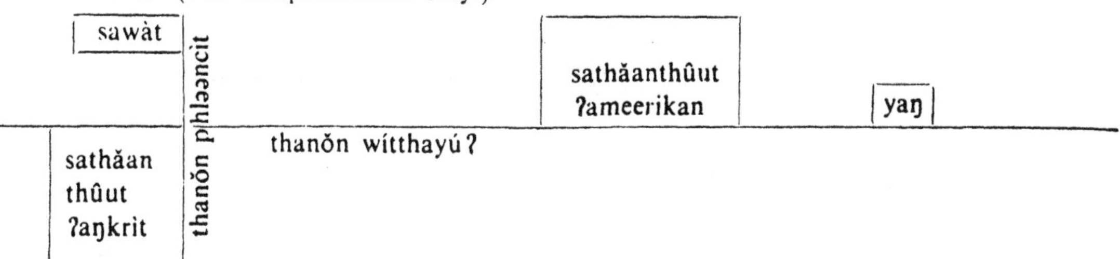


khun yaŋ pen (is) khon ʔaŋkrìt. bâan (house) kháw yùu thîi thanǒn wítthayúʔ. kháw tham ŋaan thîi sathǎanthûut ʔaŋkrìt. sathǎanthûut ʔaŋkrìt yùu thîi thanǒn phləəncìt.

khun sawàt pen khon thay. bâan kháw yùu thîi thanǒn phləəncìt. kháw tham ŋaan thîi sathǎanthûut ʔameerikan. sathǎanthûut ʔameerikan yùu thîi thanǒn wítthayúʔ.

bâan khun yaŋ rɔ́ɔn. kháw mây chɔ̂ɔp yùu bâan. kháw chɔ̂ɔp pay tham ŋaan mâak kwàa. bâan khun sawàt yen. kháw chɔ̂ɔp yùu bâan. kháw mây chɔ̂ɔp pay tham ŋaan.

ʔaahǎan thîi bâan khun yaŋ mây dii. kháw mây chɔ̂ɔp kin (eat) thîi bâan. kháw chɔ̂ɔp pay kin thîi ráan ʔaahǎan ník rʉ thîi rooŋreem ʔeerawan. ʔaahǎan thîi bâan khun sawàt dii. kháw chɔ̂ɔp kin thîi bâan. kháw mây chɔ̂ɔp kin thîi ráan ʔaahǎan.

Read the following questions and answers for comprehension only. Most of them are much too long to be used as conversation at this stage.

khun yaŋ pen khon ʔameerikan chây máy.
  mây chây. kháw pen khon ʔaŋkrìt.

khun sawàt pen khon ʔaŋkrìt chây máy.
  mây chây. kháw pen khon thay.

bâan khun yaŋ yùu thîi thanǒn phləəncìt chây máy.
  mây chây. bâan khun yaŋ yùu thîi thanǒn wítthayúʔ.

bâan khun sawàt yùu thîi thanǒn wítthayúʔ chây máy.
  mây chây. bâan khun sawàt yùu thîi thanǒn phləəncìt.

khun yaŋ tham ŋaan thîi sathǎanthûut ʔameerikan chây máy.
  mây chây. kháw tham ŋaan thîi sathǎanthûut ʔaŋkrìt.

khun sawàt tham ŋaan thîi sathǎanthûut thay chây máy.
  mây chây. kháw tham ŋaan thîi sathǎanthûut ʔameerikan.

sathǎanthûut ʔaŋkrìt yùu thîi thanǒn wítthayúʔ chây máy.
  mây chây. sathǎanthûut ʔaŋkrìt yùu thîi thanǒn phləəncìt.

sathǎanthûut ʔameerikan yùu thîi thanǒn phləəncìt chây máy.
  mây chây. sathǎanthûut ʔameerikan yùu thîi thanǒn wítthayúʔ.

bâan khun yaŋ yen kwàa bâan khun sawàt chây máy.
  mây chây. bâan khun sawàt yen kwàa bâan khun yaŋ.

bâan khun sawàt rɔ́ɔn kwàa bâan khun yaŋ chây máy.
  mây chây. bâan khun yaŋ rɔ́ɔn kwàa bâan khun sawàt.

(More.)

คุณยังชอบอยู่บ้านมากกว่าไปทำงานใช่ไหม

ไม่ใช่, เขาชอบไปทำงานมากกว่าอยู่บ้าน

คุณสวัสดิ์ชอบไปทำงานมากกว่าอยู่บ้านใช่ไหม

ไม่ใช่, เขาชอบอยู่บ้านมากกว่าไปทำงาน

อาหารที่บ้านคุณยังดีกว่าอาหารที่บ้านคุณสวัสดิ์ใช่ไหม

ไม่ใช่, อาหารที่บ้านคุณสวัสดิ์ดีกว่าอาหารที่บ้านคุณยัง

คุณยังชอบกินที่บ้านมากกว่าไปกินที่ร้านอาหารใช่ไหม

ไม่ใช่, เขาชอบไปกินที่ร้านอาหารมากกว่ากินที่บ้าน

คุณสวัสดิ์ชอบไปกินที่ร้านอาหารมากกว่าที่บ้านใช่ไหม

ไม่ใช่, เขาชอบกินที่บ้านมากกว่าที่ร้านอาหาร

คุณยังทำงานที่ไหน

คุณยังทำงานที่สถานทูตอังกฤษ

สถานทูตอังกฤษอยู่ที่ไหน

สถานทูตอังกฤษอยู่ที่ถนนเพลินจิต

อาหารที่ไหนดีกว่ากัน ที่บ้านคุณยังหรือที่บ้านคุณสวัสดิ์

อาหารที่บ้านคุณสวัสดิ์ดีกว่าอาหารที่บ้านคุณยัง

ที่ไหนเย็นกว่ากัน ที่บ้านคุณสวัสดิ์หรือที่บ้านคุณยัง

ที่บ้านคุณสวัสดิ์เย็นกว่าที่บ้านคุณยัง

ใครชอบอยู่บ้านมากกว่ากัน คุณยังหรือคุณสวัสดิ์

คุณสวัสดิ์ชอบอยู่บ้านมากกว่าคุณยัง

ใครชอบทำงานมากกว่ากัน คุณยังหรือคุณสวัสดิ์

คุณยังชอบทำงานมากกว่าคุณสวัสดิ์

**ข.**

ก. คุณครับ, ขอโทษ ที่นี่สถานทูตอเมริกันใช่ไหมครับ

ข. ใช่ครับ

ก. คุณรู้จักคุณยังไหมครับ

ข. รู้จักครับ

ก. เขาทำงานที่นี่ใช่ไหมครับ

ข. ไม่ใช่ครับ, เขาทำงานที่สถานทูตอังกฤษ

ก. สถานทูตอังกฤษอยู่ที่ไหนครับ

ข. คุณรู้จักถนนเพลินจิตไหมครับ

ก. ไม่รู้จักครับ

ข. เดินตรงไปทางโน้น ถึงสี่แยกแล้วเลี้ยวซ้าย สถานทูตอังกฤษอยู่ทางขวาครับ

ก. อ้อ, ขอโทษครับ คุณรู้จักคุณสวัสดิ์ไหมครับ

ข. รู้จักครับ

ก. เขาทำงานที่ไหนครับ

ข. เขาทำงานที่นี่ครับ เดินไปทางนี้แล้วเลี้ยวขวา ห้องเขาอยู่ทางซ้าย

ก. ขอบคุณมากครับ

ข. ไม่เป็นไรครับ

khun yaŋ chɔ̂ɔp yùu bâan mâak kwàa pay tham ŋaan chây máy.
  mây chây. kháw chɔ̂ɔp pay tham ŋaan mâak kwàa yùu bâan.

khun sawàt chɔ̂ɔp pay tham ŋaan mâak kwàa yùu bâan chây máy.
  mây chây. kháw chɔ̂ɔp yùu bâan mâak kwàa pay tham ŋaan.

ʔaahǎan thîi bâan khun yaŋ dii kwàa ʔaahǎan thîi bâan khun sawàt chây máy.
  mây chây. ʔaahǎan thîi bâan khun sawàt dii kwàa ʔaahǎan thîi bâan khun yaŋ.

khun yaŋ chɔ̂ɔp kin thîi bâan mâak kwàa pay kin thîi ráan ʔaahǎan chây máy.
  mây chây. kháw chɔ̂ɔp pay kin thîi ráan ʔaahǎan mâak kwàa kin thîi bâan.

khun sawàt chɔ̂ɔp pay kin thîi ráan ʔaahǎan mâak kwàa thîi bâan chây máy.
  mây chây. kháw chɔ̂ɔp kin thîi bâan mâak kwàa thîi ráan ʔaahǎan.

khun yaŋ tham ŋaan thîi nǎy.
  khun yaŋ tham ŋaan thîi sathǎanthûut ʔaŋkrìt.

sathǎanthûut ʔaŋkrìt yùu thîi nǎy.
  sathǎanthûut ʔaŋkrìt yùu thîi thanǒn phləəncìt.

ʔaahǎan thîi nǎy dii kwàa kan. thîi bâan khun yaŋ rʉ̌ thîi bâan khun sawàt.
  ʔaahǎan thîi bâan khun sawàt dii kwàa ʔaahǎan thîi bâan khun yaŋ.

thîi nǎy yen kwàa kan. thîi bâan khun sawàt rʉ̌ thîi bâan khun yaŋ.
  thîi bâan khun sawàt yen kwàa thîi bâan khun yaŋ.

khray chɔ̂ɔp yùu bâan mâak kwàa kan. khun yaŋ rʉ̌ khun sawàt.
  khun sawàt chɔ̂ɔp yùu bâan mâak kwàa khun yaŋ.

khray chɔ̂ɔp tham ŋaan mâak kwàa kan. khun yaŋ rʉ̌ khun sawàt.
  khun yaŋ chɔ̂ɔp tham ŋaan mâak kwàa khun sawàt.

c. **Dialog.** (For comprehension only.)

A. khun khráp. khɔ̌ɔ thôot. thîi nîi sathǎanthûut ʔameerikan, chây máy khráp.

  B. chây khráp

A. khun rúucàk khun yaŋ máy khráp.

  B. rúucàk khráp.

A. kháw tham ŋaan thîi nîi, chây máy khráp.

  B. mây chây khráp. kháw tham ŋaan thîi sathǎanthûut ʔaŋkrìt.

A. sathǎanthûut ʔaŋkrìt yùu thîi nǎy khráp.

  B. khun rúucàk thanǒn phləəncìt máy khráp.

A. mây rúucàk khráp.

  B. dəən troŋ pay thaaŋ nóon. thʉ̌ŋ sìiyɛ̂ɛk lɛ́ɛw liaw sáay.
  sathǎanthûut ʔaŋkrìt yùu thaaŋ khwǎa khráp.

A. ʔɔ̌ɔ, khɔ̌ɔ thôot khráp. khun rúucàk khun sawàt máy khráp.

  B. rúucàk khráp.

A. kháw tham ŋaan thîi nǎy khráp.

  B. kháw tham ŋaan thîi nîi khráp. dəən pay thaaŋ níi lɛ́ɛw líaw khwǎa.
  hɔ̂ŋ kháw yùu thaaŋ sáay.

A. khɔ̀ɔpkhun·mâak khráp.

  B. mây pen ray khráp.

# บทที่ ๑๑

## ๑๑.๑ คำศัพท์

จะ

เปล่า

เรียน
โรงเรียน

ประสงค์
ราช
ราชประสงค์
สี่แยกราชประสงค์

วง
เวียน
วงเวียน

สา
ศาลาแดง

ดำริห์
ราชดำริห์

เอ ยู เอ
ใกล้
ก่อน
เชิญ

พบ
พบกัน
ใหม่
พบกันใหม่

นาฬิกา

นาที

ลุง
ปู่
พี่
น้อง
หลาน
กิน
สั่ง
ทอด
ขาย

# LESSON 11

**11.1 Vocabulary and expansions.**

| | |
|---|---|
| càʔ, ca | Will. |
| plàaw | Empty. No. Used to reject a wrong assumption. |
| rian | To study. |
| rooŋrian | School. |
| prasŏŋ | Prasong. A man's name. |
| râat | |
| râatprasŏŋ | Rajprasong. |
| sìiyɛ̂ɛk râatprasŏŋ | Rajprasong Intersection. |
| woŋ | |
| wian | |
| woŋwian | A traffic circle. |
| săa | |
| săaladɛɛŋ | Saladaeng. |
| damrìʔ | |
| râatdamrìʔ | Rajdamri. |
| ʔee yuu ʔee | AUA. American University Alumni Association. |
| klây | To be near. |
| kɔ̀ɔn | Before, first. |
| chəən | To invite. Go ahead. Please do. Help yourself. Similar in meaning to the invitational, palm up, hand gesture. |
| phóp | To see, meet, find. |
| phóp kan | To meet each other. |
| mày | To be new, anew. |
| phóp kan mày | To meet again. |
| naalikaa | Watch, clock, o'clock (in the 24 hour system). |
| naathii | Minute. |
| luŋ | Older brother of father or mother, uncle. |
| pùu | Father's father, grandfather. |
| phîi | Older brother or sister, older sibling. |
| nɔ́ɔŋ | Younger brother or sister, younger sibling. |
| lăan | Nephew, niece, grandchild. |
| kin | To eat. |
| sàŋ | To order. |
| thɔ̂ɔt | To fry (in large pieces). |
| khăay | To sell. |

## ๑๑.๒ โครงสร้างของประโยค

จะไปหรือ
จะทำงานหรือ
จะเลี้ยวหรือ
จะพูดหรือ
จะซื้อหมูหรือ

จะไปโรงเรียน
จะไปห้องน้ำ
จะไปตลาด

สี่แยกราชประสงค์
สี่แยกเพลินจิต
วงเวียนศาลาแดง
วงเวียนวิทยุ

ถนนวิทยุ
ถนนเพลินจิต
ถนนราชดำริห์

โรงเรียน
โรงแรม
โรงงาน

ใกล้สี่แยก
ใกล้โรงเรียน
ใกล้สถานทูต
ที่สถานทูต

## ๑๑.๓ บทสนทนา

ก. จะไปทำงานหรือ
ข. เปล่า, จะไปโรงเรียน
ก. โรงเรียนอยู่ที่ไหน
ข. รู้จักสี่แยกราชประสงค์ไหม
ก. รู้จัก
ข. อยู่ใกล้สี่แยกราชประสงค์
ขอโทษครับ,
ผมไปก่อนนะครับ
ก. เชิญครับ, แล้วพบกันใหม่

## ๑๑.๔ แบบฝึกหัดการฟังและการออกเสียงสูงต่ำ

ก.

อ่าน เขียน ใช้ ทราบ ครัว

## 11.2 Patterns.

| | |
|---|---|
| ca pay lɔ̌ɔ. | You're going, are you? |
| ca tham ŋaan lɔ̌ɔ. | Going to work? |
| ca líaw lɔ̌ɔ. | You mean you're going to turn here? |
| ca phûut lɔ̌ɔ. | Oh, you want to say something, do you? |
| ca sɨ́ɨ mǔu lɔ̌ɔ. | You're going to buy some pork? |
| ca pay rooŋ rian. | I'm going to school. |
| ca pay hɔ̂ŋ náam. | I'm going to the bathroom. |
| ca pay talàat. | I'm going to the market. |
| sìiyɛ̂ɛk râatprasɔ̌ŋ. | Rajprasong Intersection. |
| sìiyɛ̂ɛk phləəncìt | Ploenchit Intersection. |
| woŋwian sǎaladɛɛŋ | Saladaeng Circle. |
| woŋwian wítthayúʔ | Wittayu Circle. |
| thanǒn wítthayúʔ | Wireless Road. |
| thanǒn phləəncìt | Ploenchit Road. |
| thanǒn râatdamrìʔ | Rajdamri Road. |
| rooŋ rian | School. |
| rooŋ rɛɛm | Hotel. (*rɛɛm* means to spend the night.) |
| rooŋ ŋaan | Factory. |
| klây sìiyɛ̂ɛk | Near the intersection. |
| klây rooŋ rian | Near the school. |
| klây sathǎanthûut | Near the Embassy. |
| thîi sathǎanthûut | At the Embassy. |

## 11.3 Dialog.

| | |
|---|---|
| A. ca pay tham ŋaan lɔ̌ɔ. | Going to work? |
| B. plàaw. ca pay rooŋ rian. | No, I'm going to school. |
| A. rooŋ rian yùu thîi nǎy. | Where is the school? |
| B. rúucàk sìiyɛ̂ɛk râatprasɔ̌ŋ máy. | Do you know Rajprasong Intersection? |
| A. rúucàk. | Yes. |
| B. yùu klây sìiyɛ̂ɛk râatprasɔ̌ŋ. | It's near Rajprasong Intersection. |
| khɔ̌ɔ thôot khráp. | Excuse me. |
| phǒm pay kɔ̀ɔn ná khráp. | I must be going now. (I leave first.) |
| A. chəən khráp. lɛ́ɛw phóp kan mày. | All right. We'll meet again. |

## 11.4 Tone identification and production.

**a.** Identify the tones and record the number of repetitions required.

| | | |
|---|---|---|
| To read. | *ʔaan | ........... |
| To write. | *khian | ........... |
| To use. | *chay | ........... |
| To know. | *saap | ........... |
| Kitchen. | *khrua | ........... |

ข.

ใครกิน
  ลุงกิน
ลุงกินอะไร
  ลุงกินปลา

ใครสั่ง
  ปู่สั่ง
ปู่สั่งอะไร
  ปู่สั่งไก่

ใครซื้อ
  น้องซื้อ
น้องซื้ออะไร
  น้องซื้อเนื้อ

ใครขาย
  หลานขาย
หลานขายอะไร
  หลานขายหมู

ใครทอด
  พี่ทอด
พี่ทอดอะไร
  พี่ทอดกุ้ง

**๑๑.๕ แบบฝึกหัดการสลับเสียงสูงต่ำ**

ก.

| | |
|---|---|
| ชอบกุ้งไหม | (หมู) |
| ชอบหมูไหม | (ไก่) |
| ชอบไก่ไหม | (ปลา) |
| ชอบปลาไหม | (เนื้อ) |
| ชอบเนื้อไหม | (กุ้ง) |

ข.

| | | |
|---|---|---|
| ไม่ชอบ, | ชอบกุ้ง | (หมู) |
| ไม่ชอบ, | ชอบหมู | (ไก่) |
| ไม่ชอบ, | ชอบไก่ | (ปลา) |
| ไม่ชอบ, | ชอบปลา | (เนื้อ) |
| ไม่ชอบ, | ชอบเนื้อ | (กุ้ง) |

b. **Response drill.**

| | |
|---|---|
| khray kin. | Who ate? |
| luŋ kin. | Uncle ate. |
| luŋ kin ʔaray. | What did Uncle eat? |
| luŋ kin plaa. | Uncle ate fish. |
| khray sàŋ. | Who ordered? |
| pùu sàŋ. | Grandpa ordered. |
| pùu sàŋ ʔaray. | What did Grandpa order? |
| pùu sàŋ kày. | Grandpa ordered chicken. |
| khray sɨ́ɨ. | Who bought? |
| nɔ́ɔŋ sɨ́ɨ. | Younger One bought. |
| nɔ́ɔŋ sɨ́ɨ ʔaray. | What did Younger One buy? |
| nɔ́ɔŋ sɨ́ɨ nɨ́a. | Younger One bought beef. |
| khray khǎay. | Who sold? |
| lǎan khǎay. | Nephew sold. |
| lǎan khǎay ʔaray. | What did Nephew sell? |
| lǎan khǎay mǔu. | Nephew sold pork. |
| khray thɔ̂ɔt. | Who fried? |
| phîi thɔ̂ɔt. | Older One fried. |
| phîi thɔ̂ɔt ʔaray. | What did Older One fry? |
| phîi thɔ̂ɔt kûŋ. | Older One fried shrimps. |

**11.5 Tone manipulation.**

a. **Substitution drill.**

| | | | |
|---|---|---|---|
| chɔ̂ɔp kûŋ máy. | (mǔu) | Do you like shrimps? | (pork) |
| chɔ̂ɔp mǔu máy. | (kày) | Do you like pork? | (chicken) |
| chɔ̂ɔp kày máy. | (plaa) | Do you like chicken? | (fish) |
| chɔ̂ɔp plaa máy. | (nɨ́a) | Do you like fish? | (beef) |
| chɔ̂ɔp nɨ́a máy. | (kûŋ) | Do you like beef? | (shrimps) |

b. **Substitution drill.**

| | | | |
|---|---|---|---|
| mây chɔ̂ɔp. chɔ̂ɔp kûŋ. | (mǔu) | I don't like it. I like shrimps. | (pork) |
| mây chɔ̂ɔp. chɔ̂ɔp mǔu. | (kày) | I don't like it. I like pork. | (chicken) |
| mây chɔ̂ɔp. chɔ̂ɔp kày. | (plaa) | I don't like it. I like chicken. | (fish) |
| mây chɔ̂ɔp. chɔ̂ɔp plaa. | (nɨ́a) | I don't like it. I like fish. | (beef) |
| mây chɔ̂ɔp. chɔ̂ɔp nɨ́a. | (kûŋ) | I don't like it. I like beef. | (shrimps) |

ข.

| | | | |
|---|---|---|---|
| ชอบกุ้ง | (ใส่) | ใส่ไก่ | (มี) |
| ใส่กุ้ง | (มี) | มีไก่ | (เนื้อ) |
| มีกุ้ง | (ซื้อ) | มีเนื้อ | (ซื้อ) |
| ซื้อกุ้ง | (เห็น) | ซื้อเนื้อ | (เห็น) |
| เห็นกุ้ง | (หมู) | เห็นเนื้อ | (ชอบ) |
| เห็นหมู | (ชอบ) | ชอบเนื้อ | (ใส่) |
| ชอบหมู | (ใส่) | ใส่เนื้อ | (ปลา) |
| ใส่หมู | (มี) | ใส่ปลา | (มี) |
| มีหมู | (ซื้อ) | มีปลา | (ซื้อ) |
| ซื้อหมู | (ไก่) | ซื้อปลา | (เห็น |
| ซื้อไก่ | (เห็น) | เห็นปลา | (ชอบ) |
| เห็นไก่ | (ชอบ) | ชอบปลา | |
| ชอบไก่ | (ใส่) | | |

**๑๑.๖ แบบฝึกหัดการออกเสียงสระและพยัญชนะ**

ก.

กัน เกิน กัน เกิน กัน เกิน กัน เกิน กัน เกิน

กาน กัน เกิน กัน กาน กัน เกิน กัน กาน

ข.

ใครต่อยตา
ติ๋มต่อยตา
ติ๋มต่อยตาใคร
ติ๋มต่อยตาต้อย

ใครทิ้งถุง
ทอมทิ้งถุง
ทอมทิ้งถุงใคร
ทอมทิ้งถุงแถม

ใครดึงด้าย
แดงดึงด้าย
แดงดึงด้ายใคร
แดงดึงด้ายดำ

**c. Substitution drill.** (Try for maximum speed without sacrificing tonal accuracy.)

| | | | |
|---|---|---|---|
| chɔ̂ɔp kûŋ. | (sày) | I like shrimps. | (put) |
| sày kûŋ. | (mii) | Put in some shrimps. | (have) |
| mii kûŋ. | (sʉ́ʉ) | We have shrimps. | (buy) |
| sʉ́ʉ kûŋ. | (hěn) | I want to buy shrimps. | (see) |
| hěn kûŋ. | (mǔu) | I see shrimps. | (pork) |
| hěn mǔu. | (chɔ̂ɔp) | I see pork. | (like) |
| chɔ̂ɔp mǔu. | (sày) | I like pork. | (put) |
| sày mǔu. | (mii) | Put in some pork. | (have) |
| mii mǔu. | (sʉ́ʉ) | We have pork. | (buy) |
| sʉ́ʉ mǔu. | (kày) | I want to buy pork. | (chicken) |
| sʉ́ʉ kày. | (hěn) | I want to buy chicken. | (see) |
| hěn kày. | (chɔ̂ɔp) | I see chicken. | (like) |
| chɔ̂ɔp kày. | (sày) | I like chicken. | (put) |
| sày kày. | (mii) | Put in some chicken. | (have) |
| mii kày. | (nʉ́a) | We have chicken. | (beef) |
| mii nʉ́a. | (sʉ́ʉ) | We have beef. | (buy) |
| sʉ́ʉ nʉ́a. | (hěn) | I want to buy beef. | (see) |
| hěn nʉ́a. | (chɔ̂ɔp) | I see beef. | (like) |
| chɔ̂ɔp nʉ́a. | (sày) | I like beef. | (put) |
| sày nʉ́a. | (plaa) | Put in some beef. | (fish) |
| sày plaa. | (mii) | Put in some fish. | (have) |
| mii plaa. | (sʉ́ʉ) | We have fish. | (buy) |
| sʉ́ʉ plaa. | (hěn) | I want to buy fish. | (see) |
| hěn plaa. | (chɔ̂ɔp) | I see fish. | (like) |
| chɔ̂ɔp plaa. | | I like fish. | |

### 11.6 Vowel and consonant drills.

**a. aa-a-ɔɔ alternation drill.**

kan kɔɔn kan kɔɔn kan kɔɔn kan kɔɔn kan kɔɔn
kaan kan kɔɔn kan kaan kan kɔɔn kan kaan

**b. Response drill.** (t, th, and d).

| | |
|---|---|
| khray tɔ̀y taa. | Who punched someone in the eye? |
| tim tɔ̀y taa. | Tim punched someone in the eye. |
| tim tɔ̀y taa khray. | Who did Tim punch in the eye? |
| tim tɔ̀y taa tɔ̂y. | Tim punched Toy in the eye. |
| khray thíŋ thǔŋ. | Who threw away the sack? |
| thɔɔm thíŋ thǔŋ. | Tom threw away the sack? |
| thɔɔm thíŋ thǔŋ khray. | Whose sack did Tom throw away? |
| thɔɔm thíŋ thǔŋ thɛ̌ɛm. | Tom threw away Taem's sack. |
| khray dʉŋ dâay. | Who pulled the thread? |
| dɛɛŋ dʉŋ dâay. | Daeng pulled the thread. |
| dɛɛŋ dʉŋ dâay khray. | Whose thread did Daeng pull? |
| dɛɛŋ dʉŋ dâay dam. | Daeng pulled Dum's thread. |

### ๑๑.๗ แบบฝึกหัดไวยากรณ์

ก.

จะไปทำงานหรือ
(โรงเรียน)

เปล่า, จะไปโรงเรียน
(ทำงาน)

จะไปโรงเรียนหรือ
(สถานทูตอังกฤษ)

เปล่า, จะไปทำงาน
(สถานทูตอเมริกัน)

จะไปสถานทูตอังกฤษหรือ
(ห้องน้ำ)

เปล่า, จะไปสถานทูตอเมริกัน
(ห้องอาหาร)

จะไปห้องน้ำหรือ
(ตลาด)

เปล่า, จะไปห้องอาหาร
(วงเวียนศาลาแดง)

จะไปตลาดหรือ
(ทำงาน)

เปล่า, จะไปวงเวียนศาลาแดง
(โรงเรียน)

ข.

ค.

จะไปทำงานหรือ
(โรงเรียน)
เปล่า, จะไปโรงเรียน

จะไปวงเวียนศาลาแดงหรือ
(สี่แยกราชประสงค์)
เปล่า, จะไปสี่แยกราชประสงค์

จะไปถนนเพลินจิตหรือ
(วิทยุ)
เปล่า, จะไปถนนวิทยุ

จะไปสถานทูตอเมริกันหรือ
(อังกฤษ)
เปล่า, จะไปสถานทูตอังกฤษ

จะไปตัดผมหรือ
(ทำงาน)
เปล่า, จะไปทำงาน

## 11.7 Grammar drills.

### a. Substitution drill.

| | |
|---|---|
| ca pay tham ŋaan lɔ̆ɔ. | Going to work? |
| (rooŋ rian) | (school) |
| ca pay rooŋ rian lɔ̆ɔ. | Going to school? |
| (sathǎanthûut ʔaŋkrìt) | (British Embassy) |
| ca pay sathǎanthûut ʔaŋkrìt lɔ̆ɔ. | Going to the British Embassy? |
| (hɔ̂ŋ náam) | (bathroom) |
| ca pay hɔ̂ŋ náam lɔ̆ɔ. | Going to the bathroom? |
| (talàat) | (market) |
| ca pay talàat lɔ̆ɔ. | Going to the market? |
| (tham ŋaan) | (work) |

### b. Substitution drill.

| | |
|---|---|
| plàaw. ca pay rooŋ rian. | No. I'm going to school. |
| (tham ŋaan) | (work) |
| plàaw. ca pay tham ŋaan. | No. I'm going to work. |
| (sathǎanthûut ʔameerikan) | (American Embassy) |
| plàaw. ca pay sathǎanthûut ʔameerikan. | No. I'm going to the American Embassy. |
| (hɔ̂ŋ ʔaahǎan) | (dining room) |
| plàaw. ca pay hɔ̂ŋ ʔaahǎan. | No. I'm going to the dining room. |
| (woŋwian sǎaladɛɛŋ) | (Saladaeng Circle.) |
| plàaw. ca pay woŋwian sǎaladɛɛŋ. | No. I'm going to Saladaeng Circle. |
| (rooŋ rian) | (school) |

### c. Response drill.

| | |
|---|---|
| ca pay tham ŋaan lɔ̆ɔ. | Going to work? |
| (rooŋ rian) | (school) |
| plàaw. ca pay rooŋ rian. | No. I'm going to school. |
| ca pay woŋwian sǎaladɛɛŋ lɔ̆ɔ. | Going to Saladaeng circle? |
| (siiyɛ̂ɛk râatprasɔ̌ŋ) | (Rajprasong Intersection) |
| plàaw. ca pay siiyɛ̂ɛk râatprasɔ̌ŋ. | No. I'm going to Rajprasong Intersection. |
| ca pay thanɔ̆n phlɔɔncìt lɔ̆ɔ. | Going to Ploenchit Road? |
| (wítthayúʔ) | (Wireless) |
| plàaw. ca pay thanɔ̆n wítthayúʔ. | No. I'm going to Wireless Road. |
| ca pay sathǎanthûut ʔameerikan lɔ̆ɔ. | Going to the American Embassy? |
| (ʔaŋkrìt) | (British) |
| plàaw. ca pay sathǎanthûut ʔaŋkrìt. | No. I'm going to the British Embassy. |
| ca pay tàt phǒm lɔ̆ɔ. | Going to get a haircut? |
| (tham ŋaan) | (work) |
| plàaw. ca pay tham ŋaan. | No. I'm going to work. |

ง.

โรงแรมเอราวัณอยู่ที่ไหน
(สี่แยกราชประสงค์)
รู้จักสี่แยกราชประสงค์ไหม
รู้จัก
โรงแรมเอราวัณอยู่ใกล้
สี่แยกราชประสงค์

ร้านอาหารนิคอยู่ที่ไหน
(วงเวียนวิทยุ)
รู้จักวงเวียนวิทยุไหม
รู้จัก
ร้านอาหารนิคอยู่ใกล้วงเวียนวิทยุ

สถานทูตอังกฤษอยู่ที่ไหน
(สี่แยกเพลินจิต)
รู้จักสี่แยกเพลินจิตไหม
รู้จัก
สถานทูตอังกฤษอยู่ใกล้สี่แยกเพลินจิต

เอ ยู เอ อยู่ที่ไหน
(วงเวียนศาลาแดง)
รู้จักวงเวียนศาลาแดงไหม
รู้จัก
เอ ยู เอ อยู่ใกล้
วงเวียนศาลาแดง

สถานทูตอเมริกันอยู่ที่ไหน
(ถนนวิทยุ)
รู้จักถนนวิทยุไหม
รู้จัก
สถานทูตอเมริกันอยู่ที่ถนนวิทยุ

### ๑๑.๘ เลข

๐๐๘๐ แปดนาฬิกา
๑๓๓๐ สิบสามนาฬิกาสามสิบนาที
๒๓๕๙ ยี่สิบสามนาฬิกาห้าสิบเก้านาที

| | | | | |
|---|---|---|---|---|
| ๒๐๐๕ | ๑๑๔๕ | ๑๘๓๐ | ๐๙๕๐ | ๑๖๐๐ |
| ๐๕๔๐ | ๒๔๐๐ | ๐๗๓๕ | ๒๑๑๕ | ๐๑๕๕ |
| ๑๙๓๐ | ๐๖๔๕ | ๑๓๒๕ | ๐๒๓๕ | ๒๓๕๕ |
| ๑๒๑๐ | ๐๘๕๐ | ๒๒๔๐ | ๑๕๓๐ | ๒๔๐๕ |

**d. Response drill.**

| | |
|---|---|
| rooŋrɛɛm ?eerawan yùu thîi nǎy. | Where's the Erawan Hotel? |
| (sìiyɛ̂ɛk râatprasǒŋ) | (Rajprasong Intersection) |
| rúucàk sìiyɛ̂ɛk râatprasǒŋ máy. | Do you know Rajprasong Intersection? |
| rúucàk. | Yes. |
| rooŋrɛɛm ?eerawan yùu klây sìiyɛ̂ɛk râatprasǒŋ. | The Erawan Hotel is near Rajprasong Intersection. |
| ráan ?aahǎan ník yùu thîi nǎy. | Where's Nick's Restaurant? |
| (woŋwian wítthayú?) | (Wittayu circle) |
| rúucàk woŋwian wítthayú? máy. | Do you know Wittayu circle? |
| rúucàk. | Yes. |
| ráan ?aahǎan ník yùu klây woŋwian wítthayú?. | Nick's Restaurant is near Wittayu circle. |
| sathǎanthûut ?aŋkrìt yùu thîi nǎy. | Where's the British Embassy? |
| (sìiyɛ̂ɛk phlɔɔncìt) | (Ploenchit Intersection) |
| rúucàk sìiyɛ̂ɛk phlɔɔncìt máy. | Do you know Ploenchit Intersection? |
| rúucàk. | Yes. |
| sathǎanthûut ?aŋkrìt yùu klây sìiyɛ̂ɛk phlɔɔncìt. | The British Embassy is near Ploenchit Intersection. |
| ?ee yuu ?ee yùu thîi nǎy. | Where's A.U.A.? |
| (woŋwian sǎaladɛɛŋ) | (Saladaeng circle) |
| rúucàk woŋwian sǎaladɛɛŋ máy. | Do you know Saladaeng circle? |
| rúucàk. | Yes. |
| ?ee yuu ?ee yùu klây woŋwian sǎaladɛɛŋ. | A.U.A. is near Saladaeng circle. |
| sathǎanthûut ?ameerikan yùu thîi nǎy. | Where's the American Embassy? |
| (thanǒn wítthayú?) | (Wireless Road) |
| rúucàk thanǒn wítthayú? máy. | Do you know Wireless Road? |
| rúucàk. | Yes. |
| sathǎanthûut ?ameerikan yùu thîi thanǒn wítthayú?. | The American Embassy is on Wireless Road. |

**11.8 Numbers.**

The 24 hour system for telling the time of day is used in official notices — not in ordinary conversation. It is introduced here mainly as another way of practicing numbers. The more difficult 6 hour system will appear later. In the meantime, don't be afraid to use the 24 hour system if you have need of mentioning a time. It is understood by everyone.

| | | |
|---|---|---|
| 0800 | pɛ̀ɛt naalikaa | 8:00 a.m. |
| 1330 | sìp sǎam naalikaa sǎam sìp naathii | 1:30 p.m. |
| 2359 | yîi sìp sǎam naalikaa hâa sìp kâaw naathii | 11:59 p.m. |

Practice reading the following times. Try to get the time under 50 seconds.

| | | | | |
|---|---|---|---|---|
| 2005 | 1145 | 1830 | 0950 | 1600 |
| 0540 | 2400 | 0735 | 2115 | 0155 |
| 1930 | 0645 | 1325 | 0235 | 2355 |
| 1210 | 0850 | 2240 | 1530 | 2405 |

**d. Response drill.**

| | |
|---|---|
| roonreem ?eerawan yùu thîi nǎy. | Where's the Erawan Hotel? |
| (sìiyɛ̂ɛk râatprasɔ̌ŋ) | (Rajprasong Intersection) |
| rúucàk sìiyɛ̂ɛk râatprasɔ̌ŋ máy. | Do you know Rajprasong Intersection? |
| rúucàk. | Yes. |
| rooŋrɛɛm ?eerawan yùu klây sìiyɛ̂ɛk râatprasɔ̌ŋ. | The Erawan Hotel is near Rajprasong Intersection. |
| ráan ?aahǎan ník yùu thîi nǎy. | Where's Nick's Restaurant? |
| (woŋwian wítthayú?) | (Wittayu circle) |
| rúucàk woŋwian wítthayú? máy. | Do you know Wittayu circle? |
| rúucàk. | Yes. |
| ráan ?aahǎan ník yùu klây woŋwian wítthayú?. | Nick's Restaurant is near Wittayu circle. |
| sathǎanthûut ?aŋkrìt yùu thîi nǎy. | Where's the British Embassy? |
| (sìiyɛ̂ɛk phlɔɔncìt) | (Ploenchit Intersection) |
| rúucàk sìiyɛ̂ɛk phlɔɔncìt máy. | Do you know Ploenchit Intersection? |
| rúucàk. | Yes. |
| sathǎanthûut ?aŋkrìt yùu klây sìiyɛ̂ɛk phlɔɔncìt. | The British Embassy is near Ploenchit Intersection. |
| ?ee yuu ?ee yùu thîi nǎy. | Where's A.U.A.? |
| (woŋwian sǎaladɛɛŋ) | (Saladaeng circle) |
| rúucàk woŋwian sǎaladɛɛŋ máy. | Do you know Saladaeng circle? |
| rúucàk. | Yes. |
| ?ee yuu ?ee yùu klây woŋwian sǎaladɛɛŋ. | A.U.A. is near Saladaeng circle. |
| sathǎanthûut ?ameerikan yùu thîi nǎy. | Where's the American Embassy? |
| (thanɔ̌n wítthayú?) | (Wireless Road) |
| rúucàk thanɔ̌n wítthayú? máy. | Do you know Wireless Road? |
| rúucàk. | Yes. |
| sathǎanthûut ?ameerikan yùu thîi thanɔ̌n wítthayú?. | The American Embassy is on Wireless Road. |

**11.8 Numbers.**

The 24 hour system for telling the time of day is used in official notices — not in ordinary conversation. It is introduced here mainly as another way of practicing numbers. The more difficult 6 hour system will appear later. In the meantime, don't be afraid to use the 24 hour system if you have need of mentioning a time. It is understood by everyone.

| | | |
|---|---|---|
| 0800 | pɛ̀ɛt naalikaa | 8:00 a.m. |
| 1330 | sìp sǎam naalikaa sǎam sìp naathii | 1:30 p.m. |
| 2359 | yîi sìp sǎam naalikaa hâa sìp kâaw naathii | 11:59 p.m. |

Practice reading the following times. Try to get the time under 50 seconds.

| | | | | |
|---|---|---|---|---|
| 2005 | 1145 | 1830 | 0950 | 1600 |
| 0540 | 2400 | 0735 | 2115 | 0155 |
| 1930 | 0645 | 1325 | 0235 | 2355 |
| 1210 | 0850 | 2240 | 1530 | 2405 |

## 11.9 Conversation.

**a.** Answer with any of the 4 kinds of meat not mentioned in the question.

| | |
|---|---|
| mii nʉ́a máy khá. | mây mii khráp. mii .......... . |
| sày mǔu máy khá. | mây sày khráp. sày .......... . |
| sʉ́ʉ plaa máy khá. | mây sʉ́ʉ khráp. sʉ́ʉ .......... . |
| hěn kûŋ máy khá. | mây hěn khráp. hěn .......... . |
| chɔ̂ɔp kày máy khá. | mây chɔ̂ɔp khráp. chɔ̂ɔp .......... . |

Etc.

**b.** Using the following map, practice the conversation suggested below.

woŋwian sǎaladɛɛŋ
thanǒn râatdamrìʔ
siiyɛ̂ɛk râatprasǒŋ
ʔee yuu ʔee
rooŋrɛɛm ʔeerawan
thanǒn phlɔɔncìt
sathǎanthûut ʔaŋkrìt
woŋwian wítthayúʔ
thanǒn wítthayúʔ
ráan ʔaahǎan ník
sathǎanthûut ʔameerikan
siiyɛ̂ɛk phlɔɔncìt

ca pay ............... lɔ̌ɔ khá.

    plàaw khráp. ca pay .............. .

............... yùu thîi nǎy khá.

    rúucàk ............... máy khráp.

rúucàk khâ.

    ............... yùu klây / thîi ............... khráp.

    khɔ̌ɔ thôot khráp. phǒm pay kɔ̀ɔn ná khráp.

chəən khâ. lɛ́ɛw phóp kan mày.

**๑๑.๑๐ การเขียน**

| เห็น | | เอ ยู เอ |
|---|---|---|
| เห็น | หา | อัง |
| เย็น | เห | หัง |
| เปิ่น | เอ | หง |
| เริ่น | เอง | อง |
| เร็ว | เอ็ง | อม |
| ราว | เส็ง | เอม |
| หาว | แสง | เอ็ม |
| หาย | สัง | เข็ม |

### 11.10 Writing.

| เห็น | เอ ยู เอ |
|---|---|
| hěn | ʔee yuu ʔee |
| To see. | A. U. A. |

| | | | | | |
|---|---|---|---|---|---|
| เห็น | *hěn | หา | hǎa | อัง | ʔaŋ |
| เย็น | *yen | เห | hěe | หัง | hǎŋ |
| เป็น | *pen | เอ | *ʔee | หง | hǒŋ |
| เร็น | ren | เอง | ʔeeŋ | อง | ʔoŋ |
| เร็ว | rew | เอ็ง | ʔeŋ | อม | ʔom |
| ราว | raaw | เส็ง | sěŋ | เอม | ʔeem |
| หาว | hǎaw | แสง | sěɛŋ | เอ็ม | ʔem |
| หาย | hǎay | สัง | sǎŋ | เข็ม | khěm |

# บทที่ ๑๒

## ๑๒.๑ คำศัพท์

กลับ
บ้าน
กลับบ้าน

สุ
ขุม
สุขุม
สุขุมวิท
ถนนสุขุมวิท

ซอย

ที่
ที่ห้า

เลข
เลขที่
เลขที่ห้า
บ้านเลขที่ห้า

เท่า
ไหร่
เท่าไหร่
ที่เท่าไหร่

ศูนย์

ทับ

ร้อย

คุณจอน

คุณเจน

คุณเดวิด

คุณแมรี่

## ๑๒.๒ โครงสร้างของประโยค

ที่หนึ่ง
ที่สอง
ที่สาม
ที่เท่าไหร่

เลขที่สี่
เลขที่ห้า
เลขที่หก

บ้านเลขที่เจ็ด
บ้านเลขที่แปด
บ้านเลขที่เก้า

สามทับหนึ่ง
เจ็ดทับสอง
เก้าทับสี่

# LESSON 12

## 12.1 Vocabulary and expansions.

| | |
|---|---|
| klàp | To return. |
| bâan | House. |
| klàp bâan | To go home. |
| sù? | |
| khŭm | |
| sùkhŭm | |
| sùkhŭmwít | Sukhumvit. |
| thanŏn sùkhŭmwít | Sukhumvit Road. |
| sɔɔy | Soi, lane. |
| thîi | Precedes cardinal numbers to form ordinals, -th. |
| thîi hâa | The fifth. |
| lêek | Number. |
| lêek thîi | A number used as a designation. |
| lêek thîi hâa | Number five. |
| bâan lêek thîi hâa | House number 5. |
| thâw | |
| rày | |
| thâwrày | How much, how many. |
| thîi thâwrày | The question used to elicit an ordinal number. Which number in order? The 'how manyeth' ? |
| sŭun | Zero. |
| tháp | To superimpose, lay on top, run over. |
| rɔ́ɔy | A hundred. |
| khun cɔɔn | John. |
| khun ceen | Jane. |
| khun deewít | David. |
| khun mɛɛrîi | Mary. |

## 12.2 Patterns.

| | |
|---|---|
| thîi nùŋ | First. |
| thîi sɔ̌ɔŋ | Second. |
| thîi săam | Third. |
| thîi thâwrày | Which number ? |
| lêek thîi sìi | Number four. |
| lêek thîi hâa | Number five. |
| lêek thîi hòk | Number six. |
| bâan lêek thîi cèt | House number 7. |
| bâan lêek thîi pɛ̀ɛt | House number 8. |
| bâan lêek thîi kâaw | House number 9. |
| săam tháp nùŋ | 3/1. Three slash one. |
| cèt tháp sɔ̌ɔŋ | 7/2. Seven slash two. |
| kâaw tháp sìi | 9/4. Nine slash four. |

## ๑๒.๓ บทสนทนา

ก. ไปไหน

ข. จะกลับบ้าน

ก. คุณอยู่ที่ถนนวิทยุ
ใช่ไหม

ข. ไม่ใช่
ผมอยู่ที่ถนนสุขุมวิท, ซอยหก

ก. บ้านเลขที่เท่าไหร่

ข. บ้านเลขที่,
สี่ศูนย์หนึ่งทับสอง

## ๑๒.๔ แบบฝึกหัดการฟังและการออกเสียงสูงต่ำ

**ก.**

ตอนเช้า ตอนสาย ตอนเที่ยง ตอนบ่าย ตอนเย็น

**ข.**

ลุงกินอะไร
ลุงกินปลา
ลุงกินปลาอะไร
ลุงกินปลาทู

ปู่สั่งอะไร
ปู่สั่งไก่
ปู่สั่งไก่อะไร
ปู่สั่งไก่อบ

น้องซื้ออะไร
น้องซื้อเนื้อ
น้องซื้อเนื้ออะไร
น้องซื้อเนื้อแพะ

หลานขายอะไร
หลานขายหมู
หลานขายหมูอะไร
หลานขายหมูหวาน

พี่ทอดอะไร
พี่ทอดกุ้ง
พี่ทอดกุ้งอะไร
พี่ทอดกุ้งแห้ง

**12.3 Dialog.**

| | |
|---|---|
| A. pay năy. | Where are you going? |
| B. ca klàp bâan. | I'm going home. |
| A. khun yùu thîi thanŏn wítthayúʔ, chây máy. | You live on Wireless Road, don't you? |
| B. mây chây. phŏm yùu thîi thanŏn sùkhŭmwít, sɔɔy hòk. | No. I live on Sukhumvit Road, Soi 6. |
| A. bâan lêek thîi thâwrày. | What's the house number? |
| B. bâan lêek thîi sìi sŭun nùŋ tháp sɔ̌ɔŋ. | The house number is 401/2. |

**12.4 Tone identification and production.**

**a.** Identify the tones and record the number of repetitions required.

| | | |
|---|---|---|
| Morning (especially early morning). | tɔɔn *chaaw | ........... |
| Late morning. | tɔɔn *saay | ........... |
| Noon. | tɔɔn *thiaŋ | ........... |
| Afternoon. | tɔɔn *baay | ........... |
| Late afternoon or evening. | tɔɔn *yen | ........... |

**b. Response drill.**

| | |
|---|---|
| luŋ kin ʔaray. | What did Uncle eat? |
| luŋ kin plaa. | Uncle ate fish. |
| luŋ kin plaa ʔaray. | What kind of fish did Uncle eat? |
| luŋ kin plaa thuu. | Uncle ate mackerel. |
| pùu sàŋ ʔaray. | What did Grandpa order? |
| pùu sàŋ kày. | Grandpa ordered chicken. |
| pùu sàŋ kày ʔaray. | What kind of chicken did Grandpa order? |
| pùu sàŋ kày ʔòp. | Grandpa ordered roast chicken. |
| nɔ́ɔŋ sʉ́ʉ ʔaray. | What did Younger One buy? |
| nɔ́ɔŋ sʉ́ʉ nʉ́a. | Young One bought meat. |
| nɔ́ɔŋ sʉ́ʉ nʉ́a ʔaray. | What kind of meat did Younger One buy? |
| nɔ́ɔŋ sʉ́ʉ nʉ́a phɛ́ʔ. | Younger One bought goat meat. |
| lăan khăay ʔaray. | What did Nephew sell? |
| lăan khăay mŭu. | Nephew sold pork. |
| lăan khăay mŭu ʔaray. | What kind of pork did Nephew sell? |
| lăan khăay mŭu wăan. | Nephew sold sweet pork. |
| phîi thɔ̂ɔt ʔaray. | What did Older One fry? |
| phîi thɔ̂ɔt kûŋ. | Older One fried shrimps. |
| phîi thɔ̂ɔt kûŋ ʔaray. | What kind of shrimps did Older One fry? |
| phîi thɔ̂ɔt kûŋ hɛ̂ɛŋ. | Older One fried dried shrimps. |

### ๑๒.๕ แบบฝึกหัดการสลับเสียงสูงต่ำ

ก.

ควายเตี้ยกว่าหมู,
ใช่ไหม

ไม่ใช่.
ควายสูงกว่า (หมู)

หมูผอมกว่าไก่,
ใช่ไหม

ไม่ใช่,
หมูอ้วนกว่า (ไก่)

พี่เล็กกว่าน้อง,
ใช่ไหม

ไม่ใช่,
พี่ใหญ่กว่า (น้อง)

น้องสูงกว่าพี่,
ใช่ไหม

ไม่ใช่,
น้องเตี้ยกว่า (พี่)

ไก่ใหญ่กว่าวัว,
ใช่ไหม

ไม่ใช่
ไก่เล็กกว่า (วัว)

### ๒๒.๖ แบบฝึกหัดการออกเสียงสระและพยัญชนะ

ก. กาว แกว กาว แกว กาว แกว กาว แกว กาว แกว
ลาว แลว เลว แลว ลาว แลว เลว แลว ลาว

ข.

ใครจับจาน
แจ๋วจับจาน
แจ๋วจับจานใคร
แจ๋วจับจานจิม

ใครเช็ดช้อน
ชดเช็ดช้อน
ชดเช็ดช้อนใคร
ชดเช็ดช้อนชม

### ๑๒.๗ แบบฝึกหัดไวยากรณ์

ก.

บ้านเลขที่สี่ศูนย์หนึ่ง
(เก้าศูนย์แปด)
บ้านเลขที่เก้าศูนย์แปด
(ห้าสี่สาม)

บ้านเลขที่ห้าสี่สาม
(เก้าห้าเก้า)
บ้านเลขที่เก้าห้าเก้า
(สี่ศูนย์หนึ่ง)

**12.5 Tone manipulation.**

**a. Response drill.** (Drill first without the parenthesized parts.)

| | |
|---|---|
| khwaay tîa kwàa mŭu, | The buffalo is shorter than the pig, |
| chây máy. | isn't it? |
| mây chây. | No. |
| khwaay sŭuŋ kwàa (mŭu). | The buffalo is taller (than the pig). |
| phîi lék kwàa nɔ́ɔŋ, | Older One is smaller than Younger One, |
| chây máy. | isn't he? |
| mây chây. | No. |
| phîi yày kwàa (nɔ́ɔŋ). | Older One is bigger (than Younger One). |
| kày yày kwàa wua, | The chicken is bigger than the cow, |
| chây máy. | isn't it? |
| mây chây. | No. |
| kày lék kwàa (wua). | The chicken is smaller (than the cow). |
| mŭu phɔ̌ɔm kwàa kày, | The pig is thinner than the chicken, |
| chây máy. | isn't it? |
| mây chây. | No. |
| mŭu ʔûan kwàa (kày). | The pig is fatter (than the chicken). |
| nɔ́ɔŋ sŭuŋ kwàa phîi, | Younger One is taller than Older One, |
| chây máy. | isn't she? |
| mây chây. | No. |
| nɔ́ɔŋ tîa kwàa (phîi). | Younger One is shorter (than Older One). |

**12.6 Vowel and consonant drills.**

**a. aaw-ɛɛw-eew alternation drill.**

kaaw kɛɛw kaaw kɛɛw kaaw kɛɛw kaaw kɛɛw kaaw kɛɛw

laaw lɛɛw leew lɛɛw laaw lɛɛw leew lɛɛw laaw

**b. Response drill.** (c and ch).

| | |
|---|---|
| khray càp caan. | Who grabbed the plate? |
| cɛ̌w càp caan. | Jaeo grabbed the plate. |
| cɛ̌w càp caan khray. | Whose plate did Jaeo grab? |
| cɛ̌w càp caan cim. | Jaeo grabbed Jim's plate. |
| khray chét chɔ́ɔn. | Who wiped the spoon? |
| chót chét chɔ́ɔn. | Chot wiped the spoon. |
| chót chét chɔ́ɔn khray. | Whose spoon did Chot wipe? |
| chót chét chɔ́ɔn chom. | Chot wiped Chom's spoon. |

**12.7 Grammar drills.**

**a. Substitution drill.**

| | |
|---|---|
| bâan lêek thîi sìi sŭun nʉ̀ŋ. | House number 401. |
| (kâaw sŭun pɛ̀ɛt) | (908) |
| bâan lêek thîi kâaw sŭun pɛ̀ɛt. | House number 908. |
| (hâa sìi săam) | (543) |
| bâan lêek thîi hâa sìi săam. | House number 543. |
| (kâaw hâa kâaw) | (959) |
| bâan lêek thîi kâaw hâa kâaw. | House number 959. |
| (sìi sŭun nʉ̀ŋ) | (401). |

ข.

บ้านเลขที่เท่าไหร่ (๗๔๔)
    บ้านเลขที่เจ็ดเก้าสี่

บ้านเลขที่เท่าไหร่ (๘๑๓)
    บ้านเลขที่แปดหนึ่งสาม

บ้านเลขที่เท่าไหร่ (๔๐๖)
    บ้านเลขที่เก้าศูนย์หก

บ้านเลขที่เท่าไหร่ (๕๔๕)
    บ้านเลขที่ห้าเก้าห้า

ค.

คุณจอนอยู่ที่ถนนวิทยุ, ใช่ไหม
(ซอยหก)

คุณจอนอยู่ที่ซอยหก, ใช่ไหม
(ถนนสุขุมวิท)

คุณจอนอยู่ที่ถนนสุขุมวิท, ใช่ไหม
(คุณเจน)

คุณเจนอยู่ที่ถนนสุขุมวิท, ใช่ไหม
(ถนนราชดำริห์)

คุณเจนอยู่ที่ถนนราชดำริห์, ใช่ไหม
(ซอยห้า)

คุณเจนอยู่ที่ซอยห้า, ใช่ไหม
(ถนนเพลินจิต)

คุณเจนอยู่ที่ถนนเพลินจิต, ใช่ไหม

ง.

คุณเดวิดอยู่ที่ถนนวิทยุ, ใช่ไหม
(เพลินจิต)
    ไม่ใช่, เขาอยู่ที่ถนนเพลินจิต

คุณแมรี่อยู่ที่ซอยห้า, ใช่ไหม
(สาม)
    ไม่ใช่, เขาอยู่ที่ซอยสาม

คุณแมรี่อยู่ที่ถนนเพลินจิต, ใช่ไหม
(สุขุมวิท)
    ไม่ใช่, เขาอยู่ที่ถนนสุขุมวิท

คุณเดวิดอยู่ที่ถนนราชดำริห์ ใช่ไหม
(วิทยุ)
    ไม่ใช่, เขาอยู่ที่ถนนวิทยุ

คุณจอนอยู่ที่ซอยสี่, ใช่ไหม
(หก)
    ไม่ใช่, เขาอยู่ที่ซอยหก

คุณอยู่ที่ถนนสุขุมวิท, ใช่ไหม
(ราชดำริห์)
    ไม่ใช่, ฉันอยู่ที่ถนนราชดำริห์

**b. Response drill.**

bâan lêek thîi thâwrày. (794)
  bâan lêek thîi cèt kâaw sìi.

What's the house number? (794)
  The house number is 794.

bâan lêek thîi thâwrày. (813)
  bâan lêek thîi pɛ̀ɛt nʉ̀ŋ sǎam.

What's the house number? (813)
  The house number is 813.

bâan lêek thîi thâwrày. (906)
  bâan lêek thîi kâaw sǔun hòk.

What's the house number? (906)
  The house number is 906.

bâan lêek thîi thâwrày. (595)
  bâan lêek thîi hâa kâaw hâa.

What's the house number? (595)
  The house number is 595.

**c. Substitution drill.**

khun cɔɔn yùu thîi thanǒn wítthayú?, chây máy. (sɔɔy hòk)

John lives on Wireless Road, doesn't he? (Soi 6)

khun cɔɔn yùu thîi sɔɔy hòk, chây máy. (thanǒn sùkhǔmwít)

John lives on Soi 6, doesn't he? (Sukhumvit Road)

khun cɔɔn yùu thîi thanǒn sùkhǔmwít, chây máy. (khun ceen)

John lives on Sukhumvit Road, doesn't he? (Jane)

khun ceen yùu thîi thanǒn sùkhǔmwít, chây máy. (thanǒn râatdamrì?)

Jane lives on Sukhumvit Road, doesn't she? (Rajdamri Road)

khun ceen yùu thîi thanǒn râatdamrì?, chây máy. (sɔɔy hâa)

Jane lives on Rajdamri Road, doesn't she? (Soi 5)

khun ceen yùu thîi sɔɔy hâa, chây máy. (thanǒn phləəncìt)

Jane lives on Soi 5, doesn't she? (Ploenchit Road)

khun ceen yùu thîi thanǒn phləəncìt, chây máy.

Jane lives on Ploenchit Road, doesn't she?

**d. Response drill.**

khun deewít yùu thîi thanǒn wítthayú?, chây máy. (phləəncìt)
  mây chây.
  kháw yùu thîi thanǒn phləəncìt.

David lives on Wireless Road, doesn't he? (Ploenchit)
  No.
  He lives on Ploenchit Road.

khun mɛɛrîi yùu thîi sɔɔy hâa, chây máy. (sǎam)
  mây chây. kháw yùu thîi sɔɔy sǎam.

Mary lives on Soi 5, doesn't she? (3)
  No. She lives on Soi 3.

khun mɛɛrîi yùu thîi thanǒn phləəncìt, chây máy. (sùkhǔmwít)
  mây chây.
  kháw yùu thîi thanǒn sùkhǔmwít.

Mary lives on Ploenchit Road, doesn't she? (Sukhumvit)
  No.
  She lives on Sukhumvit Road.

khun deewít yùu thîi thanǒn râatdamrì?, chây máy. (wítthayú?)
  mây chây. kháw yùu thîi thanǒn wítthayú?.

David lives on Rajdamri Road, doesn't he? (Wireless)
  No. He lives on Wireless Road.

khun cɔɔn yùu thîi sɔɔy sìi, chây máy. (hòk)
  mây chây. kháw yùu thîi sɔɔy hòk.

John lives on Soi 4, doesn't he? (6)
  No. He lives on Soi 6.

khun yùu thîi thanǒn sùkhǔmwít. chây máy. (râatdamrì?)
  mây chây.
  chán yùu thîi thanǒn râatdamrì?.

You live on Sukhumvit Road, don't you? (Rajdamri)
  No.
  I live on Rajdamri Road.

**๑๒.๘ เลข**

๑๐๐ ร้อยบาท
๑๐๑ ร้อยกะหนึ่งบาท
๑๐๒ ร้อยสองบาท
๒๐๑ สองร้อยกะหนึ่งบาท
๒๐๙ สองร้อยเก้าบาท
๓๑๑ สามร้อยสิบเอ็ดบาท

๖๔๕ หกร้อยสี่สิบห้าบาท
๗๕๖ เจ็ดร้อยห้าสิบหกบาท
๘๖๗ แปดร้อยหกสิบเจ็ดบาท
๙๗๘ เก้าร้อยเจ็ดสิบแปดบาท
๕๓๔ ห้าร้อยสามสิบสี่บาท
๔๒๓ สี่ร้อยยี่สิบสามบาท

| | | | |
|---|---|---|---|
| | ๑ บาท | ๙ บาท | ๕ บาท |
| ๘๐ บาท | ๔๑ บาท | ๕๙ บาท | ๖๕ บาท |
| ๕๘๐ บาท | ๙๔๑ บาท | ๗๕๙ บาท | ๑๖๕ บาท |
| ๒ บาท | ๖ บาท | ๘ บาท | ๑ บาท |
| ๙๒ บาท | ๗๖ บาท | | ๒๑ บาท |
| ๑๙๒ บาท | ๓๗๖ บาท | ๖๐๘ บาท | ๓๒๑ บาท |
| ๒๒๒ บาท | ๘๓๔ บาท | ๔๑๗ บาท | ๙๐๑ บาท |

**๑๒.๙ การสนทนาโต้ตอบ**

**ก.**

ดิฉันสูงกว่าคุณจอน, ใช่ไหมคะ — ไม่ใช่ครับ, คุณเตี้ยกว่าเขา
คุณจอนอ้วนกว่าคุณเจน, ใช่ไหมคะ — ใช่ครับ
คุณเล็กกว่าดิฉัน, ใช่ไหมคะ — ไม่ใช่ครับ, ผมใหญ่กว่าคุณ

**ข.**

(คุณแมรี่ซื้อหมูที่ร้าน, นะคะ)
คุณเจนซื้อหมู, ใช่ไหมคะ
ไม่ใช่ครับ
ใครซื้อคะ
คุณแมรี่ครับ
ซื้ออะไรคะ
ซื้อหมูครับ
ซื้อที่ไหนคะ
ที่ร้านครับ

(คุณจอนสูงกว่าคุณเจน, นะคะ)
คุณเจนสูงกว่าคุณจอน, ใช่ไหมคะ
ไม่ใช่ครับ
ใครสูงกว่าคะ
คุณจอนครับ
สูงกว่าใครคะ
คุณเจนครับ

**12.8 Numbers.**

| | | | |
|---|---|---|---|
| 100 | rɔ́ɔy bàat | 645 | hòk rɔ́ɔy sìi sìp hâa bàat |
| 101 | rɔ́ɔy ka nʉ̀ŋ bàat | 756 | cèt rɔ́ɔy hâa sìp hòk bàat |
| 102 | rɔ́ɔy sɔ̌ɔŋ bàat | 867 | pɛ̀ɛt rɔ́ɔy hòk sìp cèt bàat |
| 201 | sɔ̌ɔŋ rɔ́ɔy ka nʉ̀ŋ bàat | 978 | kâaw rɔ́ɔy cèt sìp pɛ̀ɛt bàat |
| 209 | sɔ̌ɔŋ rɔ́ɔy kâaw bàat | 534 | hâa rɔ́ɔy sǎam sìp sìi bàat |
| 311 | sǎam rɔ́ɔy sìp ʔèt bàat | 423 | sìi rɔ́ɔy yîi sìp sǎam bàat |

Practice reading the following amounts of money. Try to get the time under 40 seconds.

| | | | |
|---|---|---|---|
| | 1 bàat | 9 bàat | 5 bàat |
| 80 bàat | 41 bàat | 59 bàat | 65 bàat |
| 580 bàat | 941 bàat | 759 bàat | 165 bàat |
| 2 bàat | 6 bàat | 8 bàat | 1 bàat |
| 92 bàat | 76 bàat | | 21 bàat |
| 192 bàat | 376 bàat | 608 bàat | 321 bàat |
| 222 bàat | 384 bàat | 417 bàat | 901 bàat |

**12.9 Conversation.**

**a.** Compare members of the class as to height, weight, and size in the manner shown below.

| | |
|---|---|
| dichán sǔuŋ kwàa khun cɔɔn,<br>chây máy khá. | mây chây khráp.<br>khun tîa kwàa kháw. |
| khun cɔɔn ʔûan kwàa khun ceen,<br>chây máy khá. | chây khráp. |
| khun lék kwàa dichán,<br>chây máy khá. | mây chây khráp.<br>phǒm yày kwàa khun. |

**b. Questioning information.**

(khun mɛɛrîi sʉ́ʉ mǔu thîi ráan. ná khá.)

khun ceen sʉ́ʉ mǔu, chây máy khá.
  mây chây khráp.
khray sʉ́ʉ khá.
  khun mɛɛrîi khráp.
sʉ́ʉ ʔaray khá.
  sʉ́ʉ mǔu khráp.
sʉ́ʉ thîi nǎy khá.
  thîi ráan khráp.

(khun cɔɔn sǔuŋ kwàa khun ceen. ná khá.)

khun ceen sǔuŋ kwàa khun cɔɔn, chây máy khá.
  mây chây khráp.
khray sǔuŋ kwàa khá.
  khun cɔɔn khráp.
sǔuŋ kwàa khray khá.
  khun ceen khráp.

(More.)

(คุณสวัสดิ์เห็นคุณจอนที่วงเวียนศาลา
แดง, นะคะ)
คุณสวัสดิ์เห็นคุณจอนที่วงเวียนวิทยุ,
ใช่ไหมคะ
ไม่ใช่ครับ
เห็นที่ไหนคะ
ที่วงเวียนศาลาแดงครับ
ใครเห็นคะ
คุณสวัสดิ์ครับ
เห็นใครคะ
คุณจอนครับ

(คุณยังไปทำงานที่สถานทูตอังกฤษ, นะคะ)
ใครไปคะ
คุณยังครับ
ไปไหนคะ
ไปทำงานครับ
ไปทำงานที่ไหนคะ
ที่สถานทูตครับ
สถานทูตอเมริกัน, ใช่ไหมคะ
ไม่ใช่ครับ
สถานทูตอะไรคะ
สถานทูตอังกฤษครับ

## ๑๒.๑๐ การเขียน

ลุง กิน

| | | |
|---|---|---|
| ลุง | ขึ่ม | ไอ |
| หุง | ขิม | ไห |
| ยุง | กิม | โห |
| ยุย | กิน | โหม |
| คุย | อิน | โดม |
| คุม | เอ็น | ดม |
| คิม | เอน | ดุม |
| คึม | เอ | ดูม |

(khun sawàt hěn khun cɔɔn thîi woŋwian săaladɛɛŋ. ná khá.)

khun sawàt hěn khun cɔɔn thîi woŋwian wítthayú? chây máy khá.
 mây chây khráp.
hěn thîi năy khá.
 thîi woŋwian săaladɛɛŋ khráp.
khray hěn khá.
 khun sawàt khráp.
hěn khray khá.
 khun cɔɔn khráp.

(khun yaŋ pay tham ŋaan thîi sathăanthûut ʔaŋkrìt. ná khá.)

khray pay khá.
 khun yaŋ khráp.
pay năy khá.
 pay tham ŋaan khráp.
pay tham ŋaan thîi năy khá.
 thîi sathăanthûut khráp.
sathăanthûut ʔameerikan, chây máy khá.
 mây chây khráp.
sathăanthûut ʔaray khá.
 sathăanthûut ʔaŋkrìt khráp.

**12.10 Writing.**

| ลุง<br>luŋ<br>Uncle. | กิน<br>kin<br>To eat. |
|---|---|

| | | | | | |
|---|---|---|---|---|---|
| ลุง | *luŋ | ขีม | khĭim | ไอ | ʔay |
| หุง | hŭŋ | ขิม | khĭm | ไห | hăy |
| ยุง | yuŋ | กิม | kim | โห | hŏo |
| ยุย | yuy | กิน | *kin | โหม | hŏom |
| คุย | khuy | อิน | ʔin | โดม | doom |
| คุม | khum | เอ็น | ʔen | ดม | dom |
| คิม | khim | เอน | ʔeen | ดุม | dum |
| คืม | khiim | เอ | ʔee | ดูม | duum |

# บทที่ ๑๓

## ๑๓.๑ คำศัพท์

มา

หา

มาหาใคร

งาน

ทำงาน

ที่ทำงาน

ที่ทำงานเขา

ที่ที่ทำงานเขา

สับ

ระสับ

โท

โทรศัพท์

เลข

เลขที่

เบอร์

ทราบ

รู้

รู้จัก

ได้

ไม่ได้...

ไปหรือเปล่า

ไม่ได้ไป

ไปไหม

ไม่ไป

ครัว

อ่าน

เขียน

ใช้

พัน

# LESSON 13

**13.1 Vocabulary and expansions.**

| | |
|---|---|
| maa | To come. |
| hăa | To look for. |
| maa hăa khray | Who have you come looking for?<br>Who have you come to see? |
| ŋaan | Work. |
| tham ŋaan | To do work. |
| thîi tham ŋaan | Place of doing work, office. |
| thîi tham ŋaan kháw | His office. |
| thîi thîi tham ŋaan kháw | At his office. |
| sàp | |
| rasàp | |
| thoo | |
| thoorasàp | Telephone. |
| lêek | Numbers as units in arithmetic. |
| lêek thîi | Numbers in addresses and identification numbers such as insurance policy numbers, social security numbers, etc. |
| bɔɔ | Telephone numbers, license plate numbers, lottery ticket numbers, room numbers, and numbers used to indicate clothing sizes. |
| sâap | To know information (that is, something *found out*). |
| rúu | To know a subject (that is, something *learned*).<br>This can also be used in the sense of *sâap*, but it is less polite when so used. |
| rúucàk | To know a person, place, or thing (that is, to be acquainted with). |
| dây | To get, receive. |
| mây dây . . . | This denies the *occurrence* of an *action* and hence almost always refers to the past (I didn't . . .). |
| pay rú plàaw | Go or not? Did you go? (Asking for a fact.) |
| mây dây pay | Not accomplish going. I didn't go. |
| pay máy | Go? Do you want to go? (Asking for a decision.) |
| mây pay | I decide against going. |
| khrua | Kitchen. |
| ʔàan | To read. |
| khĭan | To write. |
| cháy | To use. |
| phan | A thousand. |

## ๑๓.๒ โครงสร้างของประโยค

มาหาใคร
มาหาคุณประสงค์
ไปหาคุณประสงค์

คุณประสงค์อยู่ไหม
คุณสวัสดิ์อยู่ไหม
คุณยังอยู่ไหม

เขาไปแล้ว
เขาไปทำงานแล้ว
เขาไปโรงเรียนแล้ว
เขาไปตลาดแล้ว
เขาไปหาคุณประสงค์แล้ว

มีอาหารไหม
มีตลาดไหม
มีน้ำไหม
มีห้องน้ำไหม
มีโทรศัพท์ไหม
มีมากไหม

บ้านฉัน
บ้านเขา
บ้านคุณ
บ้านคุณยัง

ไปหรือเปล่า
เขียนหรือเปล่า
อ่านหรือเปล่า
ใช้หรือเปล่า
พูดหรือเปล่า

ไม่ได้ไป
ไม่ได้เขียน
ไม่ได้อ่าน
ไม่ได้ใช้
ไม่ได้พูด

## ๑๓.๓ บทสนทนา

ก. มาหาใคร

ข. คุณประสงค์อยู่ไหม

ก. ไม่อยู่, เขาไปทำงานแล้ว

ข. ที่ทำงานเขามีโทรศัพท์ไหม

ก. มี

ข. เบอร์อะไร, ทราบไหม

ก. เบอร์ห้าสี่สามสองหนึ่ง

### 13.2 Patterns.

| | |
|---|---|
| maa hǎa khray. | Who have you come to see? |
| maa hǎa khun prasǒŋ. | I've come to see Prasong. |
| pay hǎa khun prasǒŋ. | He's gone to see Prasong. |
| | |
| khun prasǒŋ yùu máy. | Is Prasong here? |
| khun sawàt yùu máy. | Is Sawat here? |
| khun yaŋ yùu máy. | Is Mr. Young here? |
| | |
| kháw pay lɛ́ɛw. | He has already gone. |
| kháw pay tham ŋaan lɛ́ɛw. | He has gone to work. |
| kháw pay rooŋrian lɛ́ɛw. | They have gone to school. |
| kháw pay talàat lɛ́ɛw. | She has gone to the market. |
| kháw pay hǎa khun prasǒŋ lɛ́ɛw. | He has gone to see Prasong. |
| | |
| mii ʔaahǎan máy. | Is there any food? |
| mii talàat máy. | Is there a market? |
| mii náam máy. | Do you have any water? |
| mii hɔ̂ŋ náam máy. | Is there a bathroom? |
| mii thoorasàp máy. | Do you have a telephone? |
| mii mâak máy. | Is there a lot? |
| | |
| bâan chán | My house. |
| bâan kháw | His house. |
| bâan khun | Your house. |
| bâan khun yaŋ | Mr. Young's house. |
| | |
| pay rɨ́ plàaw. | Did you go or not? |
| khǐan rɨ́ plàaw. | Did you write it or not? |
| ʔàan rɨ́ plàaw. | Did you read it or not? |
| cháy rɨ́ plàaw. | Did you use it or not? |
| phûut rɨ́ plàaw. | Did you say anything or not? |
| | |
| mây dây pay. | I didn't go. |
| mây dây khǐan. | I didn't write it. |
| mây dây ʔàan. | I didn't read it. |
| mây dây cháy. | I didn't use it. |
| mây dây phûut. | I didn't say anything. |

### 13.3 Dialog.

| | |
|---|---|
| A. maa hǎa khray. | Who have you come to see? |
| B. khun prasǒŋ yùu máy. | Is Prasong here? |
| A. mây yùu.<br>kháw pay tham ŋaan lɛ́ɛw. | No.<br>He has gone to work. |
| B. thîi tham ŋaan kháw mii thoorasàp máy. | Does his office have a phone? |
| A. mii. | Yes. |
| B. bəə ʔaray. sâap máy. | Do you know the number? |
| A. bəə hâa sii sǎam sɔ̌ɔŋ nɨ̀ŋ. | It's 54321. |

### ๑๓.๔ แบบฝึกหัดการฟังและการออกเสียงสูงต่ำ

ก. วันจันทร์ วันพุธ วันศุกร์ วันเสาร์ วันแม่

ข.

ลุงกินอะไร
  ลุงกินปลา
ลุงกินปลาอะไร
  ลุงกินปลาทู
ลุงกินปลาทูที่ไหน
  ลุงกินปลาทูที่ครัว

หลานขายอะไร
  หลานขายหมู
หลานขายหมูอะไร
  หลานขายหมูหวาน
หลานขายหมูหวานที่ไหน
  หลานขายหมูหวานที่ถนน

ปู่สั่งอะไร
  ปู่สั่งไก่
ปู่สั่งไก่อะไร
  ปู่สั่งไก่อบ
ปู่สั่งไก่อบที่ไหน
  ปู่สั่งไก่อบที่ตลาด

พี่ทอดอะไร
  พี่ทอดกุ้ง
พี่ทอดกุ้งอะไร
  พี่ทอดกุ้งแห้ง
พี่ทอดกุ้งแห้งที่ไหน
  พี่ทอดกุ้งแห้งที่บ้าน

น้องซื้ออะไร
  น้องซื้อเนื้อ
น้องซื้อเนื้ออะไร
  น้องซื้อเนื้อแพะ
น้องซื้อเนื้อแพะที่ไหน
  น้องซื้อเนื้อแพะที่ร้าน

### ๑๓.๕ แบบฝึกหัดการสลับเสียงสูงต่ำ

ก. เรียนที่บ้านหรือเปล่า (อ่าน)
  อ่านที่บ้านหรือเปล่า (เขียน)
  เขียนที่บ้านหรือเปล่า (ใช้)
  ใช้ที่บ้านหรือเปล่า (พูด)
  พูดที่บ้านหรือเปล่า (เรียน)

### 13.4 Tone identification and production.

**a.** Identify the tones and record the number of repetitions required.

| | | |
|---|---|---|
| Monday. | wan *can | ........... |
| Wednesday. | wan *phut | ........... |
| Friday. | wan *suk | ........... |
| Saturday. | wan *saw | ........... |
| Mother's Day. | wan *mɛɛ | ........... |

**b. Response drill.**

| | |
|---|---|
| luŋ kin ʔaray. | What did Uncle eat? |
| luŋ kin plaa. | Uncle ate fish. |
| luŋ kin plaa ʔaray. | What kind of fish did Uncle eat? |
| luŋ kin plaa thuu. | Uncle ate mackerel. |
| luŋ kin plaa thuu thîi nǎy. | Where did Uncle eat mackerel? |
| luŋ kin plaa thuu thîi khrua. | Uncle ate mackerel in the kitchen. |
| pùu sàŋ ʔaray. | What did Grandpa order? |
| pùu sàŋ kày. | Grandpa ordered chicken. |
| pùu sàŋ kày ʔaray. | What kind of chicken did Grandpa order? |
| pùu sàŋ kày ʔòp. | Grandpa ordered roast chicken. |
| pùu sàŋ kày ʔòp thîi nǎy. | Where did Grandpa order roast chicken? |
| pùu sàŋ kày ʔòp thîi talàat. | Grandpa ordered roast chicken at the market. |
| nɔ́ɔŋ sʉ́ʉ ʔaray. | What did Younger One buy? |
| nɔ́ɔŋ sʉ́ʉ nʉ́a. | Younger One bought meat. |
| nɔ́ɔŋ sʉ́ʉ nʉ́a ʔaray. | What kind of meat did Younger One buy? |
| nɔ́ɔŋ sʉ́ʉ nʉ́a phɛ́ʔ. | Younger One bought goat meat. |
| nɔ́ɔŋ sʉ́ʉ nʉ́a phɛ́ʔ thîi nǎy. | Where did Younger One buy goat meat? |
| nɔ́ɔŋ sʉ́ʉ nʉ́a phɛ́ʔ thîi ráan. | Younger One bought goat meat at the shop. |
| lǎan khǎay ʔaray. | What did Nephew sell? |
| lǎan khǎay mǔu. | Nephew sold pork. |
| lǎan khǎay mǔu ʔaray. | What kind of pork did Nephew sell? |
| lǎan khǎay mǔu wǎan. | Nephew sold sweet pork. |
| lǎan khǎay mǔu wǎan thîi nǎy. | Where did Nephew sell sweet pork? |
| lǎan khǎay mǔu wǎan thîi thanǒn. | Nephew sold sweet pork on the street. |
| phîi thɔ̂ɔt ʔaray. | What did Older One fry? |
| phîi thɔ̂ɔt kûŋ. | Older One fried shrimps. |
| phîi thɔ̂ɔt kûŋ ʔaray. | What kind of shrimps did Older One fry? |
| phîi thɔ̂ɔt kûŋ hɛ̂ɛŋ. | Older One fried dried shrimps. |
| phîi thɔ̂ɔt kûŋ hɛ̂ɛŋ thîi nǎy. | Where did Older One fry dried shrimps? |
| phîi thɔ̂ɔt kûŋ hɛ̂ɛŋ thîi bâan. | Older One fried dried shrimps at home. |

### 13.5 Tone manipulation.

**a. Substitution drill.**

| | |
|---|---|
| rian thîi bâan rʉ́ plàaw. (ʔàan) | Did you study at home? (read) |
| ʔàan thîi bâan rʉ́ plàaw. (khǐan) | Did you read it at home? (write) |
| khǐan thîi bâan rʉ́ plàaw. (cháy) | Did you write it at home? (use) |
| cháy thîi bâan rʉ́ plàaw. (phûut) | Did you use it at home? (speak) |
| phûut thîi bâan rʉ́ plàaw. (rian) | Did you speak at home? (study) |

ข.

ไม่ได้เรียน, เรียนที่โรงเรียน
(อ่าน)

ไม่ได้อ่าน, อ่านที่โรงเรียน
(เขียน)

ไม่ได้เขียน, เขียนที่โรงเรียน
(ใช้)

ไม่ได้ใช้, ใช้ที่โรงเรียน
(พูด)

ไม่ได้พูด, พูดที่โรงเรียน
(เรียน)

ค.

เรียนที่บ้านหรือเปล่า
    ไม่ได้เรียน, เรียนที่โรงเรียน

อ่านที่บ้านหรือเปล่า
    ไม่ได้อ่าน, อ่านที่โรงเรียน

เขียนที่บ้านหรือเปล่า
    ไม่ได้เขียน, เขียนที่โรงเรียน

ใช้ที่บ้านหรือเปล่า
    ไม่ได้ใช้, ใช้ที่โรงเรียน

พูดที่บ้านหรือเปล่า
    ไม่ได้พูด, พูดที่โรงเรียน

### ๑๓.๖ แบบฝึกหัดการออกเสียงสระและพยัญชนะ

ก.

| | | |
|---|---|---|
| หนึ่งแก้ว | สี่แก้ว | เจ็ดแก้ว |
| สองแก้ว | ห้าแก้ว | แปดแก้ว |
| สามแก้ว | หกแก้ว | เก้าแก้ว |

ข.

ใครกินแกง
    โกกินแกง
โกกินแกงใคร
    โกกินแกงเกียรติ

ใครข่วนแขน
    เข็มข่วนแขน
เข็มข่วนแขนใคร
    เข็มข่วนแขนแขก

**b. Substitution drill.**

| | |
|---|---|
| mây dây rian. rian thîi rooŋrian.<br>(ʔàan) | No I didn't. I studied at school.<br>(read) |
| mây dây ʔàan. ʔàan thîi rooŋrian.<br>(khĭan) | No I didn't. I read it at school.<br>(write) |
| mây dây khĭan. khĭan thîi rooŋrian.<br>(cháy) | No I didn't. I wrote it at school.<br>(use) |
| mây dây cháy. cháy thîi rooŋrian.<br>(phûut) | No I didn't. I used it at school.<br>(speak) |
| mây dây phûut. phûut thîi rooŋrian.<br>(rian) | No I didn't. I spoke at school.<br>(study) |

**c. Response drill.**

| | |
|---|---|
| rian thîi bâan rʉ́ plàaw.<br>mây dây rian. rian thîi rooŋrian. | Did you study at home?<br>No I didn't. I studied at school. |
| ʔàan thîi bâan rʉ́ plàaw.<br>mây dây ʔàan. ʔàan thîi rooŋrian. | Did you read it at home?<br>No I didn't. I read it at school. |
| khĭan thîi bâan rʉ́ plàaw.<br>mây dây khĭan. khĭan thîi rooŋrian. | Did you write it at home?<br>No I didn't. I wrote it at school. |
| cháy thîi bâan rʉ́ plàaw.<br>mây dây cháy. cháy thîi rooŋrian. | Did you use it at home?<br>No I didn't. I used it at school. |
| phûut thîi bâan rʉ́ plàaw.<br>mây dây phûut. phûut thîi rooŋrian. | Did you speak at home?<br>No I didn't. I spoke at school. |

### 13.6 Vowel and consonant drills.

**a. aaw-ɛɛw speed drill.**

Count glasses (of something) from 1 to 9. Then practice saying '9 glasses' for greater speed.

| | | |
|---|---|---|
| nʉ̀ŋ kɛ̂ɛw | sìi kɛ̂ɛw | cèt kɛ̂ɛw |
| sɔ̆ɔŋ kɛ̂ɛw | hâa kɛ̂ɛw | pɛ̀ɛt kɛ̂ɛw |
| săam kɛ̂ɛw | hòk kɛ̂ɛw | kâaw kɛ̂ɛw |

**b. Response drill.** (k and kh).

| | |
|---|---|
| khray kin kɛɛŋ.<br>koo kin kɛɛŋ.<br>koo kin kɛɛŋ khray.<br>koo kin kɛɛŋ kìat. | Who ate the curry?<br>Ko ate the curry.<br>Whose curry did Ko eat?<br>Ko ate Kiat's curry. |
| khray khùan khɛ̆ɛn.<br>khĕm khùan khɛ̆ɛn.<br>khĕm khùan khɛ̆ɛn khray.<br>khĕm khùan khɛ̆ɛn khɛ̀ɛk. | Who scratched the arm?<br>Kem scratched the arm.<br>Whose arm did Kem scratch?<br>Kem scratched Kaek's arm. |

๑๓.๗ แบบฝึกหัดไวยากรณ์

ก.

ที่ทำงานเขามีโทรศัพท์ไหม
(บ้านเขา)

บ้านเขามีโทรศัพท์ไหม
(ร้านอาหารนี้)

ร้านอาหารนี้มีโทรศัพท์ไหม
(บ้านคุณยัง)

บ้านคุณยังมีโทรศัพท์ไหม
(สถานทูต)

สถานทูตมีโทรศัพท์ไหม
(ที่ทำงานคุณ)

ที่ทำงานคุณมีโทรศัพท์ไหม

ข.

โทรศัพท์ที่บ้านคุณเบอร์อะไร
(เอ ยู เอ)

โทรศัพท์ที่ เอ ยู เอ เบอร์อะไร
(ร้านนี้)

โทรศัพท์ที่ร้านนี้เบอร์อะไร
(สถานทูต)

โทรศัพท์ที่สถานทูตเบอร์อะไร
(บ้านเขา)

โทรศัพท์ที่บ้านเขาเบอร์อะไร
(ที่ทำงานเขา)

โทรศัพท์ที่ที่ทำงานเขาเบอร์อะไร

ค.

คุณประสงค์อยู่ไหม (ทำงาน)
ไม่อยู่, เขาไปทำงานแล้ว

คุณสวัสดิ์อยู่ไหม (โรงเรียน)
ไม่อยู่, เขาไปโรงเรียนแล้ว

คุณยังอยู่ไหม. (หาคุณประสงค์)
ไม่อยู่, เขาไปหาคุณประสงค์แล้ว

คุณเจนอยู่ไหม (ตลาด)
ไม่อยู่. เขาไปตลาดแล้ว

คุณจอนอยู่ไหม (กลับบ้าน)
ไม่อยู่, เขากลับบ้านแล้ว

### 13.7 Grammar drills.

**a. Substitution drill.**

| | |
|---|---|
| thîi tham ŋaan kháw mii thoorasàp máy.<br>(bâan kháw) | Does his office have a phone?<br>(his house) |
| bâan kháw mii thoorasàp máy.<br>(ráan ʔaahǎan níi) | Does his house have a phone?<br>(this restaurant) |
| ráan ʔaahǎan níi mii thoorasàp máy.<br>(bâan khun yaŋ) | Does this restaurant have a phone?<br>(Mr. Young's house) |
| bâan khun yaŋ mii thoorasàp máy.<br>(sathǎanthûut) | Does Mr. Young's house have a phone?<br>(Embassy) |
| sathǎanthûut mii thoorasàp máy.<br>(thîi tham ŋaan khun) | Does the Embassy have a phone?<br>(your office) |
| thîi tham ŋaan khun mii thoorasàp máy. | Does your office have a phone? |

**b. Substitution drill.**

| | |
|---|---|
| thoorasàp thîi bâan khun bɔɔ ʔaray.<br>(ʔee yuu ʔee) | What's the number of the phone at your house? (AUA) |
| thoorasàp thîi ʔee yuu ʔee bɔɔ ʔaray.<br>(ráan níi) | What's the number of the phone at AUA? (this shop) |
| thoorasàp thîi ráan níi bɔɔ ʔaray.<br>(sathǎanthûut) | What's the number of the phone at this shop? (Embassy) |
| thoorasàp thîi sathǎanthûut bɔɔ ʔaray.<br>(bâan kháw) | What's the number of the phone at the Embassy? (his house) |
| thoorasàp thîi bâan kháw bɔɔ ʔaray.<br>(thîi tham ŋaan kháw) | What's the number of the phone at his house? (his office) |
| thoorasàp thîi thîi tham ŋaan kháw bɔɔ ʔaray. | What's the number of the phone at his office? |

**c. Response drill.**

| | |
|---|---|
| khun prasɔ̌ŋ yùu máy. (tham ŋaan)<br>mây yùu. kháw pay tham ŋaan léew. | Is Prasong here? (work)<br>No. He has gone to work. |
| khun sawàt yùu máy. (rooŋrian)<br>mây yùu. kháw pay rooŋrian léew. | Is Sawat here? (school)<br>No. He has gone to school. |
| khun yaŋ yùu máy. (hǎa khun prasɔ̌ŋ)<br>mây yùu. kháw pay hǎa khun prasɔ̌ŋ léew. | Is Mr. Young here? (see Prasong)<br>No. He has gone to see Prasong. |
| khun ceen yùu máy. (talàat)<br>mây yùu. kháw pay talàat léew. | Is Jane here? (market)<br>No. She has gone to the market. |
| khun cɔɔn yùu máy. (klàp bâan)<br>mây yùu. kháw klàp bâan léew. | Is John here? (go home)<br>No. He has gone home. |

ง.

| | | | |
|---|---|---|---|
| สองหกสาม (ห้า) | ๒๖๓ (๕) | สองเก้าสาม (สาม) | ๒๙๓ (๓) |
| สองห้าสาม (สอง) | ๒๕๓ (๒) | สองสามสาม (เจ็ด) | ๒๓๓ (๗) |
| สองสองสาม (สี่) | ๒๒๓ (๔) | สองเจ็ดสาม (หนึ่ง) | ๒๗๓ (๑) |
| สองสี่สาม (เก้า) | ๒๔๓ (๙) | สองหนึ่งสาม | ๒๑๓ |

**๑๓.๘ เลข**

| | |
|---|---|
| ๑,๐๐๐ บาท | พันบาท |
| ๑,๐๐๑ บาท | พันกะหนึ่งบาท |
| ๑,๐๐๒ บาท | พันสองบาท |
| ๑,๐๑๐ บาท | พันสิบบาท |
| ๓,๐๐๕ บาท | สามพันห้าบาท |
| ๔,๗๐๐ บาท | สี่พันเจ็ดร้อยบาท |
| ๕,๑๙๐ บาท | ห้าพันหนึ่งร้อยเก้าสิบบาท |
| ๙,๘๓๒ บาท | เก้าพันแปดร้อยสามสิบสองบาท |

| | | |
|---|---|---|
| ๑ บาท | ๙ บาท | ๗ บาท |
| ๙๑ บาท | ๘๙ บาท | ๑๗ บาท |
| ๒๙๑ บาท | ๕๘๙ บาท | ๓๑๗ บาท |
| ๘,๒๙๑ บาท | ๔,๕๘๙ บาท | ๕,๓๑๗ บาท |

| | | |
|---|---|---|
| ๔ บาท | ๖ บาท | |
| ๓๔ บาท | ๕๖ บาท | ๗๐ บาท |
| ๖๓๔ บาท | | ๘๗๐ บาท |
| ๑,๖๓๔ บาท | ๒,๐๕๖ บาท | ๓,๘๗๐ บาท |
| ๖,๙๒๘ บาท | ๙,๑๐๕ บาท | ๗,๔๖๒ บาท |

**๑๓.๙ การสนทนาโต้ตอบ**

ก.

อ่านที่บ้านหรือเปล่าคะ
 ไม่ได้อ่านครับ, อ่านที่โรงเรียนครับ

เขียนที่บ้านหรือเปล่าคะ
 ไม่ได้เขียนครับ, เขียนที่โรงเรียนครับ

พูดที่โรงเรียนหรือเปล่าคะ
 ไม่ได้พูดครับ, พูดที่บ้านครับ

ใช้ที่โรงเรียนหรือเปล่าคะ
 ไม่ได้ใช้ครับ, ใช้ที่บ้านครับ

เรียนที่บ้านหรือเปล่าคะ
 ไม่ได้เรียนครับ, เรียนที่โรงเรียนครับ

**d. Substitution drill.**

| | | | | | |
|---|---|---|---|---|---|
| sɔ̌ɔŋ hòk sǎam | (hâa) | 263 (5) | sɔ̌ɔŋ kâaw sǎam | (sǎam) | 293 (3) |
| sɔ̌ɔŋ hâa sǎam | (sɔ̌ɔŋ) | 253 (2) | sɔ̌ɔŋ sǎam sǎam | (cèt) | 233 (7) |
| sɔ̌ɔŋ sɔ̌ɔŋ sǎam | (sìi) | 223 (4) | sɔ̌ɔŋ cèt sǎam | (nɯ̀ŋ) | 273 (1) |
| sɔ̌ɔŋ sìi sǎam | (kâaw) | 243 (9) | sɔ̌ɔŋ nɯ̀ŋ sǎam | | 213 |

## 13.8 Numbers.

| | |
|---|---|
| 1,000 baht | phan bàat |
| 1,001 baht | phan ka nɯ̀ŋ bàat |
| 1,002 baht | phan sɔ̌ɔŋ bàat |
| 1,010 baht | phan sìp bàat |
| 3,005 baht | sǎam phan hâa bàat |
| 4,700 baht | sìi phan cèt rɔ́ɔy bàat |
| 5,190 baht | hâa phan nɯ̀ŋ rɔ́ɔy kâaw sìp bàat |
| 9,832 baht | kâaw phan pɛ̀ɛt rɔ́ɔy sǎam sìp sɔ̌ɔŋ bàat |

Practice reading the following amounts of money. Try to get the time under 50 seconds.

| | | |
|---|---|---|
| 1 bàat | 9 bàat | 7 bàat |
| 91 bàat | 89 bàat | 17 bàat |
| 291 bàat | 589 bàat | 317 bàat |
| 8,291 bàat | 4,589 bàat | 5,317 bàat |
| 4 bàat | 6 bàat | |
| 34 bàat | 56 bàat | 70 bàat |
| 634 bàat | | 870 bàat |
| 1,634 bàat | 2,056 bàat | 3,870 bàat |
| 6,928 bàat | 9,105 bàat | 7,462 bàat |

## 13.9 Conversation.

**a.** Answer the questions with 'at school' instead of 'at home', and vice versa.

ʔàan thîi bâan rɯ́ plàaw khá.
mây dây ʔàan khráp. ʔàan thîi rooŋrian khráp.

khǐan thîi bâan rɯ́ plàaw khá.
mây dây khǐan khráp. khǐan thîi rooŋrian khráp.

phûut thîi rooŋrian rɯ́ plàaw khá.
mây dây phûut khráp. phûut thîi bâan khráp.

cháy thîi rooŋrian rɯ́ plàaw khá.
mây dây cháy khráp. cháy thîi bâan khráp.

rian thîi bâan rɯ́ plàaw khá.
mây dây rian khráp. rian thîi rooŋrian khráp.

ข.

มาหาใครคะ

คุณ .................... อยู่ไหมครับ

ไม่อยู่ค่ะ, เขา ...................... แล้ว

ที่ .......................... มีโทรศัพท์ไหมครับ

มีค่ะ

เบอร์อะไร, ทราบไหมครับ

เบอร์ ...................... ค่ะ

## ๑๓.๑๐ การเขียน

| ถึง | | ซอย |
|---|---|---|
| ซอย | ถีน | เซ็ม |
| ซุย | ถุน | เชม |
| ซุง | ถิน | แซม |
| สุง | ทิน | แบม |
| สูง | ลิน | แบน |
| สึง | ลิม | แสน |
| ทึง | ผิม | แซน |
| ถึง | ชิม | ซัน |

**b.** Use the following information to practice the suggested conversation.
Sawat has gone to work. His office phone number is 57067.
Mr. Young has gone home. His home phone number is 910 252.
Prasong has gone to school. The phone number there is 911 459.
John has gone to Jane's house. Her phone number is 50330.

maa hǎa khray khá.

khun ................. yùu máy khráp.

mây yùu khâ. kháw ................................... lɛ́ɛw.

thîi ........................... mii thoorasàp máy khráp.

mii khâ.

bɔɔ ʔaray. sâap máy khráp.

bɔɔ ..................... khâ.

**13.10 Writing.**

| ถึง | | ซอย | |
|---|---|---|---|
| thʉ̌ŋ | | sɔɔy | |
| To reach. | | Lane, Soi. | |

| | | | | | |
|---|---|---|---|---|---|
| ซอย | *sɔɔy | ถีน | thʉ̌n | เช็ม | chem |
| ซุย | suy | ถุน | thǔn | เชม | cheem |
| ซุง | suŋ | ถิน | thǐn | แชม | chɛɛm |
| สุง | sǔŋ | ทิน | thin | แบม | bɛɛm |
| สูง | *sǔuŋ | ลิน | lin | แบน | bɛɛn |
| สึง | sʉ̌ŋ | ลิม | lim | แสน | sɛ̌ɛn |
| ทึง | thʉŋ | ผิม | phǐm | แซน | sɛɛn |
| ถึง | *thʉ̌ŋ | ชิม | chim | ซัน | san |

# บทที่ ๑๔

## ๑๔.๑ คำศัพท์

ภาษา
ภาษาอังกฤษ

ไทย

จีน

พม่า

เวียดนาม

นิด
หน่อย
นิดหน่อย

เรียก
ว่า

เรียกว่า
เรียกว่าอะไร

นัง
สือ
หนังสือ

บุหรี่

นะ

เท่าไหร่
เท่าไหร่นะ

ช้า
ช้าช้า

หน่อย

ตอน
เช้า
ตอนเช้า

สาย

เที่ยง

บ่าย

เย็น
ตอนเย็น

กี่
กี่คน

# LESSON 14

**14.1 Vocabulary and expansions.**

| | |
|---|---|
| phasǎa | Language. |
| phasǎa ʔaŋkrìt | English language. |
| thay | Thai. |
| ciin | Chinese. |
| phamâa | Burmese. |
| wîatnaam | Vietnamese. |
| | |
| nít | |
| nɔ̀y | A little. |
| nítnɔ̀y | A little bit. |
| | |
| rîak | To call. |
| wâa | A quotation signal. Its use is similar to the English *that* (He told me *that*...), *if* (He asked me *if*...), or quotation marks (It's called '...', the word '...'). |
| rîak wâa | |
| rîak wâa ʔaray | What's it called? |
| | |
| naŋ | |
| sɯ̌ɯ | |
| naŋsɯ̌ɯ | Book. |
| burìi | Cigaret. |
| ná | With questions, this is similar to the shifted stress and rising intonation used in English when a question is repeated. |
| thâwrày | How much? (Said with falling intonation and stress on *much*.) |
| thâwrày ná | *How* much? (Said with rising intonation and stress on *how*.) |
| cháa | Slow (used to express a fact). |
| chácháa | Slow (used to express one's feelings or judgement: slow *down*). This kind of reduplication will be clarified further in Book 2. |
| nɔ̀y | Using this word with imperatives has much the same effect as using *please* in English: it softens the order and thus makes it more polite. With *nɔ̀y* the softening is accomplished by minimizing the request. It is more polite to ask for a little than a lot. |
| tɔɔn | A section or period. |
| cháaw | Morning (especially early morning). |
| tɔɔn cháaw | In the morning. |
| sǎay | Late morning. |
| thîaŋ | Noon. |
| bàay | Afternoon. |
| yen | Cold (of things), cool (of weather). |
| tɔɔn yen | In the evening. This refers to the daylight hours after the sun has gone down far enough to lose its midday force. |
| kìi | How many? |
| kìi khon | How many people? |

## ๑๔.๒ โครงสร้างของประโยค

ภาษาอังกฤษ
ภาษาไทย
ภาษาจีน
ภาษาพม่า
ภาษาเวียดนาม

ใส่นิดหน่อย
มีนิดหน่อย
ซื้อนิดหน่อย

เรียกว่าอะไร
พูดว่าอะไร
เขียนว่าอะไร

เรียกว่าบ้าน
เรียกว่าตลาด
เรียกว่าหนังสือ

พูดช้าช้าหน่อย
เขียนดีดีหน่อย
ใส่มากมากหน่อย

พูดหน่อยได้ไหม
ทำงานหน่อยได้ไหม
ซื้อหมูหน่อยได้ไหม

ไปตอนเช้า
ไปตอนสาย
ไปตอนเที่ยง
ไปตอนบ่าย
ไปตอนเย็น

## ๑๔.๓ บทสนทนา

ก. ขอโทษ

คุณพูดภาษาอังกฤษได้ไหม

ข. พูดได้นิดหน่อย

ก. คุณรู้จัก book ไหม

ข. รู้จัก

ก. ภาษาไทยเรียก book ว่าอะไร

ข. เรียกว่า หนังสือ

ก. อะไรนะ

พูดช้าช้าหน่อยได้ไหม

ข. เรียกว่า หนังสือ

ก. ขอบคุณ

### 14.2 Patterns.

| | |
|---|---|
| phasǎa ʔaŋkrìt | English. |
| phasǎa thay | Thai. |
| phasǎa ciin | Chinese. |
| phasǎa phamâa | Burmese. |
| phasǎa wiatnaam | Vietnamese. |
| sày nítnɔ̀y. | Put in just a little. |
| mii nítnɔ̀y. | I have just a little. |
| sʉ́ʉ nítnɔ̀y. | Buy just a little. |
| rîak wâa ʔaray. | What's it called? |
| phûut wâa ʔaray. | What did he say? |
| khǐan wâa ʔaray. | What did he write? |
| rîak wâa bâan. | It's called *bâan*. |
| rîak wâa talàat. | It's called *talàat*. |
| rîak wâa naŋsʉ̌ʉ. | It's called *naŋsʉ̌ʉ*. |
| phûut cháchâa nɔ̀y. | Please speak a little slower. |
| khǐan didii nɔ̀y. | Please write a little better. |
| sày mâkmâak nɔ̀y. | Please put in a lot. |
| phûut nɔ̀y dây máy. | Can you please speak? |
| tham ŋaan nɔ̀y dây máy. | Can you please do some work? |
| sʉ́ʉ mǔu nɔ̀y dây máy. | Can you please buy some pork? |
| pay tɔɔn cháaw. | Go in the early morning. |
| pay tɔɔn sǎay. | Go in the late morning. |
| pay tɔɔn thîaŋ. | Go around noon time. |
| pay tɔɔn bàay. | Go in the afternoon. |
| pay tɔɔn yen. | Go in the evening. |

### 14.3 Dialog.

| | | |
|---|---|---|
| A. | khɔ̌ɔ thôot.<br>khun phûut phasǎa ʔaŋkrìt dây máy. | Excuse me.<br>Can you speak English? |
| B. | phûut dây nítnɔ̀y. | I can speak a little. |
| A. | khun rúucàk *book* máy. | Do you know *book*? |
| B. | rúucàk. | Yes. |
| A. | phasǎa thay rîak *book* wâa ʔaray. | What is *book* called in Thai? |
| B. | rîak wâa naŋsʉ̌ʉ. | It's called *naŋsʉ̌ʉ*. |
| A. | ʔaray ná.<br>phûut cháchâa nɔ̀y dây máy. | What was that?<br>Could you speak a little slower? |
| B. | rîak wâa n-a-ŋ-s-ʉ̌ʉ. | It's called *n-a-ŋ-s-ʉ̌ʉ*. |
| A. | khɔ̀ɔpkhun. | Thank you. |

## ๑๔.๔ แบบฝึกหัดการฟังและการออกเสียงสูงต่ำ

ก.

สีดำ สีขาว สีแดง สีเขียว สีฟ้า สีแสด สีเหลือง สีม่วง

ข.

ลุงกินอะไร
ลุงกินปลา
ลุงกินปลาอะไร
ลุงกินปลาทู
ลุงกินปลาทูตอนไหน
ลุงกินปลาทูตอนเย็น
ปู่สั่งอะไร
ปู่สั่งไก่
ปู่สั่งไก่อะไร
ปู่สั่งไก่อบ
ปู่สั่งไก่อบตอนไหน
ปู่สั่งไก่อบตอนบ่าย
หลานขายอะไร
หลานขายหมู
หลานขายหมูอะไร
หลานขายหมูหวาน
หลานขายหมูหวานตอนไหน
หลานขายหมูหวานตอนสาย

น้องซื้ออะไร
น้องซื้อเนื้อ
น้องซื้อเนื้ออะไร
น้องซื้อเนื้อแพะ
น้องซื้อเนื้อแพะตอนไหน
น้องซื้อเนื้อแพะตอนเช้า
พี่ทอดอะไร
พี่ทอดกุ้ง
พี่ทอดกุ้งอะไร
พี่ทอดกุ้งแห้ง
พี่ทอดกุ้งแห้งตอนไหน
พี่ทอดกุ้งแห้งตอนเที่ยง

## ๑๔.๕ แบบฝึกหัดการสลับเสียงสูงต่ำ

ก.

ทำที่ตลาดหรือเปล่า (ขาย)
ขายที่ตลาดหรือเปล่า (สั่ง)
สั่งที่ตลาดหรือเปล่า (พูด)
พูดที่ตลาดหรือเปล่า (ซื้อ)
ซื้อที่ตลาดหรือเปล่า (ทำ)

## 14.4 Tone identification and production.

**a.** Identify the tones and record the number of repetitions required.

| | | |
|---|---|---|
| Black. | sǐi *dam | ........... |
| White. | sǐi *khaaw | ........... |
| Red. | sǐi *dɛɛŋ | ........... |
| Green. | sǐi *khiaw | ........... |
| Sky blue. | sǐi *faa | ........... |
| Orange. | sǐi *sɛɛt | ........... |
| Yellow. | sǐi *lʉaŋ | ........... |
| Purple. | sǐi *muaŋ | ........... |

**b. Response drill.**

| | |
|---|---|
| luŋ kin ʔaray. | What did Uncle eat? |
| luŋ kin plaa. | Uncle ate fish. |
| luŋ kin plaa ʔaray. | What kind of fish did Uncle eat? |
| luŋ kin plaa thuu. | Uncle ate mackerel. |
| luŋ kin plaa thuu tɔɔn nǎy. | When did Uncle eat mackerel? |
| luŋ kin plaa thuu tɔɔn yen. | Uncle ate mackerel in the evening. |

pùu sàŋ ʔaray.
pùu sàŋ kày.
pùu sàŋ kày ʔaray.
pùu sàŋ kày ʔòp.
pùu sàŋ kày ʔòp tɔɔn nǎy.
pùu sàŋ kày ʔòp tɔɔn bàay.

nɔ́ɔŋ sʉ́ʉ ʔaray.
nɔ́ɔŋ sʉ́ʉ nʉ́a.
nɔ́ɔŋ sʉ́ʉ nʉ́a ʔaray.
nɔ́ɔŋ sʉ́ʉ nʉ́a phɛ́ʔ.
nɔ́ɔŋ sʉ́ʉ nʉ́a phɛ́ʔ tɔɔn nǎy.
nɔ́ɔŋ sʉ́ʉ nʉ́a phɛ́ʔ tɔɔn cháaw.

lǎan khǎay ʔaray.
lǎan khǎay mǔu.
lǎan khǎay mǔu ʔaray.
lǎan khǎay mǔu wǎan.
lǎan khǎay mǔu wǎan tɔɔn nǎy.
lǎan khǎay mǔu wǎan tɔɔn sǎay.

phîi thɔ̂ɔt ʔaray.
phîi thɔ̂ɔt kûŋ.
phîi thɔ̂ɔt kûŋ ʔaray.
phîi thɔ̂ɔt kûŋ hɛ̂ɛŋ.
phîi thɔ̂ɔt kûŋ hɛ̂ɛŋ tɔɔn nǎy.
phîi thɔ̂ɔt kûŋ hɛ̂ɛŋ tɔɔn thiaŋ.

## 14.5 Tone manipulation.

**a. Substitution drill.**

| | |
|---|---|
| tham thîi talàat rʉ́ plàaw. (khǎay) | Did you get it made at the market? (sell) |
| khǎay thîi talàat rʉ́ plàaw. (sàŋ) | Did you sell it at the market? (order) |
| sàŋ thîi talàat rʉ́ plàaw. (phûut) | Did you order it at the market? (speak) |
| phûut thîi talàat rʉ́ plàaw. (sʉ́ʉ) | Did you speak at the market? (buy) |
| sʉ́ʉ thîi talàat rʉ́ plàaw. (tham) | Did you buy it at the market? (get made) |

**ข.**

ไม่ได้ทำ, ทำที่ร้าน
(ขาย)

ไม่ได้ขาย, ขายที่ร้าน
(สั่ง)

ไม่ได้สั่ง, สั่งที่ร้าน
(พูด)

ไม่ได้พูด, พูดที่ร้าน
(ซื้อ)

ไม่ได้ซื้อ, ซื้อที่ร้าน
(ทำ)

**ค.**

ทำที่ตลาดหรือเปล่า
    ไม่ได้ทำ, ทำที่ร้าน

ซื้อที่ตลาดหรือเปล่า
    ไม่ได้ซื้อ, ซื้อที่ร้าน

สั่งที่ตลาดหรือเปล่า
    ไม่ได้สั่ง, สั่งที่ร้าน

ขายที่ตลาดหรือเปล่า
    ไม่ได้ขาย, ขายที่ร้าน

พูดที่ตลาดหรือเปล่า
    ไม่ได้พูด, พูดที่ร้าน

## ๑๔.๖ แบบฝึกหัดการออกเสียงสระและพยัญชนะ

**ก.**

กี่แก้ว    กี่ก้าว
    แปดแก้ว    แปดก้าว
กี่แก้ว    กี่ก้าว
    เก้าแก้ว    เก้าก้าว

**ข.**

สงวนเป็นอะไร
    สงวนง่วงนอน
แล้วเสงี่ยมล่ะ, เป็นอะไร
    เสงี่ยมก็ง่วงนอน

**b. Substitution drill.**

| | |
|---|---|
| mây dây tham. tham thîi ráan. | No. I got it made at the shop. |
| (khǎay) | (sell) |
| mây dây khǎay. khǎay thîi ráan. | No. I sold it at the shop. |
| (sàŋ) | (order) |
| mây dây sàŋ. sàŋ thîi ráan. | No. I ordered it at the shop. |
| (phûut) | (speak) |
| mây dây phûut. phûut thîi ráan. | No. I spoke at the shop. |
| (sʉ́ʉ) | (buy) |
| mây dây sʉ́ʉ. sʉ́ʉ thîi ráan. | No. I bought it at the shop. |
| (tham) | (get made) |

**c. Response drill.**

| | |
|---|---|
| tham thîi talàat rʉ́ plàaw. | Did you get it made at the market? |
| mây dây tham. tham thîi ráan. | No. I got it made at the shop. |
| sʉ́ʉ thîi talàat rʉ́ plàaw. | Did you buy it at the market? |
| mây dây sʉ́ʉ. sʉ́ʉ thîi ráan. | No. I bought it at the shop. |
| sàŋ thîi talàat rʉ́ plàaw. | Did you order it at the market? |
| mây dây sàŋ. sàŋ thîi ráan. | No. I ordered it at the shop. |
| khǎay thîi talàat rʉ́ plàaw. | Did you sell it at the market? |
| mây dây khǎay. khǎay thîi ráan. | No. I sold it at the shop. |
| phûut thîi talàat rʉ́ plàaw. | Did you speak at the market? |
| mây dây phûut. phûut thîi ráan. | No. I spoke at the shop. |

**14.6 Vowel and consonant drills.**

**a. Response drill.** (aaw–ɛɛw).

Answer 'eight' to the following two questions asked repeatedly in random order by the teacher.

| | | | |
|---|---|---|---|
| kìi kɛ̂ɛw. | How many glasses? | kìi kâaw. | How many steps? |
| pɛ̀ɛt kɛ̂ɛw. | Eight glasses. | pɛ̀ɛt kâaw. | Eight steps. |

Now answer 'nine'.

| | | | |
|---|---|---|---|
| kìi kɛ̂ɛw. | How many glasses? | kìi kâaw. | How many steps? |
| kâaw kɛ̂ɛw. | Nine glasses. | kâaw kâaw. | Nine steps. |

**b. Response drill.** (ŋ).

| | |
|---|---|
| saŋǔan pen ʔaray. | What's the matter with Sanguan? |
| saŋǔan ŋûaŋ nɔɔn. | Sanguan is sleepy. |
| lɛ́ɛw saŋìam lâ. pen ʔaray. | And Sangiam? What's wrong with her? |
| saŋìam kɔ̂ ŋûaŋ nɔɔn. | Sangiam is sleepy, too. |

(*kɔ̂*, as used in the above pattern, means 'also' or 'too'.)

๑๔.๗ แบบฝึกหัดไวยากรณ์

ก.

คุณพูดภาษาอังกฤษได้ไหม
(ไทย)

คุณพูดภาษาไทยได้ไหม
(จีน)

คุณพูดภาษาจีนได้ไหม
(พม่า)

คุณพูดภาษาพม่าได้ไหม
(เวียดนาม)

คุณพูดภาษาเวียดนามได้ไหม
(เขียน)

คุณเขียนภาษาเวียดนามได้ไหม
(จีน)

คุณเขียนภาษาจีนได้ไหม
(อ่าน)

คุณอ่านภาษาจีนได้ไหม
(ไทย)

คุณอ่านภาษาไทยได้ไหม
(เขียน)

คุณเขียนภาษาไทยได้ไหม
(อังกฤษ)

คุณเขียนภาษาอังกฤษได้ไหม
(อ่าน)

คุณอ่านภาษาอังกฤษได้ไหม

ข.

พูดภาษาไทยไม่ได้ (อ่าน)
อ่านภาษาไทยไม่ได้ (เขียน)
เขียนภาษาไทยไม่ได้ (จีน)
เขียนภาษาจีนไม่ได้ (อ่าน)
อ่านภาษาจีนไม่ได้ (พูด)
พูดภาษาจีนไม่ได้ (อังกฤษ)
พูดภาษาอังกฤษไม่ได้

ค.

เรียกว่าหนังสือ (โรงแรม)
เรียกว่าโรงแรม (ห้องน้ำ)
เรียกว่าห้องน้ำ (สี่แยก)
เรียกว่าสี่แยก (ควาย)
เรียกว่าควาย (นาฬิกา)
เรียกว่านาฬิกา

## 14.7 Grammar drills.

### a. Substitution drill.

| | |
|---|---|
| khun phûut phasǎa ʔaŋkrìt dây máy.<br>(thay) | Can you speak English?<br>(Thai) |
| khun phûut phasǎa thay dâay máy.<br>(ciin) | Can you speak Thai?<br>(Chinese) |
| khun phûut phasǎa ciin dâay máy.<br>(phamâa) | Can you speak Chinese?<br>(Burmese) |
| khun phûut phasǎa phamâa dâay máy.<br>(wîatnaam) | Can you speak Burmese?<br>(Vietnamese) |
| khun phûut phasǎa wîatnaam dâay máy.<br>(khǐan) | Can you speak Vietnamese?<br>(write) |
| khun khǐan phasǎa wîatnaam dâay máy.<br>(ciin) | Can you write Vietnamese?<br>(Chinese) |
| khun khǐan phasǎa ciin dâay máy.<br>(ʔàan) | Can you write Chinese?<br>(read) |
| khun ʔàan phasǎa ciin dâay máy.<br>(thay) | Can you read Chinese?<br>(Thai) |
| khun ʔàan phasǎa thay dâay máy.<br>(khǐan) | Can you read Thai?<br>(write) |
| khun khǐan phasǎa thay dâay máy.<br>(ʔaŋkrìt) | Can you write Thai?<br>(English) |
| khun khǐan phasǎa ʔaŋkrìt dâay máy.<br>(ʔàan) | Can you write English?<br>(read) |
| khun ʔàan phasǎa ʔaŋkrìt dâay máy. | Can you read English? |

### b. Substitution drill.

| | |
|---|---|
| phûut phasǎa thay mây dâay. (ʔàan) | I can't speak Thai (read) |
| ʔàan phasǎa thay mây dâay. (khǐan) | I can't read Thai. (write) |
| khǐan phasǎa thay mây dâay. (ciin) | I can't write Thai. (Chinese) |
| khǐan phasǎa ciin mây dâay. (ʔàan) | I can't write Chinese. (read) |
| ʔàan phasǎa ciin mây dâay. (phûut) | I can't read Chinese. (speak) |
| phûut phasǎa ciin mây dâay. (ʔaŋkrìt) | I can't speak Chinese. (English) |
| phûut phasǎa ʔaŋkrìt mây dâay. | I can't speak English. |

### c. Substitution drill.

| | |
|---|---|
| rîak wâa naŋsʉ̌ʉ. (rooŋrɛɛm) | It's called a book. (hotel) |
| rîak wâa rooŋrɛɛm. (hɔ̂ŋ náam) | It's called a hotel. (bathroom) |
| rîak wâa hɔ̂ŋ náam. (sìiyɛ̂ɛk) | It's called a bathroom. (intersection) |
| rîak wâa sìiyɛ̂ɛk. (khwaay) | It's called an intersection. (buffalo) |
| rîak wâa khwaay. (naalikaa) | It's called a buffalo. (clock) |
| rîak wâa naalikaa. | It's called a clock. |

ง.

book เรียกว่าอะไร
เรียกว่าหนังสือ

hotel เรียกว่าอะไร
เรียกว่าโรงแรม

cow เรียกว่าอะไร
เรียกว่าวัว

radio เรียกว่าอะไร
เรียกว่าวิทยุ

cigaret เรียกว่าอะไร
เรียกว่าบุหรี่

จ.

| | | | | | |
|---|---|---|---|---|---|
| ห้าหนึ่งเก้า | (สอง) | ๕๑๙ (๒) | ห้าห้าเก้า | (สาม) | ๕๕๙ (๓) |
| ห้าสองเก้า | (สี่) | ๕๒๙ (๔) | ห้าสามเก้า | (เก้า) | ๕๓๙ (๙) |
| ห้าสี่เก้า | (ห้า) | ๕๔๙ (๕) | ห้าเก้าเก้า | (หนึ่ง) | ๕๙๙ (๑) |

**๑๔.๘ เลข**

| | | | | | | | |
|---|---|---|---|---|---|---|---|
| ค.ศ. | ๑๗๘๒ | พ.ศ. | ๒๓๒๕ | ค.ศ. | ๑๙๕๓ | พ.ศ. | ๒๔๙๖ |
| ค.ศ. | ๑๘๐๙ | พ.ศ. | ๒๓๕๒ | ค.ศ. | ๑๙๕๖ | พ.ศ. | ๒๔๙๙ |
| ค.ศ. | ๑๘๒๔ | พ.ศ. | ๒๓๖๗ | ค.ศ. | ๑๙๕๗ | พ.ศ. | ๒๕๐๐ |
| ค.ศ. | ๑๘๕๑ | พ.ศ. | ๒๓๙๔ | ค.ศ. | ๑๙๖๐ | พ.ศ. | ๒๕๐๓ |
| ค.ศ. | ๑๘๖๘ | พ.ศ. | ๒๔๑๑ | ค.ศ. | ๑๙๖๒ | พ.ศ. | ๒๕๐๕ |
| ค.ศ. | ๑๙๑๐ | พ.ศ. | ๒๔๕๓ | ค.ศ. | ๑๙๖๕ | พ.ศ. | ๒๕๐๘ |
| ค.ศ. | ๑๙๒๕ | พ.ศ. | ๒๔๖๘ | ค.ศ. | ๑๙๖๗ | พ.ศ. | ๒๕๑๐ |
| ค.ศ. | ๑๙๓๔ | พ.ศ. | ๒๔๗๗ | ค.ศ. | ๑๙๖๙ | พ.ศ. | ๒๕๑๒ |
| ค.ศ. | ๑๙๔๖ | พ.ศ. | ๒๔๘๙ | ค.ศ. | ๑๙๗๑ | พ.ศ. | ๒๕๑๔ |

**๑๔.๙ การสนทนาโต้ตอบ**

ก.

| | |
|---|---|
| ซื้อที่ร้านหรือเปล่าคะ | ไม่ได้ซื้อครับ, ซื้อที่ตลาด |
| สั่งที่ตลาดหรือเปล่าคะ | ไม่ได้สั่งครับ, สั่งที่ร้าน |
| ขายที่ร้านหรือเปล่าคะ | ไม่ได้ขายครับ, ขายที่ตลาด |
| ทำที่ตลาดหรือเปล่าคะ | ไม่ได้ทำครับ, ทำที่ร้าน |
| พูดที่ตลาดหรือเปล่าคะ | ไม่ได้พูดครับ, พูดที่ร้าน |

**d. Response drill.**

| | |
|---|---|
| *book* rîak wâa ʔaray. | What do you call a book? |
| rîak wâa naŋsɨ̌ɨ. | It's called a *naŋsɨ̌ɨ*. |
| *hotel* rîak wâa ʔaray. | What do you call a hotel? |
| rîak wâa rooŋrɛɛm. | It's called a *rooŋrɛɛm*. |
| *cow* rîak wâa ʔaray. | What do you call a cow? |
| rîak wâa wua. | It's called a *wua*. |
| *radio* rîak wâa ʔaray. | What do you call a radio? |
| rîak wâa wítthayúʔ. | It's called a *wítthayúʔ*. |
| *cigaret* rîak wâa ʔaray. | What do you call a cigaret? |
| rîak wâa burìi. | It's called a *burìi*. |

**e. Substitution drill.**

| | | | | | |
|---|---|---|---|---|---|
| hâa nɨ̀ŋ kâaw | (sɔ̌ɔŋ) | 519 (2) | hâa hâa kâaw | (sǎam) | 559 (3) |
| hâa sɔ̌ɔŋ kâaw | (sìi) | 529 (4) | hâa sǎam kâaw | (kâaw) | 539 (9) |
| hâa sìi kâaw | (hâa) | 549 (5) | hâa kâaw kâaw | (nɨ̀ŋ) | 599 (1) |

**14.8 Numbers.**

Practice reading the following years of the Christian (khɔɔ sɔ̌ɔ) and Buddhist (phɔɔ sɔ̌ɔ) eras. 2325, for example, is to be read *sɔ̌ɔŋ phan sǎam rɔ́ɔy yîi sìp hâa*. Try to get the time under a minute and a half. (The first column gives the years that the nine kings of the present dynasty ascended to the throne.

| | | | |
|---|---|---|---|
| khɔɔ sɔ̌ɔ 1782 | phɔɔ sɔ̌ɔ 2325 | khɔɔ sɔ̌ɔ 1953 | phɔɔ sɔ̌ɔ 2496 |
| khɔɔ sɔ̌ɔ 1809 | phɔɔ sɔ̌ɔ 2352 | khɔɔ sɔ̌ɔ 1956 | phɔɔ sɔ̌ɔ 2499 |
| khɔɔ sɔ̌ɔ 1824 | phɔɔ sɔ̌ɔ 2367 | khɔɔ sɔ̌ɔ 1957 | phɔɔ sɔ̌ɔ 2500 |
| khɔɔ sɔ̌ɔ 1851 | phɔɔ sɔ̌ɔ 2394 | khɔɔ sɔ̌ɔ 1960 | phɔɔ sɔ̌ɔ 2503 |
| khɔɔ sɔ̌ɔ 1868 | phɔɔ sɔ̌ɔ 2411 | khɔɔ sɔ̌ɔ 1962 | phɔɔ sɔ̌ɔ 2505 |
| khɔɔ sɔ̌ɔ 1910 | phɔɔ sɔ̌ɔ 2453 | khɔɔ sɔ̌ɔ 1965 | phɔɔ sɔ̌ɔ 2508 |
| khɔɔ sɔ̌ɔ 1925 | phɔɔ sɔ̌ɔ 2468 | khɔɔ sɔ̌ɔ 1967 | phɔɔ sɔ̌ɔ 2510 |
| khɔɔ sɔ̌ɔ 1934 | phɔɔ sɔ̌ɔ 2477 | khɔɔ sɔ̌ɔ 1969 | phɔɔ sɔ̌ɔ 2512 |
| khɔɔ sɔ̌ɔ 1946 | phɔɔ sɔ̌ɔ 2489 | khɔɔ sɔ̌ɔ 1971 | phɔɔ sɔ̌ɔ 2514 |

**14.9 Conversation.**

**a.** Answer the questions with 'at the shop' instead of 'at the market', and vice versa.

| | | |
|---|---|---|
| sɨ́ɨ thîi ráan rɨ́ plàaw khá. | mây dây sɨ́ɨ khráp. | sɨ́ɨ thîi talàat. |
| sàŋ thîi talàat rɨ́ plàaw khá. | mây dây sàŋ khráp. | sàŋ thîi ráan. |
| khǎay thîi ráan rɨ́ plàaw khá. | mây dây khǎay khráp. | khǎay thîi talàat. |
| tham thîi talàat rɨ́ plàaw khá. | mây dây tham khráp. | tham thîi ráan. |
| phûut thîi talàat rɨ́ plàaw khá. | mây dây phûut khráp. | phûut thîi ráan. |

Etc.

ข.

คุณรู้จัก..........................ไหมครับ

        รู้จักค่ะ

ภาษาไทยเรียก..........................ว่าอะไรครับ

        เรียกว่า..........................ค่ะ

อะไรนะครับ, พูดช้าช้าหน่อยได้ไหม

        เรียกว่า......................................ค่ะ

ขอบคุณครับ

**๑๔.๑๐ การเขียน**

วัว สวย

| | | |
|---|---|---|
| วัว | ซวย | แทม |
| หัว | ซอย | แถม |
| งัว | ซาย | ถวม |
| ผัว | ขาย | ถัว |
| ผวน | ขาว | บัว |
| กวน | คาว | บัง |
| สวน | ทาว | ปง |
| สวย | แทว | ลง |

**b.** Use the suggested dialog to ask the teacher the Thai names for various things you don't know.

khun rúucàk....................máy khráp.

rúucàk khâ.

phasǎa thay rîak....................wâa ʔaray khráp.

rîak wâa......................khâ.

ʔaray ná khráp. phûut cháchá nɔ̀y dây máy.

rîak wâa........................... ......khâ.

khɔ̀ɔpkhun khráp.

### 14.10 Writing.

| วัว | สวย |
|---|---|
| wua | sǔay |
| Cow. | Pretty. |

| | | | | | |
|---|---|---|---|---|---|
| วัว | *wua | ซวย | suay | แทม | thɛɛm |
| หัว | hǔa | ซอย | *sɔɔy | แถม | thɛ̌ɛm |
| งัว | ŋua | ซาย | saay | ถวม | thǔam |
| ผัว | phǔa | ขาย | *khǎay | ถัว | thǔa |
| ผวน | phǔan | ขาว | *khǎaw | ปัว | pua |
| กวน | kuan | คาว | khaaw | ปัง | paŋ |
| สวน | sǔan | ทาว | thaaw | ปง | poŋ |
| สวย | *sǔay | แทว | thɛɛw | ลง | loŋ |

# บทที่ ๑๕

ข.

คุณประสงค์เป็นคนไทย เขาเรียนภาษาอังกฤษที่ เอ ยู เอ เขาอ่านภาษาอังกฤษได้และเขียนได้ แต่เขาพูดได้นิดหน่อยเท่านั้น คุณประสงค์ทำงานที่สถานทูตจีน และพูดภาษาจีนได้ดี ลูกชายเขาพูดภาษาอังกฤษไม่ได้เลย

คุณเดวิดเป็นคนอเมริกัน เขาเรียนภาษาไทยที่ เอ ยู เอ เขาพูดภาษาไทยได้นิดหน่อย แต่เขาอ่านหรือเขียนไม่ได้เลย ก่อนนี้เขาอยู่ที่ฮ่องกงและพูดภาษาจีนได้เก่ง ลูกสาวเขาพูดภาษาไทยไม่ได้เลย

คุณเดวิดกับลูกเขาไปหาคุณประสงค์ที่บ้าน คุณเดวิดกับคุณประสงค์พูดภาษาจีนกัน คุณเดวิดกับลูกคุณประสงค์ พูดภาษาไทยกัน คุณประสงค์กับลูกคุณเดวิดพูดภาษาอังกฤษกัน แต่ลูกคุณประสงค์กับลูกคุณเดวิดพูดกันไม่เข้าใจเลย

คุณประสงค์เป็นคนจีนใช่ไหม
　ไม่ใช่, เขาเป็นคนไทย

เขาพูดภาษาอังกฤษเก่งใช่ไหม
　ไม่ใช่, เขาพูดได้นิดหน่อยเท่านั้น

เขาเรียนภาษาไทยที่ เอ ยู เอ ใช่ไหม
　ไม่ใช่, เขาเรียนภาษาอังกฤษ

เขารู้ภาษาอังกฤษมากใช่ไหม
　รู้มากเขาอ่านได้ เขียนได้ แต่เขาพูดได้นิดหน่อยเท่านั้น

เขาทำงานที่ไหน
　ที่สถานทูตจีน

เขาพูดภาษาจีนได้หรือเปล่า
　ได้

เขาเขียนภาษาจีนได้ไหม
　ไม่ทราบ

# LESSON 15
## (Review)

a. **Review sections 3, 5, 7, and 9 of lessons 11 - 14.**

b. **Narrative.** (For comprehension only).

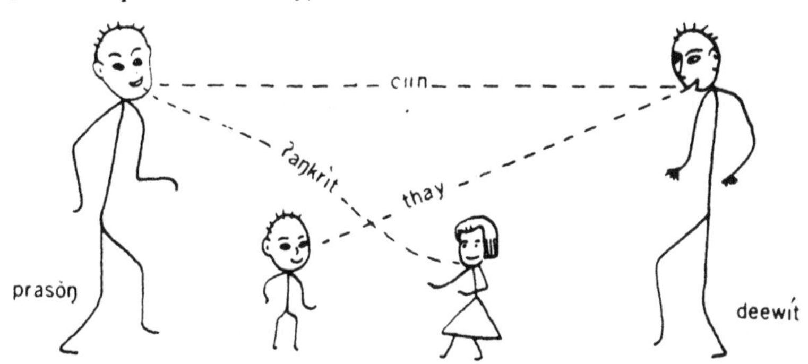


khun prasǒŋ pen khon thay. kháw rian phasǎa ʔaŋkrìt thîi ʔee yuu ʔee. kháw ʔàan phasǎa ʔaŋkrìt dây lɛ́ʔ (and) khǐan dây, tɛ̀ɛ (but) kháw phûut dây nítnɔ̀y thâwnán (only). khun prasǒŋ tham ŋaan thîi sathǎanthûut ciin, lɛ́ʔ phûut phasǎa ciin dây dii. lûuk chaay (son) kháw phûut phasǎa ʔaŋkrìt mây dây lǝǝy.

khun deewít pen khon ʔameerikan. kháw rian phasǎa thay thîi ʔee yuu ʔee. kháw phûut phasǎa thay dây nítnɔ̀y, tɛ̀ɛ kháw ʔàan rʉ́ khǐan mây dây lǝǝy. kɔ̀ɔn níi kháw yùu thîi hɔ̂ŋkoŋ lɛ́ʔ phûut phasǎa ciin dây kèŋ (well, skillfully). lûuk sǎaw (daughter) kháw phûut phasǎa thay mây dây lǝǝy.

khun deewít kàp lûuk kháw pay hǎa khun prasǒŋ thîi bâan. khun deewít kàp khun prasǒŋ phûut phasǎa ciin kan. khun deewít kàp lûuk khun prasǒŋ phûut phasǎa thay kan. khun prasǒŋ kàp lûuk khun deewít phûut phasǎa ʔaŋkrìt kan. tɛ̀ɛ lûuk khun prasǒŋ kàp lûuk khun deewít phûut kan mây khâwcay lǝǝy.

Read the following questions and answers for comprehension. Then, without looking, listen for comprehension as the teacher reads them.

khun prasǒŋ pen khon ciin chây máy.
  mây chây. kháw pen khon thay.

kháw phûut phasǎa ʔaŋkrìt kèŋ chây máy.
  mây chây. kháw phûut dây nítnɔ̀y thâwnán.

kháw rian phasǎa thay thîi ʔee yuu ʔee chây máy.
  mây chây. kháw rian phasǎa ʔaŋkrìt.

kháw rúu phasǎa ʔaŋkrìt mâak chây máy.
  rúu mâak. kháw ʔàan dây, khǐan dây, tɛ̀ɛ kháw phûut dây nítnɔ̀y thâwnán.

kháw tham ŋaan thîi nǎy.
  thîi sathǎanthûut ciin.

kháw phûut phasǎa ciin dây rʉ́ plàaw.
  dây.

kháw khǐan phasǎa ciin dây máy.
  mây sâap.

(More.)

เขาพูดภาษาอังกฤษได้เก่งกว่าภาษาจีน ใช่ไหม

ไม่ใช่, เขาพูดภาษาจีนได้เก่งกว่าภาษาอังกฤษ

ลูกเขาเป็นผู้หญิงใช่ไหม

ไม่ใช่, เป็นผู้ชาย

ลูกพูดภาษาอังกฤษได้เก่งกว่าพ่อใช่ไหม

ไม่ใช่, ลูกพูดภาษาอังกฤษไม่ได้เลย

คุณเดวิดเป็นคนอังกฤษใช่ไหม

ไม่ใช่, เป็นคนอเมริกัน

เขาเรียนภาษาจีนที่ เอ ยู เอ ใช่ไหม

ไม่ใช่, เขาเรียนภาษาไทย

เขารู้ภาษาไทยมากไหม

ไม่มาก, เขาอ่านไม่ได้เลย และพูดได้นิดหน่อยเท่านั้น

เขาพูดภาษาจีนได้ไหม

ได้, ก่อนนี้เขาอยู่ที่ฮ่องกง

ลูกคุณเดวิดเป็นผู้หญิงหรือผู้ชาย

ผู้หญิง

ลูกเขาพูดภาษาไทยไม่ได้ใช่ไหม

ใช่, พูดไม่ได้เลย

คุณเดวิดรู้จักคุณประสงค์หรือเปล่า

รู้จัก

คุณเดวิดกับคุณประสงค์พูดภาษาอะไรกัน

ภาษาจีน

คุณเดวิดพูดภาษาอังกฤษกับลูกคุณประสงค์ใช่ไหม

ไม่ใช่, เขาพูดภาษาไทย ลูกคุณประสงค์พูดภาษาอังกฤษไม่ได้เลย

ลูกคุณเดวิดพูดภาษาไทยกับคุณประสงค์ใช่ไหม

ไม่ใช่เขาพูดภาษาไทยไม่ได้

ลูกคุณประสงค์กับลูกคุณเดวิดพูดภาษาอะไรกัน

เปล่า, เขาไม่ได้พูดกัน

ใครพูดภาษาอังกฤษกัน

คุณประสงค์กับลูกคุณเดวิด

และใครอีก

คุณเดวิดกับลูกเขา

ใครพูดภาษาไทยกัน

คุณเดวิดกับลูกคุณประสงค์

และใครอีก

คุณประสงค์กับลูกเขา

ใครพูดภาษาจีนกัน

คุณประสงค์กับคุณเดวิด

และใครอีก

เท่านั้น

ก่อนนี้คุณเดวิดอยู่ที่ไหน

ที่ฮ่องกง

เขาทำอะไรที่นั่น

ไม่ทราบ

เขาพูดภาษาจีนเก่งหรือภาษาไทยเก่ง

เขาพูดภาษาจีนเก่ง

kháw phûut phasǎa ʔaŋkrìt dây kèŋ kwàa phasǎa ciin chây máy.
  mây chây. kháw phûut phasǎa ciin dây kèŋ kwàa phasǎa ʔaŋkrìt.
lûuk kháw pen phûu yǐŋ châay máy.
  mây châay. pen phûu chaay.
lûuk phûut phasǎa ʔaŋkrìt dây kèŋ kwàa phɔ̂ɔ châay máy.
  mây châay. lûuk phûut phasǎa ʔaŋkrìt mây dây lǝǝy.
khun deewít pen khon ʔaŋkrìt châay máy.
  mây châay. pen khon ʔameerikan.
kháw rian phasǎa ciin thîi ʔee yuu ʔee châay máy.
  mây châay. kháw rian phasǎa thay.
kháw rúu phasǎa thay mâak máy.
  mây mâak. kháw ʔàan mây dây lǝǝy, lɛ́ʔ phûut dây nítnɔ̀y thâwnán.
kháw phûut phasǎa ciin dây máy.
  dây. kɔ̀ɔn níi kháw yùu thîi hɔ̂ŋkoŋ.
lûuk khun deewít pen phûu yǐŋ rɨ̌ phûu chaay.
  phûu yǐŋ.
lûuk kháw phûut phasǎa thay mây dây châay máy.
  châay. phûut mây dây lǝǝy.
khun deewít rúucàk khun prasɔ̌ŋ rɨ̌ plàaw.
  rúucàk.
khun deewít ka khun prasɔ̌ŋ phûut phasǎa ʔaray kan.
  phasǎa ciin.
khun deewít phûut phasǎa ʔaŋkrìt ka lûuk khun prasɔ̌ŋ châay máy.
  mây châay. kháw phûut phasǎa thay. lûuk khun prasɔ̌ŋ phûut phasǎa ʔaŋkrìt mây dây lǝǝy.
lûuk khun deewít phûut phasǎa thay ka khun prasɔ̌ŋ châay máy.
  mây châay. kháw phûut phasǎa thay mây dây.
lûuk khun prasɔ̌ŋ ka lûuk khun deewít phûut phasǎa ʔaray kan.
  plàaw. kháw mây dây phûut kan.
khray phûut phasǎa ʔaŋkrìt kan.
  khun prasɔ̌ŋ ka lûuk khun deewít.
lɛ́ʔ khray ʔìik.
  khun deewít ka lûuk kháw.
khray phûut phasǎa thay kan.
  khun deewít ka lûuk khun prasɔ̌ŋ.
lɛ́ʔ khray ʔìik.
  khun prasɔ̌ŋ ka lûuk kháw.
khray phûut phasǎa ciin kan.
  khun prasɔ̌ŋ ka khun deewít.
lɛ́ʔ khray ʔìik.
  thâwnán.

kɔ̀ɔn níi khun deewít yùu thîi nǎy.
  thîi hɔ̂ŋkoŋ.
kháw tham ʔaray thîi nân.
  mây sâap.
kháw phûut phasǎa ciin kèŋ rɨ̌ phûut phasǎa thay kèŋ.
  kháw phûut phasǎa ciin kèŋ.

# บทที่ ๑๖

## ๑๖.๑ คำศัพท์

| | |
|---|---|
| ดิน | วัน |
| สอ | จันทร์ |
| ดินสอ | วันจันทร์ |
| ดาด | พุด |
| กระดาษ | วันพุธ |
| ถูก | สุก |
| | วันศุกร์ |
| ตู | |
| ประตู | เสา |
| ต่าง | วันเสาร์ |
| หน้าต่าง | แม่ |
| ไฟ | วันแม่ |
| พัด | หมื่น |
| ลม | |
| พัดลม | |

## ๑๖.๒ โครงสร้างของประโยค

| | |
|---|---|
| เรียกถูกไหม | เรียกไม่ถูก |
| พูดถูกไหม | พูดไม่ถูก |
| ไปถูกไหม | ไปไม่ถูก |

# LESSON 16

**16.1 Vocabulary and expansions.**

| | |
|---|---|
| din | |
| sɔ̌ɔ | |
| dinsɔ̌ɔ | Pencil. |
| dàat | |
| kradàat | Paper. |
| thùuk | To be correct. From the dialog, this might appear to be similar to *chây*. The function of these two words, however, is quite different. (See below.) |
| tuu | |
| pratuu | Door. |
| tàaŋ | |
| nâatàaŋ | Window (the opening and shutters, not the glass). |
| fay | Fire, light, electricity. |
| phát | To blow (as the wind). |
| lom | Wind, air (in motion or under pressure). |
| phátlom | Electric fan. |
| wan | Day (either daylight period or 24 hour period). |
| can | |
| wan can | Monday. |
| phút | |
| wan phút | Wednesday. |
| sùk | |
| wan sùk | Friday. |
| sǎw | |
| wan sǎw | Saturday. |
| mɛ̂ɛ | Mother. |
| wan mɛ̂ɛ | Mother's Day. |
| mùun | Ten thousand. |

**16.2 Patterns.**

| | |
|---|---|
| rîak thùuk máy. | Have I called it correctly? |
| phûut thùuk máy. | Did I say it right? |
| pay thùuk máy. | Can you go correctly? (Do you know the way?) |
| rîak mây thùuk. | You called it incorrectly. |
| phûut mây thùuk. | You said it incorrectly. |
| pay mây thùuk. | I can't go correctly. (I don't know the way.) |

(More.)

| | |
|---|---|
| เรียกว่าไฟใช่ไหม<br>เรียกว่าไฟถูกไหม | ดีแล้ว |
| | สวยแล้ว |
| ไป, ใช่ไหม<br>ไปถูกไหม | ถูกแล้ว |

**๑๖.๓ บทสนทนา**

ก. นี่เรียกว่าอะไร

ข. เรียกว่าดินสอ

ก. นั่นเรียกว่ากระดาษ, ถูกไหม

ข. ถูกแล้ว

ก. แล้วนั่นประตูใช่ไหม

ข. ไม่ใช่, ประตูอยู่โน่น
นั่นหน้าต่าง

ก. แล้วข้างบนนั่นล่ะ, เรียกว่าอะไร

ข. เรียกว่าไฟ

ก. แล้วโน่นล่ะ

ข. พัดลม

**๑๖.๔ แบบฝึกหัดการฟังและการออกเสียงสูงต่ำ**

ก.

| | |
|---|---|
| หัว | มือ |
| หู | นิ้ว |
| แก้ม | ขา |
| ปาก | เท้า |

**Different** patterns. Notice the different rhythm and spacing.

| | |
|---|---|
| rîak wâa fay chây máy. | It's called *fay*. Is my statement right? |
| rîak wâa fay, thùuk máy. | It's called *fay*. Have I called it right? |
| pay, chây máy. | He has gone. Is that right? |
| pay thùuk máy. | Did he go the right way? |
| dii léɛw. | Now it's good (after making a change). |
| Or: | It's good as it is (don't change it). |
| sǔay léɛw. | Now (that she has put on lipstick) she's pretty. |
| Or: | She's already pretty (don't put on lipstick). |
| thùuk léɛw. | That's right. Now you've got it. *léɛw* marks a change point (see section 8.1). Whenever a judgement of correct or incorrect is called for, presumably there is the chance that the person might be wrong and will have to try again. After several failures (mây thùuk), the force of *léɛw* is 'That's it. *Now* you've got it.' If the person is right on his first attempt, the implication is 'That's right. You don't have to try again.' It simply marks the point when success is achieved. In this use, *thùuk* is almost always accompanied by léɛw, and *thùuk léɛw* should be learned as a set phrase. |

## 16.3 Dialog.

| | |
|---|---|
| A. nîi rîak wâa ʔaray. | What's this called? |
| B. rîak wâa dinsɔ̌ɔ. | It's called a pencil. |
| A. nân rîak wâa kradàat, thùuk máy. | That's called paper. Am I correct? |
| B. thùuk léɛw. | That's correct. |
| A. léɛw nân pratuu chây máy. | And that's a door, isn't it? |
| B. mây chây. pratuu yùu nôon. nân nâatàaŋ. | No. The door is over there. That's a window. |
| A. léɛw khâŋ bon nân lâ. rîak wâa ʔaray. | And what about that up there? What's it called? |
| B. rîak wâa fay. | It's called a light. |
| A. léɛw nôon lâ. | And how about that over there. |
| B. phátlom. | An electric fan. |

## 16.4 Tone identification and production.

**a.** Identify the tones and record the number of repetitions required.

| | | | | | |
|---|---|---|---|---|---|
| Head. | *hua | ........... | Hands. | *mʉʉ | ........... |
| Ears. | *huu | ........... | Fingers. | *niw | ........... |
| Cheeks. | *kɛɛm | ........... | Legs. | *khaa | ........... |
| Mouth. | *paak | ........... | Feet. | *thaaw | ........... |

ข.

ใครเรียน
    แดงเรียน
แดงเรียนวันไหน
    แดงเรียนวันจันทร์

ใครอ่าน
    หน่อยอ่าน
หน่อยอ่านวันไหน
    หน่อยอ่านวันศุกร์

ใครใช้
    น้อยใช้
น้อยใช้วันไหน
    น้อยใช้วันพุธ

ใครเขียน
    ต๋อยเขียน
ต๋อยเขียนวันไหน
    ต๋อยเขียนวันเสาร์

ใครพูด
    ต้อยพูด
ต้อยพูดวันไหน
    ต้อยพูดวันแม่

**๑๖.๕ แบบฝึกหัดการสลับเสียงสูงต่ำ**

อ่านที่ถนน (ซื้อ)
ซื้อที่ถนน (เขียน)
เขียนที่ถนน (ร้าน)
เขียนที่ร้าน (โรงเรียน)
เขียนที่โรงเรียน (ซื้อ)
ซื้อที่โรงเรียน (ตลาด)
ซื้อที่ตลาด (พูด)
พูดที่ตลาด (บ้าน)
พูดที่บ้าน (อ่าน)
อ่านที่บ้าน (ร้าน)
อ่านที่ร้าน (กิน)
กินที่ร้าน (โรงเรียน)
กินที่โรงเรียน (อ่าน)
อ่านที่โรงเรียน (ตลาด)
อ่านที่ตลาด (เขียน)
เขียนที่ตลาด (บ้าน)
เขียนที่บ้าน (ซื้อ)
ซื้อที่บ้าน (ร้าน)
ซื้อที่ร้าน (พูด)
พูดที่ร้าน (โรงเรียน)
พูดที่โรงเรียน (ถนน)
พูดที่ถนน (กิน)
กินที่ถนน (บ้าน)
กินที่บ้าน (ตลาด)
กินที่ตลาด

b. **Response drill.**

| | |
|---|---|
| khray rian. | Who studied? |
| dɛɛŋ rian. | Daeng studied. |
| dɛɛŋ rian wan nǎy. | On what day did Daeng study? |
| dɛɛŋ rian wan can. | Daeng studied on Monday. |
| khray ʔàan. | Who read it? |
| nɔ̀y ʔàan. | Noy Low read it. |
| nɔ̀y ʔàan wan nǎy. | On what day did Noy Low read it? |
| nɔ̀y ʔàan wan sùk. | Noy Low read it on Friday. |
| khray cháy. | Who used it? |
| nɔ́ɔy cháy. | Noy High used it. |
| nɔ́ɔy cháy wan nǎy. | On what day did Noy High use it? |
| nɔ́ɔy cháy wan phút. | Noy High used it on Wednesday. |
| khray khǐan. | Who wrote it? |
| tɔ̌y khǐan. | Toy Rise wrote it. |
| tɔ̌y khǐan wan nǎy. | On what day did Toy Rise write it? |
| tɔ̌y khǐan wan sǎw. | Toy Rise wrote it on Saturday. |
| khray phûut. | Who spoke? |
| tɔ̂y phûut. | Toy Fall spoke. |
| tɔ̂y phûut wan nǎy. | On what day did Toy Fall speak? |
| tɔ̂y phûut wan mɛ̂ɛ. | Toy Fall spoke on Mother's Day. |

## 16.5 Tone manipulation.

a. **Substitution drill.**

| | |
|---|---|
| ʔàan thîi thanɔ̌n. (sʉ́ʉ) | I read it on the street. (buy) |
| sʉ́ʉ thîi thanɔ̌n. (khǐan) | I bought it on the street. (write) |
| khǐan thîi thanɔ̌n. (ráan) | I wrote it on the street. (shop) |
| khǐan thîi ráan. (rooŋrian) | I wrote it at the shop. (school) |
| khǐan thîi rooŋrian. (sʉ́ʉ) | I wrote it at school. (buy) |
| sʉ́ʉ thîi rooŋrian. (talàat) | I bought it at school. (market) |
| sʉ́ʉ thîi talàat. (phûut) | I bought it at the market. (talk) |
| phûut thîi talàat. (bâan) | I talked at the market. (home) |
| phûut thîi bâan. (ʔàan) | I talked at home. (read) |
| ʔàan thîi bâan. (ráan) | I read it at home. (shop) |
| ʔàan thîi ráan. (kin) | I read it at the shop. (eat) |
| kin thîi ráan. (rooŋrian) | I ate at the shop. (school) |
| kin thîi rooŋrian. (ʔàan) | I ate at school. (read) |
| ʔàan thîi rooŋrian. (talàat) | I read it at school. (market) |
| ʔàan thîi talàat. (khǐan) | I read it at the market. (write) |
| khǐan thîi talàat. (bâan) | I wrote it at the market. (home) |
| khǐan thîi bâan. (sʉ́ʉ) | I wrote it at home. (buy) |
| sʉ́ʉ thîi bâan. (ráan) | I bought it at home. (shop) |
| sʉ́ʉ thîi ráan. (phûut) | I bought it at the shop. (talk) |
| phûut thîi ráan. (rooŋrian) | I talked at the shop. (school) |
| phûut thîi rooŋrian. (thanɔ̌n) | I talked at school. (street) |
| phûut thîi thanɔ̌n. (kin) | I talked on the street. (eat) |
| kin thîi thanɔ̌n. (bâan) | I ate on the street. (home) |
| kin thîi bâan. (talàat) | I ate at home. (market) |
| kin thîi talàat. | I ate at the market. |

## ๑๖.๖ แบบฝึกหัดการออกเสียงสระและพยัญชนะ

ก.

หลังดำ (น้ำเงิน) หลังน้ำเงิน (ดำ)

ข.

ปู่เป่าปี่ป๋า
ป๋าก็เป่าปี่ปู่

ป๋าเป่าปี่ปู่
ปู่ก็เป่าปี่ป๋า

พ่อพบผ้าพี่
พี่ก็พบผ้าพ่อ

พี่พบผ้าพ่อ
พ่อก็พบผ้าพี่

บิ๋มบีบบ่าเบิ้ม
เบิ้มก็บีบบ่าบิ๋ม

เบิ้มบีบบ่าบิ๋ม
บิ๋มก็บีบบ่าเบิ้ม

## ๑๖.๗ แบบฝึกหัดไวยากรณ์

ก.

นั่นเรียกว่าดินสอ, ถูกไหม (กระดาษ)
นั่นเรียกว่ากระดาษ, ถูกไหม (หนังสือ )
นั่นเรียกว่าหนังสือ, ถูกไหม (ประตู)
นั่นเรียกว่าประตู, ถูกไหม (หน้าต่าง)
นั่นเรียกว่าหน้าต่าง, ถูกไหม (ไฟ)
นั่นเรียกว่าไฟถูกไหม

ข.

แล้วนั่นหน้าต่างใช่ไหม (หนังสือ)
แล้วนั่นหนังสือใช่ไหม (ดินสอ)
แล้วนั่นดินสอใช่ไหม (กระดาษ)
แล้วนั่นกระดาษใช่ไหม (บุหรี่)
แล้วนั่นบุหรี่ใช่ไหม (พัดลม)
แล้วนั่นพัดลมใช่ไหม

## 16.6 Vowel and consonant drills.

**a. Substitution drill.**

| | |
|---|---|
| lăŋ dam. (námŋən) | Behind the black. (blue) |
| lăŋ námŋən. (dam) | Behind the blue. (black) |

**b. Response drill.** (p, ph, and b).

It is assumed here (and in all similar drills that follow) that the student can pronounce the problem sounds correctly. The purpose is merely to slightly increase the speed of production. Whenever a student cannot pronounce a sound correctly, he should not even attempt the drill containing it. He should go back to the appropriate contrast drills.

| | |
|---|---|
| pùu pàw pìi păa. | Grandpa played Papa's horn. |
| păa kɔ̂ pàw pìi pùu. | Papa played Grandpa's horn, too. |
| phɔ̂ɔ phóp phâa phîi. | Father saw Older One's cloth. |
| phîi kɔ̂ phóp phâa phɔ̂ɔ. | Older One saw Father's cloth, too. |
| bǐm bìip bàa bə̂m. | Bim squeezed Berm's shoulder. |
| bə̂m kɔ̂ bìip bàa bǐm. | Berm squeezed Bim's shoulder, too. |
| păa pàw pìi pùu. | Papa played Grandpa's horn. |
| pùu kɔ̂ pàw pìi păa. | Grandpa played Papa's horn, too. |
| phîi phóp phâa phɔ̂ɔ. | Older One saw Father's cloth. |
| phɔ̂ɔ kɔ̂ phóp phâa phîi. | Father saw Older One's cloth, too. |
| bə̂m bìip bàa bǐm. | Berm squeezed Bim's shoulder. |
| bǐm kɔ̂ bìip bàa bə̂m. | Bim squeezed Berm's shoulder, too. |

## 16.7 Grammar drills.

**a. Substitution drill.**

| | |
|---|---|
| nân rîak wâa dinsɔ̌ɔ, thùuk máy. (kradàat) | Is it correct to call that a pencil? (paper) |
| nân rîak wâa kradàat, thùuk máy. (naŋsʉ̌ʉ) | Is it correct to call that paper? (book) |
| nân rîak wâa naŋsʉ̌ʉ, thùuk máy. (pratuu) | Is it correct to call that a book? (door) |
| nân rîak wâa pratuu, thùuk máy. (nâatàaŋ) | Is it correct to call that a door? (window) |
| nân rîak wâa nâatàaŋ, thùuk máy. (fay) | Is it correct to call that a window? (light) |
| nân rîak wâa fay, thùuk máy. | Is it correct to call that a light? |

**b. Substitution drill.**

| | |
|---|---|
| lɛ́ɛw nân nâatàaŋ chây máy. (naŋsʉ̌ʉ) | And that's a window, isn't it? (book) |
| lɛ́ɛw nân naŋsʉ̌ʉ chây máy. (dinsɔ̌ɔ) | And that's a book, isn't it? (pencil) |
| lɛ́ɛw nân dinsɔ̌ɔ châу máy. (kradàat) | And that's a pencil, isn't it? (paper) |
| lɛ́ɛw nân kradàat châу máy. (burìi) | And that's paper, isn't it? (cigaret) |
| lɛ́ɛw nân burìi châу máy. (phátlom) | And that's a cigaret, isn't it? (fan) |
| lɛ́ɛw nân phátlom châу máy. | And that's a fan, isn't it? |

ค.

แล้วนี่ล่ะ เรียกว่าอะไร (นั่น)
แล้วนั่นล่ะ, เรียกว่าอะไร (โน่น)
แล้วโน่นล่ะ, เรียกว่าอะไร (ข้างบนนั่น)
แล้วข้างบนนั่นล่ะ, เรียกว่าอะไร (ข้างบนโน่น)
แล้วข้างบนโน่นล่ะ, เรียกว่าอะไร

ง.

แล้วนั่นบุหรี่ใช่ไหม
ไม่ใช่, บุหรี่อยู่โน่น
แล้วนั่นกระดาษใช่ไหม
ไม่ใช่, กระดาษอยู่โน่น
แล้วนั่นหนังสือใช่ไหม
ไม่ใช่, หนังสืออยู่โน่น
แล้วนั่นหน้าต่างใช่ไหม
ไม่ใช่, หน้าต่างอยู่โน่น
แล้วนั่นพัดลมใช่ไหม
ไม่ใช่, พัดลมอยู่โน่น
แล้วนั่นดินสอใช่ไหม
ไม่ใช่, ดินสออยู่โน่น
แล้วนั่นไฟใช่ไหม
ไม่ใช่, ไฟอยู่โน่น

**๑๖.๘ เลข**

๑๐,๐๐๐ บาท หมื่นบาท
๑๐,๐๐๑ บาท หมื่นกับหนึ่งบาท
๑๐,๐๐๕ บาท หมื่นห้าบาท
๓๔,๐๐๐ บาท สามหมื่นสี่พันบาท
๙๗,๕๓๑ บาท เก้าหมื่นเจ็ดพันห้าร้อยสามสิบเอ็ดบาท

๘๐ บาท
๖๘๐ บาท
๔,๖๘๐ บาท
๕๔,๖๘๐ บาท
๕ บาท
๔๕ บาท
๓๔๕ บาท
๖๐,๓๔๕ บาท
๘๗,๔๖๑ บาท

๒ บาท
๒๒ บาท
๒๒๒ บาท
๒,๒๒๒ บาท
๒๒,๒๒๒ บาท
๓ บาท
๗๓ บาท
๘,๐๗๓ บาท
๙๘,๐๗๓ บาท
๕๓,๑๓๘ บาท

๗ บาท
๕๐๗ บาท
๑,๕๐๗ บาท
๔๑,๕๐๗ บาท
๙ บาท
๑๙ บาท
๙๑๙ บาท
๕,๙๑๙ บาท
๓๕,๙๑๙ บาท
๗๙,๘๕๖ บาท

**c. Substitution drill.**

| | |
|---|---|
| lɛ́ɛw nîi lâ. rîak wâa ʔaray. | And this? What's it called? |
| (nân) | (that) |
| lɛ́ɛw nân lâ. rîak wâa ʔaray. | And that? What's it called? |
| (nôon) | (that over there) |
| lɛ́ɛw nôon lâ. rîak wâa ʔaray. | And that over there? What's it called? |
| (khâŋbon nân) | (that up there) |
| lɛ́ɛw khâŋbon nân lâ. rîak wâa ʔaray. | And that up there? What's it called? |
| (khâŋbon nôon) | (that up there beyond the other one) |
| lɛ́ɛw khâŋbon nôon lâ. rîak wâa ʔaray. | And beyond it? What's that called? |

**d. Response drill.**

| | |
|---|---|
| lɛ́ɛw nân burìi chây máy. | And that's a cigaret, isn't it? |
| mây chây. burìi yùu nôon. | No. That's a cigaret over there. |
| lɛ́ɛw nân kradàat chây máy. | And that's paper, isn't it? |
| mây chây. kradàat yùu nôon. | No. That's paper over there. |
| lɛ́ɛw nân naŋsɨ̌ɨ chây máy. | And that's a book, isn't it? |
| mây chây. naŋsɨ̌ɨ yùu nôon. | No. That's a book over there. |
| lɛ́ɛw nân nâatàaŋ chây máy. | And that's a window, isn't it? |
| mây chây. nâatàaŋ yùu nôon. | No. That's a window over there. |
| lɛ́ɛw nân phátlom chây máy. | And that's a fan, isn't it? |
| mây chây. phátlom yùu nôon. | No. That's a fan over there. |
| lɛ́ɛw nân dinsɔ̌ɔ chây máy. | And that's a pencil, isn't it? |
| mây chây. dinsɔ̌ɔ yùu nôon. | No. That's a pencil over there. |
| lɛ́ɛw nân fay chây máy. | And that's a light, isn't it? |
| mây chây. fay yùu nôon. | No. That's a light over there. |

**16.8 Numbers.**

| | |
|---|---|
| 10,000 baht | mɨ̀ɨn bàat |
| 10,001 baht | mɨ̀ɨn ka nɨ̀ŋ bàat |
| 10,005 baht | mɨ̀ɨn hâa bàat |
| 34,000 baht | sǎam mɨ̀ɨn sìi phan bàat |
| 97,531 baht | kâaw mɨ̀ɨn cèt phan hâa rɔ́ɔy sǎam sìp ʔèt bàat |

Practice reading the following amounts of money. Try to get the time under 1 minute and 15 seconds.

| | | |
|---|---|---|
| | 2 bàat | 7 bàat |
| 80 bàat | 22 bàat | |
| 680 bàat | 222 bàat | 507 bàat |
| 4,680 bàat | 2,222 bàat | 1,507 bàat |
| 54,680 bàat | 22,222 bàat | 41,507 bàat |
| 5 bàat | 3 bàat | 9 bàat |
| 45 bàat | 73 bàat | 19 bàat |
| 345 bàat | | 919 bàat |
| | 8,073 bàat | 5,919 bàat |
| 60,345 bàat | 98,073 bàat | 35,919 bàat |
| 87,461 bàat | 53,138 bàat | 79,856 bàat |

## ๑๖.๔ การสนทนาโต้ตอบ

ก.

| | |
|---|---|
| ทำงานที่ถนนหรือเปล่าคะ | ไม่ได้ทำครับ, ทำที่ที่ทำงาน |
| ซื้อที่โรงแรมหรือเปล่าคะ | ไม่ได้ซื้อครับ, ซื้อที่ตลาด |
| เรียนที่ร้านตัดผมหรือเปล่าคะ | ไม่ได้เรียนครับ, เรียนที่โรงเรียน |
| ตัดผมที่สถานทูตหรือเปล่าคะ | ไม่ได้ตัดครับ, ตัดที่ร้านตัดผม |

ข.

(คุณสวัสดิ์ไปหาคุณประสงค์ที่ที่ทำงานตอนบ่าย, นะคะ)

คุณสวัสดิ์ไปหาคุณประสงค์ที่บ้านใช่ไหมคะ

ไม่ใช่ครับ

ไปหาที่ไหนคะ

ที่ที่ทำงานครับ

คุณจอนไปหาใช่ไหมคะ

ไม่ใช่ครับ

ใครไปหาคะ

คุณสวัสดิ์ครับ

ไปหาคุณยังใช่ไหมคะ

ไม่ใช่ครับ

ไปหาใครคะ

คุณประสงค์ครับ

ไปหาตอนเช้าใช่ไหมคะ

ไม่ใช่ครับ

ไปหาตอนไหนคะ

ตอนบ่ายครับ

คุณประสงค์ไปหาคุณสวัสดิ์ใช่ไหมคะ

ไม่ใช่ครับ

ใครไปหาใครคะ

คุณสวัสดิ์ไปหาคุณประสงค์ครับ

**16.9 Conversation.**

a. The teacher asks whether one of the actions at the left took place at one of the places at the right. The student says that it didn't. It took place somewhere else. Try for *logical* answers, not *original* ones.

| | |
|---|---|
| To make something or get something made. | At the shop. |
| To study. | At the office. |
| To read something. | At the Embassy. |
| To work. | At the barber shop. |
| To eat. | At the intersection. |
| To order something. | In the dining room. |
| To buy something. | At the restaurant. |
| To get one's hair cut. | At school. |
| To meet someone. | At the hotel. |
| To write something. | At home. |
| To sell something. | At the market. |

| | |
|---|---|
| tham ŋaan thîi thanǒn rɨ́ plàaw khá. | **mây dây tham khráp.**<br>**tham thîi thîi tham ŋaan.** |
| sɨ́ɨ thîi rooŋrɛɛm rɨ́ plàaw khá. | **mây dây sɨ́ɨ khráp.**<br>**sɨ́ɨ thîi talàat.** |
| rian thîi ráan tàt phǒm rɨ́ plàaw khá. | **mây dây rian khráp.**<br>**rian thîi rooŋrian.** |
| tàt phǒm thîi sathǎanthûut rɨ́ plàaw khá. | **mây dây tàt khráp.**<br>**tàt thîi ráan tàt phǒm.** |

Etc.

**b. Questioning information.**

**(khun sawàt pay hǎa khun prasǒŋ thîi thîi tham ŋaan tɔɔn bàay. ná khá.)**

**khun sawàt pay hǎa khun prasǒŋ thîi bâan chây máy khá.**
**mây chây khráp.**
**pay hǎa thîi nǎy khá.**
**thîi thîi tham ŋaan khráp.**
**khun cɔɔn pay hǎa chây máy khá.**
**mây chây khráp.**
**khray pay hǎa khá.**
**khun sawàt khráp.**
**pay hǎa khun yaŋ chây máy khá.**
**mây chây khráp.**
**pay hǎa khray khá.**
**khun prasǒŋ khráp.**
**pay hǎa tɔɔn cháaw chây máy khá.**
**mây chây khráp.**
**pay hǎa tɔɔn nǎy khá.**
**tɔɔn bàay khráp.**
**khun prasǒŋ pay hǎa khun sawàt chây máy khá.**
**mây chây khráp.**
**khray pay hǎa khray khá.**
**khun sawàt pay hǎa khun prasǒŋ khráp.**

(More.)

(ลูกคุณประสงค์เรียนภาษาอังกฤษที่บ้านคุณยังตอนเย็น, นะคะ)

ลูกคุณสวัสดิ์เรียนใช่ไหมคะ

ไม่ใช่ครับ

ลูกใครคะ

ลูกคุณประสงค์ครับ

เรียนอะไรคะ

เรียนภาษาครับ

ภาษาอะไรคะ

ภาษาอังกฤษครับ

เรียนที่บ้านหรือที่โรงเรียนคะ

ที่บ้านครับ

บ้านใครคะ

บ้านคุณยังครับ

เรียนตอนเที่ยงใช่ไหมคะ

ไม่ใช่ครับ

เรียนตอนไหนคะ

ตอนเย็นครับ

ลูกคุณประสงค์ทำอะไรตอนเย็นคะ

เรียนภาษาอังกฤษครับ

## ๑๖.๑๐ การเขียน

ปลา ขวา ควาย ตรง

| | | |
|---|---|---|
| ปลา | กลัว | ตรึง |
| ขลา | ปลัว | ขรึง |
| ขวา | ปลวน | กรึง |
| ขวาย | ปลวง | กรุง |
| ควาย | ปลอง | ครุง |
| กวาย | ปลง | ครุม |
| กลาย | ปรง | คลุม |
| กลวย | ตรง | คุม |

(lûuk khun prasɔ̌ŋ rian phasǎa ʔaŋkrìt thîi bâan khun yaŋ tɔɔn yen. ná khá.)

lûuk khun sawàt rian chây máy khá.
  mây chây khráp.
lûuk khray khá.
  lûuk khun prasɔ̌ŋ khráp.
rian ʔaray khá.
  rian phasǎa khráp.
phasǎa ʔaray khá.
  phasǎa ʔaŋkrìt khráp.
rian thîi bâan rʉ́ thîi rooŋrian khá.
  thîi bâan khráp.
bâan khray khá.
  bâan khun yaŋ khráp.
rian tɔɔn thîaŋ chây máy khá.
  mây chây khráp.
rian tɔɔn nǎy khá.
  tɔɔn yen khráp.
lûuk khun prasɔ̌ŋ tham ʔaray tɔɔn yen khá.
  rian phasǎa ʔaŋkrìt khráp.

**16.10 Writing.**

| ปลา | ขวา | ควาย | ตรง |
|---|---|---|---|
| plaa | khwǎa | khwaay | troŋ |
| Fish. | Right. | Buffalo. | Straight. |

| | | | | | |
|---|---|---|---|---|---|
| ปลา | *plaa | กลัว | klua | ตรึง | trʉŋ |
| ขลา | khlǎa | ปลัว | plua | ขรึง | khrʉ̌ŋ |
| ขวา | *khwǎa | ปลวน | pluan | กรึง | krʉŋ |
| ขวาย | khwǎay | ปลวง | pluaŋ | กรุง | kruŋ |
| ควาย | *khwaay | ปลอง | plɔɔŋ | ครุง | khruŋ |
| กวาย | kwaay | ปลง | ploŋ | ครุม | khrum |
| กลาย | klaay | ปรง | proŋ | คลุม | khlum |
| กลวย | kluay | ตรง | *troŋ | คุม | khum |

# บทที่ ๑๗

ลืม

เอา
เอามา
เอาไป

บ้าง
มีบ้าง

ไม้
ขีด
ไม้ขีด

ด้วย

ช่วย

ส่ง
ไปส่ง
ส่งไป
ไปส่งเขาที่นั่น
ส่งเขาไปที่นั่น

ให้
ให้เขา
ฉันให้เขา
ฉันให้บุหรี่เขา
ฉันให้เขาไป
ฉันทำให้เขา
ฉันให้เขาทำให้ฉัน

เขี่ย
เขี่ยบุหรี่
ที่
ที่เขี่ยบุหรี่

พหลโยธิน
ถนนพหลโยธิน

สนาม

# LESSON 17

## 17.1 Vocabulary and expansions.

| | |
|---|---|
| lɯɯm | To forget. |
| ʔaw | To take (as when offered something), to accept. |
| ʔaw maa | To bring (take and come). |
| ʔaw pay | To take (take and go). |
| bâaŋ | Some. This word is used to pluralize question words very much like *all* is used in some dialects of English: *sɯ́ɯ ʔaray bâaŋ*. 'What all did you buy?' |
| mii bâaŋ | To have some. |
| máay | Wood, stick. |
| khìit | To scratch a mark or line, to strike. |
| máykhìit | Matches. |
| dûay | Also, too (in the meaning of 'in addition' not in the meaning 'in like manner'). |
| chûay | To help. This word is used to make a request more polite: 'Help me out by...', 'Do me a favor'. It is thus similar in function to *please*. |
| sòŋ | To send. |
| pay sòŋ | 'To go sending'. To take. |
| sòŋ pay | 'To send going'. To send. |
| pay sòŋ kháw thîi nân | Take him there. |
| sòŋ kháw pay thîi nân | Send him there. |
| hây | To give. This word marks the transfer of things, influence, etc. from subject to object. The *direction* of the transfer is its central meaning. It is shown below by an arrow. |
| hây kháw | → him. Give him, to him, for him. |
| chán hây kháw | I → him. I gave it to him. |
| chán hây burìi kháw | I → cigaret him. I gave him a cigaret. |
| chán hây kháw pay | I → him go. I had him go I let him go. |
| chán tham hây kháw | I do → him. I did it for him. |
| chán hây kháw tham hây chán | I → him do → me. I had him do it for me. |
| khìa | To remove or dislodge something with light stroking movements of the finger or some instrument. |
| khìa burìi | To brush the ash off of a cigaret. |
| thîi | A place. |
| thîi khìa burìi | Ash tray. |
| phahǒnyoothin | Paholyothin. |
| thanǒn phahǒnyoothin | Paholyothin Road. |
| sanǎam | Yard, field, court. |

## ๑๗.๒ โครงสร้างของประโยค

เขาเอาดินสอ
เขาเอากระดาษ

ฉันเอาบุหรี่มา
ฉันเอาไม้ขีดมา

เขาเอาหนังสือไป
เขาเอาวิทยุไป

เขาเอาไปบ้าน
เขาเอาไปตลาด

เขาเอาไปให้พ่อ
เขาเอาไปให้คุณยัง

เขาเอาหนังสือไปบ้าน
เขาเอากระดาษไปโรงเรียน

เขาเอาบุหรี่ไปให้พ่อ
เขาเอาดินสอมาให้ฉัน

เขาเอาบุหรี่ไปบ้านให้พ่อ
ฉันเอาดินสอไปโรงเรียนให้ลูก

เขาส่งลูกไปอเมริกา
เขาส่งหนังสือไปสถานทูต

เขาไปส่งลูกที่อเมริกา
เขาไปส่งหนังสือที่สถานทูต

เขาส่งดินสอให้ลูก
เขาส่งบุหรี่ให้ฉัน
ช่วยส่งไม้ขีดให้ฉัน

เขาเอาหนังสือไปบ้านให้พ่อ
เขาเอาไปให้
เขาส่งดินสอไปโรงเรียนให้ลูก
เขาส่งไปให้

เอาไหม
เอาบุหรี่ไหม

เอาบุหรี่,แล้วเอาไม้ขีดด้วย
เอาดินสอ,แล้วเอากระดาษด้วย

เอาบุหรี่ด้วยไหม
เอาไม้ขีดด้วยไหม

ไม่เอากระดาษ
ไม่เอาดินสอ

ซื้ออะไรบ้าง
ไปไหนบ้าง
พบใครบ้าง

มีไหม
มีบุหรี่ไหม
มีบ้างไหม
มีบุหรี่บ้างไหม

### 17.2 Patterns.

| | |
|---|---|
| kháw ʔaw dinsɔ̌ɔ. | He took a pencil. |
| kháw ʔaw kradàat. | He took some paper. |
| chán ʔaw burìi maa.<br>chán ʔaw máykhìit maa. | I brought cigarets with me.<br>I brought matches with me. |
| kháw ʔaw naŋsɯ̌ɯ pay.<br>kháw ʔaw wítthayúʔ pay. | He took a book with him.<br>He took a radio with him. |
| kháw ʔaw pay bâan.<br>kháw ʔaw pay talàat. | He took it home.<br>He took it to the market. |
| kháw ʔaw pay hây phɔ̂ɔ.<br>kháw ʔaw pay hây khun yaŋ. | He took it to his father.<br>He took it to Mr. Young. |
| kháw ʔaw naŋsɯ̌ɯ pay bâan.<br>kháw ʔaw kradàat pay rooŋrian. | He took his book home.<br>He took some paper to school. |
| kháw ʔaw burìi pay hây phɔ̂ɔ.<br>kháw ʔaw dinsɔ̌ɔ maa hây chán. | He took some cigarets to his father.<br>He brought me a pencil. |
| kháw ʔaw burìi pay bâan hây phɔ̂ɔ.<br>chán ʔaw dinsɔ̌ɔ pay rooŋrian hây lûuk. | He took some cigarets home to his father.<br>I took a pencil to school for my child. |
| kháw sòŋ lûuk pay ʔameerikaa.<br>kháw sòŋ naŋsɯ̌ɯ pay sathǎanthûut. | He sent his child to America.<br>He sent a book to the Embassy. |
| kháw pay sòŋ lûuk thîi ʔameerikaa.<br>kháw pay sòŋ naŋsɯ̌ɯ thîi sathǎanthûut. | He took his child to America.<br>He took a book to the Embassy. |
| kháw sòŋ dinsɔ̌ɔ hây lûuk.<br>kháw sòŋ burìi hây chán.<br>chûay sòŋ máykhìit hây chán. | He sent (or passed) his child a pencil.<br>He sent (or passed) me some cigarets.<br>Please pass me the matches. |
| kháw ʔaw naŋsɯ̌ɯ pay bâan hây phɔ̂ɔ.<br>kháw ʔaw pay hây.<br>kháw sòŋ dinsɔ̌ɔ pay rooŋrian hây lûuk.<br>kháw sòŋ pay hây. | He took a book home to his father.<br>He took (it) to (there) for (him).<br>He sent a pencil to school for his son.<br>He sent (it) to (there) for (him). |
| ʔaw máy.<br>ʔaw burìi máy. | Do you want it? Will you accept it?<br>Do you want a cigaret? |
| ʔaw burìi, lɛ́ɛw ʔaw máykhìit dûay.<br>ʔaw dinsɔ̌ɔ, lɛ́ɛw ʔaw kradàat dûay. | I'll have a cigaret and a match too.<br>I'll have pencil and some paper too. |
| ʔaw burìi dûay máy.<br>ʔaw máykhìit dûay máy. | Do you want a cigaret, too?<br>Do you want some matches, too? |
| mây ʔaw kradàat.<br>mây ʔaw dinsɔ̌ɔ. | I don't want any paper.<br>I don't want a pencil. |
| sɯ́ɯ ʔaray bâaŋ.<br>pay nǎy bâaŋ.<br>phóp khray bâaŋ. | What all did you buy?<br>Where all did you go?<br>Who all did you see? |
| mii máy.<br>mii burìi máy.<br>mii bâaŋ máy.<br>mii burìi bâaŋ máy. | Do you have (it)?<br>Do you have cigarets?<br>Do you have any?<br>Do you have any cigarets? |

๑๗.๓ บทสนทนา

ก. ฉันลืมเอาบุหรี่มา คุณมีบ้างไหม

ข. มี, เอาไม้ขีดด้วยไหม

ก. ไม่เอา, มีแล้ว ช่วยส่งที่เขี่ยบุหรี่ให้ฉันหน่อย

ข. นี่

ก. ขอบคุณมาก

ข. ไม่เป็นไร

**๑๗.๔ แบบฝึกหัดการฟังและการออกเสียงสูงต่ำ**

**ก.** ฝน เมฆ พอ หนาว แดด ฉาย

**ข.**

ใครเรียน
  แดงเรียน
แดงเรียนที่ไหน
  แดงเรียนที่โรงเรียน
แดงเรียนที่โรงเรียนวันไหน
  แดงเรียนที่โรงเรียนวันจันทร์

ใครอ่าน
  หน่อยอ่าน
หน่อยอ่านที่ไหน
  หน่อยอ่านที่ตลาด
หน่อยอ่านที่ตลาดวันไหน
  หน่อยอ่านที่ตลาดวันศุกร์

ใครใช้
  น้อยใช้
น้อยใช้ที่ไหน
  น้อยใช้ที่ร้าน
น้อยใช้ที่ร้านวันไหน
  น้อยใช้ที่ร้านวันพุธ

ใครเขียน
  ต๋อยเขียน
ต๋อยเขียนที่ไหน
  ต๋อยเขียนที่สนาม
ต๋อยเขียนที่สนามวันไหน
  ต๋อยเขียนที่สนามวันเสาร์

ใครพูด
  ต้อยพูด
ต้อยพูดที่ไหน
  ต้อยพูดที่บ้าน
ต้อยพูดที่บ้านวันไหน
  ต้อยพูดที่บ้านวันแม่

**17.3 Dialog.**

| | |
|---|---|
| A. chán lʉʉm ʔaw burìi maa. | I forgot to bring cigarets. |
| khun mii bâaŋ máy. | Have you got any? |
| B. mii. | Yes. |
| ʔaw máykhìit dûay máy. | Do you want some matches, too? |
| A. mây ʔaw. mii lɛ́ɛw. | No. I already have some. |
| chûay sòŋ thîi khìa burìi hây chán nɔ̀y. | Please pass me the ash tray. |
| B. nîi. | Here. |
| A. khɔ̀ɔpkhun mâak. | Thanks a lot. |
| B. mây pen ray. | You're welcome. |

**17.4 Tone identification and production.**

**a.** Identify the tones and record the number of repetitions required.

| | | | | | |
|---|---|---|---|---|---|
| Rain. | *fon | ......... | Cold (weather). | *naaw | ......... |
| Clouds. | *meek | ......... | Sunlight. | *dɛɛt | ......... |
| Enough. | *phɔɔ | ......... | To shine a light. | *chaay | ......... |

**b. Response drill.**

| | |
|---|---|
| khray rian. | Who studied? |
| dɛɛŋ rian. | Daeng studied. |
| dɛɛŋ rian thîi nǎy. | Where did Daeng study? |
| dɛɛŋ rian thîi rooŋrian. | Daeng studied at school. |
| dɛɛŋ rian thîi rooŋrian wan nǎy. | On what day did Daeng study at school? |
| dɛɛŋ rian thîi rooŋrian wan can. | Daeng studied at school on Monday. |
| khray ʔàan. | Who read it? |
| nɔ̀y ʔàan. | Noy Low read it. |
| nɔ̀y ʔàan thîi nǎy. | Where did Noy Low read it? |
| nɔ̀y ʔàan thîi talàat. | Noy Low read it at the market. |
| nɔ̀y ʔàan thîi talàat wan nǎy. | On what day did Noy Low read it at the market? |
| nɔ̀y ʔàan thîi talàat wan sùk. | Noy Low read it at the market on Friday. |
| khray cháy. | Who used it? |
| nɔ́ɔy cháy. | Noy High used it. |
| nɔ́ɔy cháy thîi nǎy. | Where did Noy High use it? |
| nɔ́ɔy cháy thîi ráan. | Noy High used it at the shop. |
| nɔ́ɔy cháy thîi ráan wan nǎy. | On what day did Noy High use it at the shop? |
| nɔ́ɔy cháy thîi ráan wan phút. | Noy High used it at the shop on Wednesday. |
| khray khǐan. | Who wrote it? |
| tɔ̌y khǐan. | Toy Rise wrote it. |
| tɔ̌y khǐan thîi nǎy. | Where did Toy Rise write it? |
| tɔ̌y khǐan thîi sanǎam. | Toy Rise wrote it in the yard. |
| tɔ̌y khǐan thîi sanǎam wan nǎy. | On what day did Toy Rise write it in the yard? |
| tɔ̌y khǐan thîi sanǎam wan sǎw. | Toy Rise wrote it in the yard on Saturday. |
| khray phûut. | Who spoke? |
| tɔ̂y phûut. | Toy Fall spoke. |
| tɔ̂y phûut thîi nǎy. | Where did Toy Fall speak? |
| tɔ̂y phûut thîi bâan. | Toy Fall spoke at home. |
| tɔ̂y phûut thîi bâan wan nǎy. | On what day did Toy Fall speak at home? |
| tɔ̂y phûut thîi bâan wan mɛ̂ɛ. | Toy Fall spoke at home on Mother's Day. |

๑๗.๕ แบบฝึกหัดการสลับเสียงสูงต่ำ

ไก่สูงกว่าควายใช่ไหม
    ไม่ใช่, ควายสูงกว่าไก่

พี่เล็กกว่าน้องใช่ไหม
    ไม่ใช่, น้องเล็กกว่าพี่

วัวเตี้ยกว่าหมูใช่ไหม
    ไม่ใช่, หมูเตี้ยกว่าวัว

น้องใหญ่กว่าพี่ใช่ไหม
    ไม่ใช่, พี่ใหญ่กว่าน้อง

หมูผอมกว่าไก่ใช่ไหม
    ไม่ใช่, ไก่ผอมกว่าหมู

๑๗.๖ แบบฝึกหัดการออกเสียงสระและพยัญชนะ

ก.

ใครปัด
    พันปัด

ใครปัด
    เพลินปัด

ใครเปิด
    พันเปิด

ใครเปิด
    เพลินเปิด

ข.

ต้อยต่อยตาติ๋ม
    ติ๋มก็ต่อยตาต้อย

แถมทิ้งถุงทอม
    ทอมก็ทิ้งถุงแถม

ดำดึงด้ายแดง
    แดงก็ดึงด้ายดำ

ติ๋มต่อยตาต้อย
    ต้อยก็ต่อยตาติ๋ม

ทอมทิ้งถุงแถม
    แถมก็ทิ้งถุงทอม

แดงดึงด้ายดำ
    ดำก็ดึงด้ายแดง

### 17.5 Tone manipulation.

**a. Response drill.**

| | |
|---|---|
| kày sǔuŋ kwàa khwaay,<br>chây máy.<br>  mây chây.<br>  khwaay sǔuŋ kwàa kày. | The chicken is taller than the buffalo,<br>isn't it?<br>  No.<br>  The buffalo is taller than the chicken. |
| phîi lék kwàa nɔ́ɔŋ,<br>chây máy.<br>  mây chây.<br>  nɔ́ɔŋ lék kwàa phîi. | Older One is smaller than Younger One,<br>isn't he?<br>  No.<br>  Younger One is smaller than Older One. |
| wua tîa kwàa mǔu,<br>chây máy.<br>  mây chây.<br>  mǔu tîa kwàa wua. | The cow is shorter than the pig,<br>isn't it?<br>  No.<br>  The pig is shorter than the cow. |
| nɔ́ɔŋ yày kwàa phîi,<br>chây máy.<br>  mây chây.<br>  phîi yày kwàa nɔ́ɔŋ. | Younger One is bigger than Older One,<br>isn't he?<br>  No.<br>  Older One is bigger than Younger One. |
| mǔu phɔ̌ɔm kwàa kày,<br>chây máy.<br>  mây chây.<br>  kày phɔ̌ɔm kwàa mǔu. | The pig is thinner than the chicken,<br>isn't it?<br>  No.<br>  The chicken is thinner than the pig. |

### 17.6 Vowel and consonant drills.

**a. Response drill.** (a-ɔɔ).

Answer 'Pun' to the following two questions asked repeatedly by the teacher.

| | | | |
|---|---|---|---|
| khray pàt. | Who brushed it off? | khray pɔ̀ɔt. | Who opened it? |
|   phan pàt. | Pun brushed it off. |   phan pɔ̀ɔt. | Pun opened it. |

Now answer 'Ploen'.

| | | | |
|---|---|---|---|
| khray pàt. | Who brushed it off? | khray pɔ̀ɔt. | Who opened it? |
|   phlɔɔn pàt. | Ploen brushed it off. |   phlɔɔn pɔ̀ɔt. | Ploen opened it. |

**b. Response drill.** (t, th, and d).

| | |
|---|---|
| tɔ̂y tɔ̀y taa tǐm.<br>  tǐm kɔ̂ tɔ̀y taa tɔ̂y. | Toy punched Tim in the eye.<br>  Tim punched Toy in the eye, too. |
| thɛ̌ɛm thíŋ thǔŋ thɔɔm.<br>  thɔɔm kɔ̂ thíŋ thǔŋ thɛ̌ɛm. | Taem threw away Tom's sack.<br>  Tom threw away Taem's sack, too. |
| dam dɯŋ dâay dɛɛŋ.<br>  dɛɛŋ kɔ̂ dɯŋ dâay dam. | Dum pulled Daeng's thread.<br>  Daeng pulled Dum's thread, too. |
| tǐm tɔ̀y taa tɔ̂y.<br>  tɔ̂y kɔ̂ tɔ̀y taa tǐm. | Tim punched Toy in the eye.<br>  Toy punched Tim in the eye, too. |
| thɔɔm thíŋ thǔŋ thɛ̌ɛm.<br>  thɛ̌ɛm kɔ̂ thíŋ thǔŋ thɔɔm. | Tom threw away Taem's sack.<br>  Taem threw away Tom's sack, too |
| dɛɛŋ dɯŋ dâay dam.<br>  dam kɔ̂ dɯŋ dâay dɛɛŋ. | Daeng pulled Dum's thread.<br>  Dum pulled Daeng's thread, too. |

## ๑๗.๗ แบบฝึกหัดไวยากรณ์

ก.

เขาลืมเอาหนังสือมา (ดินสอ)
เขาลืมเอาดินสอมา (กระดาษ)
เขาลืมเอากระดาษมา (บุหรี่)
เขาลืมเอาบุหรี่มา (ไป)
เขาลืมเอาบุหรี่ไป (ไม้ขีด)
เขาลืมเอาไม้ขีดไป (อาหาร)
เขาลืมเอาอาหารไป

ข.

เอาไม้ขีดด้วยไหม (บุหรี่)
เอาบุหรี่ด้วยไหม (กระดาษ)
เอากระดาษด้วยไหม (ดินสอ)
เอาดินสอด้วยไหม (หนังสือ)
เอาหนังสือด้วยไหม (พัดลม)
เอาพัดลมด้วยไหม

ค.

ช่วยส่งกระดาษให้ฉันหน่อย (ดินสอ)
ช่วยส่งดินสอให้ฉันหน่อย (เอามา)
ช่วยเอาดินสอมาให้ฉันหน่อย (หนังสือ)
ช่วยเอาหนังสือมาให้ฉันหน่อย (หา)
ช่วยหาหนังสือให้ฉันหน่อย (บุหรี่)
ช่วยหาบุหรี่ให้ฉันหน่อย (ส่ง)
ช่วยส่งบุหรี่ให้ฉันหน่อย (ไม้ขีด)
ช่วยส่งไม้ขีดให้ฉันหน่อย (เอามา)
ช่วยเอาไม้ขีดมาให้ฉันหน่อย (เอาไปให้เขา)
ช่วยเอาไม้ขีดไปให้เขาหน่อย (ส่ง)
ช่วยส่งไม้ขีดให้เขาหน่อย

17.7 **Grammar drills.**

a. **Substitution drill.**

| | |
|---|---|
| kháw lʉʉm ʔaw naŋsʉ̌ʉ maa. (dinsɔ̌ɔ) | He forgot to bring a book. (pencil) |
| kháw lʉʉm ʔaw dinsɔ̌ɔ maa. (kradàat) | He forgot to bring a pencil. (paper) |
| kháw lʉʉm ʔaw kradàat maa. (burìi) | He forgot to bring paper. (cigarets) |
| kháw lʉʉm ʔaw burìi maa. (pay) | He forgot to bring cigarets. (go) |
| kháw lʉʉm ʔaw burìi pay. (máykhìit) | He forgot to take cigarets. (matches) |
| kháw lʉʉm ʔaw máykhìit pay. (ʔaahǎan) | He forgot to take matches. (food) |
| kháw lʉʉm ʔaw ʔaahǎan pay. | He forgot to take food. |

b. **Substitution drill.**

| | |
|---|---|
| ʔaw máykhìit dûay máy. (burìi) | Do you want matches, too? (cigarets) |
| ʔaw burìi dûay máy. (kradàat) | Do you want cigarets, too? (paper) |
| ʔaw kradàat dûay máy. (dinsɔ̌ɔ) | Do you want paper, too? (pencil) |
| ʔaw dinsɔ̌ɔ dûay máy. (naŋsʉ̌ʉ) | Do you want a pencil, too? (book) |
| ʔaw naŋsʉ̌ʉ dûay máy. (phátlom) | Do you want a book, too? (fan) |
| ʔaw phátlom dûay máy. | Do you want a fan, too? |

c. **Substitution drill.**

| | |
|---|---|
| chûay sòŋ kradàat hây chán nɔ̀y.<br>(dinsɔ̌ɔ) | Please pass me some paper.<br>(pencil) |
| chûay sòŋ dinsɔ̌ɔ hây chán nɔ̀y.<br>(ʔaw maa) | Please pass me a pencil.<br>(bring) |
| chûay ʔaw dinsɔ̌ɔ maa hây chán nɔ̀y.<br>(naŋsʉ̌ʉ) | Please bring me a pencil.<br>(book) |
| chûay ʔaw naŋsʉ̌ʉ maa hây chán nɔ̀y.<br>(hǎa) | Please bring me a book.<br>(look for) |
| chûay hǎa naŋsʉ̌ʉ hây chán nɔ̀y.<br>(burìi) | Please find a book for me.<br>(cigaret) |
| chûay hǎa burìi hây chán nɔ̀y.<br>(sòŋ) | Please find me a cigaret.<br>(pass) |
| chûay sòŋ burìi hây chán nɔ̀y.<br>(máykhìit) | Please pass me a cigaret.<br>(matches) |
| chûay sòŋ máykhìit hây chán nɔ̀y.<br>(ʔaw maa) | Please pass me the matches.<br>(bring) |
| chûay ʔaw máykhìit maa hây chán nɔ̀y.<br>(ʔaw pay hây kháw) | Please bring me the matches.<br>(take him) |
| chûay ʔaw máykhìit pay hây kháw nɔ̀y.<br>(sòŋ) | Please take him the matches.<br>(pass) |
| chûay sòŋ máykhìit hây kháw nɔ̀y. | Please pass him the matches. |

ง.

ส่งอะไร
    ส่งหนังสือ
ส่งให้ใคร
    ส่งให้สวัสดิ์
ส่งอะไรให้สวัสดิ์
    ส่งหนังสือให้เขา

เอาอะไรมา
    เอาหนังสือมา
เอามาให้ใคร
    เอามาให้สวัสดิ์
เอาอะไรมาให้สวัสดิ์
    เอาหนังสือมาให้เขา

เอาอะไรไป
    เอาหนังสือไป
เอาไปให้ใคร
    เอาไปให้สวัสดิ์
เอาอะไรไปให้สวัสดิ์
    เอาหนังสือไปให้เขา

ให้อะไร
    ให้หนังสือ
ให้ใคร
    ให้สวัสดิ์
ให้อะไรสวัสดิ์
    ให้หนังสือเขา

### ๑๗.๘ เลข

๔๒๗/๑ ซอย ๑๒ ถนนพหลโยธิน
บ้านเลขที่สี่สองเจ็ดทับหนึ่งซอยสิบสองถนนพหลโยธิน

ถนนสุขุมวิท
ซอย ๕๗ ถนนสุขุมวิท
๖๑๘ ซอย ๕๗ ถนนสุขุมวิท

ถนนพหลโยธิน
ซอย ๑๕ ถนนพหลโยธิน
๑๐๓/๔ ซอย ๑๕ ถนนพหลโยธิน

ถนนพหลโยธิน
ซอย ๒๑ ถนนพหลโยธิน
๗๖๔/๓ ซอย ๒๑ ถนนพหลโยธิน

ถนนสุขุมวิท
ซอย ๖๔ ถนนสุขุมวิท
๕๓๐/๒ ซอย ๖๔ ถนนสุขุมวิท

### ๑๗.๙ การสนทนาโต้ตอบ

คุณเจนสูงกว่าคุณจอน
ใช่ไหมคะ
    ไม่ใช่ครับ,
    คุณจอนสูงกว่าคุณเจน

คุณยังผอมกว่าดิฉัน
ใช่ไหมคะ
    ไม่ใช่ครับ,
    คุณผอมกว่าคุณยัง

ผมเล็กกว่าคุณ
ใช่ไหมครับ
    ไม่ใช่ค่ะ
    ดิฉันเล็กกว่าคุณ

**d. Response drill.**

| | |
|---|---|
| sòŋ ʔaray. | What did you pass? |
| sòŋ naŋsʉ̌ʉ. | I passed a book. |
| sòŋ hây khray. | Who did you pass it to? |
| sòŋ hây sawàt. | I passed it to Sawat. |
| sòŋ ʔaray hây sawàt. | What did you pass to Sawat? |
| sòŋ naŋsʉ̌ʉ hây kháw. | I passed him a book. |
| ʔaw ʔaray pay. | What did you take? |
| ʔaw naŋsʉ̌ʉ pay. | I took a book. |
| ʔaw pay hây khray. | Who did you take it to? |
| ʔaw pay hây sawàt. | I took it to Sawat. |
| ʔaw ʔaray pay hây sawàt. | What did you take to Sawat? |
| ʔaw naŋsʉ̌ʉ pay hây kháw. | I took him a book. |
| ʔaw ʔaray maa. | What did you bring? |
| ʔaw naŋsʉ̌ʉ maa. | I brought a book. |
| ʔaw maa hây khray. | Who did you bring it for? |
| ʔaw maa hây sawàt. | I brought it for Sawat. |
| ʔaw ʔaray maa hây sawàt. | What did you bring for Sawat? |
| ʔaw naŋsʉ̌ʉ maa hây kháw. | I brought a book for him. |
| hây ʔaray. | What did you give? |
| hây naŋsʉ̌ʉ. | I gave a book. |
| hây khray. | Who did you give it to? |
| hây sawàt. | I gave it to Sawat. |
| hây ʔaray sawàt. | What did you give to Sawat? |
| hây naŋsʉ̌ʉ kháw. | I gave him a book. |

**17.8 Numbers.**

427/1 Soi 12, Paholyothin Road.
bâan lêek thîi sìi sɔ̌ɔŋ cèt tháp nʉ̀ŋ sɔɔy sìp sɔ̌ɔŋ thanǒn phahǒnyoothin.

Practice reading the following addresses in Thai. Try to get the time under 45 seconds.

Sukhumvit Road.
Soi 57, Sukhumvit Road.
918 Soi 57, Sukhumvit Road.
Paholyothin Road.
Soi 21, Paholyothin Road.
764/3 Soi 21, Paholyothin Road.

Paholyothin Road.
Soi 15, Paholyothin Road.
103/4 Soi 15, Paholyothin Road.
Sukhumvit Road.
Soi 64, Sukhumvit Road.
530/2 Soi 64, Sukhumvit Road.

**17.9 Conversation.**

**a.** Compare members of the class as to height, weight, and size in the manner shown below.

| | |
|---|---|
| khun ceen sǔuŋ kwàa khun cɔɔn, chây máy khá. | mây chây khràp. khun cɔɔn sǔuŋ kwàa khun ceen. |
| khun yaŋ phɔ̌ɔm kwàa dichán, chây máy khá. | mây chây khráp. khun phɔ̌ɔm kwàa khun yaŋ. |
| phǒm lék kwàa khun, chây máy khráp. | mây chây khâ. dichán lék kwàa khun. |

ข.

ฉันลืมเอา...........................................มา, คุณมีบ้างไหมคะ

มีครับ, เอา.................................ด้วยไหมครับ

ไม่เอาค่ะ, มีแล้ว ช่วยส่ง..............................ให้ฉันหน่อย

นี่ครับ

ขอบคุณมากค่ะ

ไม่เป็นไรครับ

**๑๗.๑๐ การเขียน**

จีน ไฟ พอ

| | | |
|---|---|---|
| จีน | จูง | จน |
| จอน | ฟูง | เจน |
| พอน | ฟัง | เขน |
| พอ | พัง | เข็น |
| ไพ | พัน | โขน |
| ไฟ | พน | โยน |
| ฟู | หน | โคน |
| จู | ตน | โคลน |

b. Use the following items to practice the conversation suggested below.

Cigarets, matches, ash tray. Pencil, paper, book.

chán lʉʉm ʔaw..................maa. khun mii bâaŋ máy khá.

mii khráp. ʔaw..................dûay máy khráp.

mây ʔaw khâ. mii lɛ́ɛw. chûay sòŋ..................hây chán nɔ̀y.

nîi khráp.

khɔ̀ɔpkhun mâak khâ.

mây pen ray khráp.

### 17.10 Writing.

| จีน | ไฟ | พอ |
|---|---|---|
| ciin | fay | phɔɔ |
| Chinese. | Fire. | Enough. |

| | | | | | |
|---|---|---|---|---|---|
| จีน | *ciin | จูง | cuuŋ | จน | con |
| จอน | *cɔɔn | ฟูง | fuuŋ | เจน | *ceen |
| พอน | phɔɔn | ฟั่ง | faŋ | เขน | khěen |
| พอ | *phɔɔ | พัง | phaŋ | เข็น | khěn |
| ไพ | phay | พัน | *phan | โขน | khǒon |
| ไฟ | *fay | พน | phon | โยน | yoon |
| ฟู | fuu | หน | hǒn | โคน | khoon |
| จู | cuu | ตน | ton | โคลน | khloon |

# บทที่ ๑๘

## ๑๘.๑ คำศัพท์

ถาม
ถามอะไร
จะถามอะไรไหม

ถ้า

อยาก
อยากจะอ่านหนังสือ
ได้
อยากได้หนังสือ

แต่

มืด
มืดไป

ต้อง
บอก
ต้องบอกเขา

ใช้
คนใช้

อย่าง
อย่างไร
ยังไร
ยังไง
ไง

ชื่อ
ชื่ออะไร

เปิด
เปิดไฟ

ซิ

ฟัง

แสน

# LESSON 18

**18.1 Vocabulary and expansions.**

| | |
|---|---|
| thǎam | To ask. |
| thǎam ʔaray | Ask what? What did he ask you? |
| ca thǎam ʔaray máy | Ask something? Do you want to ask me anything? In Thai, the same word is used for both the interrogative (what, who, where) and its corresponding indefinite (something, someone, somewhere). |
| thâa | If. |
| yàak | To want. |
| yàak ca ʔàan naŋsʉ̌ʉ | To want to read a book. |
| dây | To get, receive. |
| yàak dây naŋsʉ̌ʉ | To want (to get) a book. |
| tɛ̀ɛ | But. |
| mʉ̂ʉt | To be dark. |
| mʉ̂ʉt pay | To be too dark (*pay* suggests 'going' in the excessive direction). |
| tɔ̂ŋ | To have to, must. |
| bɔ̀ɔk | To tell. |
| tɔ̂ŋ bɔ̀ɔk kháw | You must tell him. |
| cháy | To use. |
| khon cháay | Servant (a person that one can use). |
| yàaŋ | Kind, sort, variety. |
| yàaŋray | In what way? How? (Usually shortened as shown below.) |
| yaŋray | |
| yaŋŋay | |
| ŋay | |
| chʉ̂ʉ | Name, to be named. |
| chʉ̂ʉ ʔaray | What's his name? |
| pə̀ət | To open, turn on. |
| pə̀ət fay | To turn on the light. |
| si | A particle used to request an action when the result of the action, not the action itself, is the point of the request. |
| faŋ | To listen to. |
| sɛ̌ɛn | A hundred thousand. |

## ๑๘.๒ โครงสร้างของประโยค

ไม่ได้ถามอะไร
ไม่ได้บอกใคร
ไม่ได้ไปไหน

อยากจะไป
อยากจะกลับบ้าน
อยากจะอ่านหนังสือ

ต้องไป
ต้องกลับบ้าน
ต้องอ่านหนังสือ

ไม่อยากจะพูดกับเขา
ไม่อยากจะบอกเขา
ไม่ต้องพูดกับเขา
ไม่ต้องบอกเขา

ไม่อยากจะไป แต่ต้องไป
ไม่ต้องไป แต่อยากจะไป

มืดไปแล้ว
ร้อนไปแล้ว
มากไปแล้ว

ถ้าเขาอยากไป
ถ้าเขาไม่ไป
ถ้าเขาไม่ได้ไป

เรียกว่ายังไง
พูดว่ายังไง
บอกว่ายังไง
ถามว่ายังไง

เรียกเขาว่ายังไง
พูดกับเขาว่ายังไง
บอกเขาว่ายังไง
ถามเขาว่ายังไง

ถนนนี้ชื่ออะไร
โรงแรมนี้ชื่ออะไร
ร้านอาหารนี้ชื่ออะไร
คุณชื่ออะไร

เปิดไฟซิ
เปิดหน้าต่างซิ
เปิดประตูซิ
เปิดน้ำซิ
เปิดพัดลมซิ

18.2 **Patterns.**

| | |
|---|---|
| mây dây thǎam ʔaray. | I didn't ask anything. |
| mây dây bɔ̀ɔk khray. | I didn't tell anyone. |
| mây dây pay nǎy. | I didn't go anywhere. |
| | |
| yàak ca pay. | I want to go. |
| yàak ca klàp bâan. | I want to go home. |
| yàak ca ʔàan naŋsʉ̌ʉ. | I want to read a book. |
| | |
| tɔ̂ŋ pay. | I have to go. |
| tɔ̂ŋ klàp bâan. | I have to go home. |
| tɔ̂ŋ ʔàan naŋsʉ̌ʉ. | I have to read a book. |
| | |
| mây yàak ca phûut ka kháw. | I don't want to talk to him. |
| mây yàak ca bɔ̀ɔk kháw. | I don't want to tell him. |
| mây tɔ̂ŋ phûut ka kháw. | I don't have to talk to him. |
| mây tɔ̂ŋ bɔ̀ɔk kháw. | I don't have to tell him. |
| | |
| mây yàak ca pay, tɛ̀ɛ tɔ̂ŋ pay. | I don't want to go, but I have to. |
| mây tɔ̂ŋ pay, tɛ̀ɛ yàak ca pay. | I don't have to go, but I want to. |
| | |
| mʉ̂ʉt pay lɛ́ɛw. | It's too dark now. |
| rɔ́ɔn pay lɛ́ɛw. | It's too hot now. (You've overheated it.) |
| mâak pay lɛ́ɛw. | That's too much. (You've gone too far.) |
| | |
| thâa kháw yàak pay, | If he wants to go, |
| thâa kháw mây pay, | If he doesn't go, |
| thâa kháw mây dây pay, | If he hadn't gone, |
| | |
| rîak wâa yaŋŋay. | How do you call (him)? |
| phûut wâa yaŋŋay. | How do you say it? |
| bɔ̀ɔk wâa yaŋŋay. | What did you tell (him)? |
| thǎam wâa yaŋŋay. | What did you ask (him)? |
| | |
| rîak kháw wâa yaŋŋay. | How do you call him? |
| phûut ka kháw wâa yaŋŋay. | What did you say to him? |
| bɔ̀ɔk kháw wâa yaŋŋay. | What did you tell him? |
| thǎam kháw wâa yaŋŋay. | What did you ask him? |
| | |
| thanǒn níi chʉ̂ʉ ʔaray. | What's the name of this street? |
| rooŋrɛɛm níi chʉ̂ʉ ʔaray. | What's the name of this hotel? |
| ráan ʔaahǎan níi chʉ̂ʉ ʔaray. | What's the name of this restaurant? |
| khun chʉ̂ʉ ʔaray. | What's your name? |
| | |
| pə̀ət fay sí. | Turn on the light! |
| pə̀ət nâatàaŋ sí. | Open the window! |
| pə̀ət pratuu sí. | Open the door! |
| pə̀ət náam sí. | Turn on the water! |
| pə̀ət phátlom sí. | Turn on the fan! |

### ๑๘.๓ บทสนทนา

ก. ฉันถามอะไรหน่อยได้ไหม

ข. เชิญ

ก. ถ้าฉันอยากจะอ่านหนังสือ
แต่ห้อง มืดไป
ต้องบอกคนใช้ว่ายังไง

ข. คนใช้ชื่ออะไร

ก. ชื่อต้อย

ข. บอกว่าเปิดไฟซิ, ต้อย

### ๑๘.๔ แบบฝึกหัดการฟังและการออกเสียงสูงต่ำ

**ก.** ทอง ไม้ ผ้า หิน เงิน เหล็ก

**ข.**

ใครเรียน
แดงเรียน
แดงเรียนที่ไหน
แดงเรียนที่โรงเรียน

แดงเรียนที่โรงเรียนวันไหน
แดงเรียนที่โรงเรียนวันจันทร์
แดงเรียนที่โรงเรียนวันจันทร์ตอนไหน
แดงเรียนที่โรงเรียนวันจันทร์ตอนเย็น

---

ใครอ่าน
หน่อยอ่าน
หน่อยอ่านที่ไหน
หน่อยอ่านที่ตลาด

หน่อยอ่านที่ตลาดวันไหน
หน่อยอ่านที่ตลาดวันศุกร์
หน่อยอ่านที่ตลาดวันศุกร์ตอนไหน
หน่อยอ่านที่ตลาดวันศุกร์ตอนบ่าย

---

ใครใช้
น้อยใช้
น้อยใช้ที่ไหน
น้อยใช้ที่ร้าน

น้อยใช้ที่ร้านวันไหน
น้อยใช้ที่ร้านวันพุธ
น้อยใช้ที่ร้านวันพุธตอนไหน
น้อยใช้ที่ร้านวันพุธตอนเช้า

---

ใครเขียน
ต๋อยเขียน
ต๋อยเขียนที่ไหน
ต๋อยเขียนที่สนาม

ต๋อยเขียนที่สนามวันไหน
ต๋อยเขียนที่สนามวันเสาร์
ต๋อยเขียนที่สนามวันเสาร์ตอนไหน
ต๋อยเขียนที่สนามวันเสาร์ตอนสาย

---

ใครพูด
ต้อยพูด
ต้อยพูดที่ไหน
ต้อยพูดที่บ้าน

ต้อยพูดที่บ้านวันไหน
ต้อยพูดที่บ้านวันแม่
ต้อยพูดที่บ้านวันแม่ตอนไหน
ต้อยพูดที่บ้านวันแม่ตอนเที่ยง

## 18.3 Dialog.

| | |
|---|---|
| A. chán thǎam ʔaray nɔ̀y dây máy. | May I ask you something? |
| B. chəən. | Go ahead. |
| A. thâa chán yàak ca ʔàan naŋsʉ̌ʉ, | If I want to read a book, |
| tɛ̀ɛ hɔ̂ŋ mʉʉt pay, | but the room is too dark, |
| tɔ̂ŋ bɔ̀ɔk khon cháay wâa yaŋŋay. | what should I tell the servant? |
| B. khon cháay chʉ̂ʉ ʔaray. | What's your servant's name? |
| A. chʉ̂ʉ tɔ̌y. | Her name is Toy. |
| B. bɔ̀ɔk wâa pə̀ət fay sí, tɔ̌y. | Tell her, 'Turn on the light, Toy'. |

## 18.4 Tone identification and production.

**a.** Identify the tones and record the number of repetitions required.

| | | | | | |
|---|---|---|---|---|---|
| Gold. | *thɔɔŋ | ........... | Rock. | *hin | ........... |
| Wood. | *maay | ........... | Silver. | *ŋən | ........... |
| Cloth. | *phaa | ........... | Iron. | *lek | ........... |

**b. Response drill.** (Each item has eight lines : 4—4.)

khray rian.
  dɛɛŋ rian.
dɛɛŋ rian thîi nǎy.
  dɛɛŋ rian thîi rooŋrian.
dɛɛŋ rian thîi rooŋrian wan nǎy.
  dɛɛŋ rian thîi rooŋrian wan can.
dɛɛŋ rian thîi rooŋrian wan can tɔɔn nǎy.
  dɛɛŋ rian thîi rooŋrian wan can tɔɔn yen.

---

khray ʔàan.
  nɔ̀y ʔàan.
nɔ̀y ʔàan thîi nǎy.
  nɔ̀y ʔàan thîi talàat.
nɔ̀y ʔàan thîi talàat wan nǎy.
  nɔ̀y ʔàan thîi talàat wan sùk.
nɔ̀y ʔàan thîi talàat wan sùk tɔɔn nǎy.
  nɔ̀y ʔàan thîi talàat wan sùk tɔɔn bàay.

---

khray cháy.
  nɔ́ɔy cháy.
nɔ́ɔy cháy thîi nǎy.
  nɔ́ɔy cháy thîi ráan.
nɔ́ɔy cháy thîi ráan wan nǎy.
  nɔ́ɔy cháy thîi ráan wan phút.
nɔ́ɔy cháy thîi ráan wan phút tɔɔn nǎy.
  nɔ́ɔy cháy thîi ráan wan phút tɔɔn cháaw.

---

khray khǐan.
  tɔ̌y khǐan.
tɔ̌y khǐan thîi nǎy.
  tɔ̌y khǐan thîi sanǎam.
tɔ̌y khǐan thîi sanǎam wan nǎy.
  tɔ̌y khǐan thîi sanǎam wan sǎw.
tɔ̌y khǐan thîi sanǎam wan sǎw tɔɔn nǎy.
  tɔ̌y khǐan thîi sanǎam wan sǎw tɔɔn sǎay.

---

khray phûut.
  tɔ̂y phûut.
tɔ̂y phûut thîi nǎy.
  tɔ̂y phûut thîi bâan.
tɔ̂y phûut thîi bâan wan nǎy.
  tɔ̂y phûut thîi bâan wan mɛ̂ɛ.
tɔ̂y phûut thîi bâan wan mɛ̂ɛ tɔɔn nǎy.
  tɔ̂y phûut thîi bâan wan mɛ̂ɛ tɔɔn thîaŋ.

### ๑๘.๕ แบบฝึกหัดการสลับเสียงสูงต่ำ

ก.

| | | | |
|---|---|---|---|
| เขียนตอนสาย | (อ่าน) | กินตอนสาย | (ทอด) |
| อ่านตอนสาย | (เช้า ) | ทอดตอนสาย | (ซื้อ) |
| อ่านตอนเช้า | (ทอด) | ซื้อตอนสาย | (ขาย) |
| ทอดตอนเช้า | (เที่ยง) | ขายตอนสาย | (เช้า) |
| ทอดตอนเที่ยง | (กิน) | ขายตอนเช้า | (เขียน) |
| กินตอนเที่ยง | (บ่าย) | เขียนตอนเช้า | (เที่ยง) |
| กินตอนบ่าย | (ซื้อ) | เขียนตอนเที่ยง | (อ่าน) |
| ซื้อตอนบ่าย | (เย็น) | อ่านตอนเที่ยง | (บ่าย) |
| ซื้อตอนเย็น | (ขาย) | อ่านตอนบ่าย | (พูด) |
| ขายตอนเย็น | (บ่าย) | พูดตอนบ่าย | (เย็น) |
| ขายตอนบ่าย | (เที่ยง) | พูดตอนเย็น | (ฟัง) |
| ขายตอนเที่ยง | (ซื้อ) | ฟังตอนเย็น | (อ่าน) |
| ซื้อตอนเที่ยง | (เช้า) | อ่านตอนเย็น | (เขียน) |
| ซื้อตอนเช้า | (กิน) | เขียนตอนเย็น | (บ่าย) |
| กินตอนเช้า | (สาย) | เขียนตอนบ่าย | |

**18.5 Tone manipulation.**

**a. Substitution drill.**

| | |
|---|---|
| khĭan tɔɔn săay. (ʔàan) | Write in the late morning. (read) |
| ʔàan tɔɔn săay. (cháaw) | Read in the late morning. (early morning) |
| ʔàan tɔɔn cháaw. (thɔ̂ɔt) | Read in the early morning. (fry) |
| thɔ̂ɔt tɔɔn cháaw. (thîaŋ) | Fry it in the early morning. (noon) |
| thɔ̂ɔt tɔɔn thîaŋ. (kin) | Fry it at noon. (eat) |
| kin tɔɔn thîaŋ. (bàay) | Eat it at noon. (afternoon) |
| kin tɔɔn bàay. (sʉ́ʉ) | Eat it in the afternoon. (buy) |
| sʉ́ʉ tɔɔn bàay. (yen) | Buy it in the afternoon. (evening) |
| sʉ́ʉ tɔɔn yen. (khăay) | Buy it in the evening. (sell) |
| khăay tɔɔn yen. (bàay) | Sell it in the evening. (afternoon) |
| khăay tɔɔn bàay. (thîaŋ) | Sell it in the afternoon. (noon) |
| khăay tɔɔn thîaŋ. (sʉ́ʉ) | Sell it at noon. (buy) |
| sʉ́ʉ tɔɔn thîaŋ. (cháaw) | Buy it at noon. (early morning) |
| sʉ́ʉ tɔɔn cháaw. (kin) | Buy it in the early morning. (eat) |
| kin tɔɔn cháaw. (săay) | Eat it in the early morning. (late morning) |
| kin tɔɔn săay. (thɔ̂ɔt) | Eat it in the late morning. (fry) |
| thɔ̂ɔt tɔɔn săay. (sʉ́ʉ) | Fry it in the late morning. (buy) |
| sʉ́ʉ tɔɔn săay. (khăay) | Buy it in the late morning. (sell) |
| khăay tɔɔn săay. (cháaw) | Sell it in the late morning. (early morning) |
| khăay tɔɔn cháaw. (khĭan) | Sell it in the early morning. (write) |
| khĭan tɔɔn cháaw. (thîaŋ) | Write in the early morning. (noon) |
| khĭan tɔɔn thîaŋ. (ʔàan) | Write at noon. (read) |
| ʔàan tɔɔn thîaŋ. (bàay) | Read at noon. (afternoon) |
| ʔàan tɔɔn bàay. (phûut) | Read in the afternoon. (talk) |
| phûut tɔɔn bàay. (yen) | Talk in the afternoon. (evening) |
| phûut tɔɔn yen. (faŋ) | Talk in the evening. (listen) |
| faŋ tɔɔn yen. (ʔàan) | Listen in the evening. (read) |
| ʔàan tɔɔn yen. (khĭan) | Read in the evening. (write) |
| khĭan tɔɔn yen. (bàay) | Write in the evening. (afternoon) |
| khĭan tɔɔn bàay. | Write in the afternoon. |

## ๑๘.๖ แบบฝึกหัดการออกเสียงสระและพยัญชนะ

ก.

พันเพิ่งบีด (เบี๊ด)
พันเพิ่งเบี๊ด (เพลิน)

เพลินเพิ่งเบี๊ด (บีด)
เพลินเพิ่งบีด (พัน)

ข.

จิมจับจานแจ๋ว
  แจ๋วก็จับจานจิม

ชมเช็ดช้อนชด
  ชดก็เช็ดช้อนชม

แจ๋วจับจานจิม
  จิมก็จับจานแจ๋ว

ชดเช็ดช้อนชม
  ชมก็เช็ดช้อนชด

## ๑๘.๗ แบบฝึกหัดไวยากรณ์

ก.

ถามอะไร
  ไม่ได้ถามอะไร

พบใคร
  ไม่ได้พบใคร

ทำอะไร
  ไม่ได้ทำอะไร

ไปไหน
  ไม่ได้ไปไหน

พูดกับใคร
  ไม่ได้พูดกับใคร

ข.

อยากจะกลับบ้าน (ต้อง)

ต้องกลับบ้าน (เรียนภาษาไทย)

ต้องเรียนภาษาไทย (อยาก)

อยากจะเรียนภาษาไทย (พูดกับคนใช้)

อยากจะพูดกับคนใช้ (ต้อง)

ต้องพูดกับคนใช้ (ถามอะไรเขา)

ต้องถามอะไรเขา (อยาก)

อยากจะถามอะไรเขา

**18.6 Vowel and consonant drills.**

**a. Substitution drill.** (a-ə-əə).

| | |
|---|---|
| phan phôŋ pàt. (pə̀ət) | Pun just now brushed it off. (open) |
| phan phôŋ pə̀ət. (phləən) | Pun just now opened it. (Ploen) |
| phləən phôŋ pə̀ət. (pàt) | Ploen just now opened it. (brush off) |
| phləən phôŋ pàt. (phan) | Ploen just now brushed it off. (Pun) |

**b. Response drill.** (c and ch).

| | |
|---|---|
| cim càp caan cɛ̌w. | Jim grabbed Jaeo's plate. |
| cɛ̌w kɔ̂ càp caan cim. | Jaeo grabbed Jim's plate, too. |
| chom chét chɔ́ɔn chót. | Chom wiped Chot's spoon. |
| chót kɔ̂ chét chɔ́ɔn chom. | Chot wiped Chom's spoon, too. |
| cɛ̌w càp caan cim. | Jaeo grabbed Jim's plate. |
| cim kɔ̂ càp caan cɛ̌w. | Jim grabbed Jaeo's plate, too. |
| chót chét chɔ́ɔn chom. | Chot wiped Chom's spoon. |
| chom kɔ̂ chét chɔ́ɔn chót. | Chom wiped Chot's spoon, too. |

**18.7 Grammar drills.**

**a. Response drill.**

| | |
|---|---|
| thǎam ʔaray. | What did you ask? |
| mây dây thǎam ʔaray. | I didn't ask anything. |
| phóp khray. | Who did you meet? |
| mây dây phóp khray. | I didn't meet anyone. |
| tham ʔaray. | What did you do? |
| mây dây tham ʔaray. | I didn't do anything. |
| pay nǎy. | Where did you go? |
| mây dây pay nǎy. | I didn't go anywhere. |
| phûut ka khray. | Who did you talk to? |
| mây dây phûut ka khray. | I didn't talk to anyone. |

**b. Substitution drill.**

| | |
|---|---|
| yàak ca klàp bâan. (tɔ̂ŋ) | I want to go home. (have to) |
| tɔ̂ŋ klàp bâan. (rian phasǎa thay) | I have to go home. (study Thai) |
| tɔ̂ŋ rian phasǎa thay. (yàak) | I have to study Thai. (want) |
| yàak ca rian phasǎa thay. (phûut ka khon cháay) | I want to study Thai. (speak with the servant) |
| yàak ca phûut ka khon cháay. (tɔ̂ŋ) | I want to speak with the servant. (have to) |
| tɔ̂ŋ phûut ka khon cháay. (thǎam ʔaray kháw) | I have to speak with the servant. (ask her something) |
| tɔ̂ŋ thǎam ʔaray kháw. (yàak) | I have to ask her something. (want) |
| yàak ca thǎam ʔaray kháw. | I want to ask her something. |

ค.

| | |
|---|---|
| อยากจะไปหรือเปล่า | อยากจะเอาไปให้เขาหรือเปล่า |
| ไม่อยากจะไป | ไม่อยากจะเอาไปให้เขา |
| แต่ต้องไป | แต่ต้องเอาไป |
| ต้องบอกเขาหรือเปล่า | ต้องช่วยแม่หรือเปล่า |
| ไม่ต้องบอกเขา | ไม่ต้องช่วยเขา |
| แต่อยากจะบอก | แต่อยากจะช่วย |

ง.

| | | | |
|---|---|---|---|
| เรียกคนใช้ว่ายังไง | (บอก) | ถามแม่เขาว่ายังไง | (คุณยัง) |
| บอกคนใช้ว่ายังไง | (แม่เขา) | ถามคุณยังว่ายังไง | (พูด) |
| บอกแม่เขาว่ายังไง | (ถาม) | พูดกับคุณยังว่ายังไง | |

**๑๘.๘ เลข**

| | | |
|---|---|---|
| ๑๐๐,๐๐๐ | บาท | แสนบาท |
| ๒๐๐,๐๐๐ | บาท | สองแสนบาท |
| ๕๐๐,๐๐๕ | บาท | ห้าแสนห้าบาท |
| ๘๔๐,๐๐๐ | บาท | แปดแสนสี่หมื่นบาท |
| ๖๖๖,๖๖๖ | บาท | หกแสนหกหมื่นหกพันหกร้อยหกสิบหกบาท |

| | | | | | |
|---|---|---|---|---|---|
| ๓ | บาท | ๔ | บาท | ๒ | บาท |
| ๗๓ | บาท | ๕๔ | บาท | ๖๒ | บาท |
| ๖๗๓ | บาท | | | ๗๖๒ | บาท |
| | | ๓,๐๕๔ | บาท | ๙,๗๖๒ | บาท |
| ๑๐,๖๗๓ | บาท | ๗๓,๐๕๔ | บาท | ๒๙,๗๖๒ | บาท |
| ๕๑๐,๖๗๓ | บาท | ๘๗๓,๐๕๔ | บาท | ๑๒๙,๗๖๒ | บาท |
| ๒๐๕,๙๒๑ | บาท | ๔๕๘,๑๙๐ | บาท | ๙๖๔,๓๐๗ | บาท |

**c. Response drill.**

| | |
|---|---|
| yàak ca pay rɯ́ plàaw. | Do you want to go, or not? |
| mây yàak ca pay, | I don't want to go, |
| tɛ̀ɛ tɔ̂ŋ pay. | but I have to. |
| tɔ̂ŋ bɔ̀ɔk kháw rɯ́ plàaw. | Do you have to tell him, or not? |
| mây tɔ̂ŋ bɔ̀ɔk kháw, | I don't have to tell him, |
| tɛ̀ɛ yàak ca bɔ̀ɔk. | but I want to. |
| yàak ca ʔaw pay hây kháw rɯ́ plàaw. | Do you want to take it to him, or not? |
| mây yàak ca ʔaw pay hây kháw, | I don't want to take it to him, |
| tɛ̀ɛ tɔ̂ŋ ʔaw pay. | but I have to. |
| tɔ̂ŋ chûay mɛ̂ɛ rɯ́ plàaw. | Do you have to help your mother, or not? |
| mây tɔ̂ŋ chûay kháw, | I don't have to help her, |
| tɛ̀ɛ yàak ca chûay. | but I want to. |

**d. Substitution drill.**

| | |
|---|---|
| rîak khon cháay wâa yaŋŋay. (bɔ̀ɔk) | What do you call the servant? (tell) |
| bɔ̀ɔk khon cháay wâa yaŋŋay. (mɛ̂ɛ kháw) | What did you tell the servant? (his mother) |
| bɔ̀ɔk mɛ̂ɛ kháw wâa yaŋŋay. (thǎam) | What did you tell his mother? (ask) |
| thǎam mɛ̂ɛ kháw wâa yaŋŋay. (khun yaŋ) | What did you ask his mother? (Mr. Young) |
| thǎam khun yaŋ wâa yaŋŋay. (phûut) | What did you ask Mr. Young? (say) |
| phûut ka khun yaŋ wâa yaŋŋay. | What did you say to Mr. Young? |

**18.8 Numbers.**

| | | |
|---|---|---|
| 100,000 | baht | sɛ̌ɛn bàat |
| 200,000 | baht | sɔ̌ɔŋ sɛ̌ɛn bàat |
| 500,005 | baht | hâa sɛ̌ɛn hâa bàat |
| 840,000 | baht | pɛ̀ɛt sɛ̌ɛn sìi mɯ̀ɯn bàat |
| 666,666 | baht | hòk sɛ̌ɛn hòk mɯ̀ɯn hòk phan hòk rɔ́ɔy hòk sìp hòk bàat |

Practice reading the following amounts of money. Try to get the time under a minute.

| | | |
|---|---|---|
| 3 bàat | 4 bàat | 2 bàat |
| 73 bàat | 54 bàat | 62 bàat |
| 673 bàat | | 762 bàat |
| | 3,054 bàat | 9,762 bàat |
| 10,673 bàat | 73,054 bàat | 29,762 bàat |
| 510,673 bàat | 873,054 bàat | 129,762 bàat |
| 205,921 bàat | 458,190 bàat | 964,307 bàat |

## ๑๘.๕ การสนทนาโต้ตอบ

**ก.**

| | |
|---|---|
| เขียนตอนเที่ยงหรือเปล่าคะ | ไม่ได้เขียนครับ, เขียนตอน .............. |
| ฟังตอนสายหรือเปล่าคะ | ไม่ได้ฟังครับ, ฟังตอน .............. |
| พูดตอนเช้าหรือเปล่าคะ | ไม่ได้พูดครับ, พูดตอน .............. |
| อ่านตอนเย็นหรือเปล่าคะ | ไม่ได้อ่านครับ, อ่านตอน .............. |

**ข.**

(พ่อเอาหนังสือไปบ้านให้ลูก, นะคะ)

แม่เอาไปใช่ไหมคะ

ไม่ใช่ครับ

ใครเอาไปคะ

พ่อครับ

เอากระดาษไปใช่ไหมคะ

ไม่ใช่ครับ

เอาอะไรไปคะ

หนังสือครับ

เอาไปร้านอาหารใช่ไหมคะ

ไม่ใช่ครับ

เอาไปไหนคะ

เอาไปบ้านครับ

เอาไปให้พี่ใช่ไหมคะ

ไม่ใช่ครับ

เอาไปให้ใครคะ

ให้ลูกครับ

ใครเอาอะไรไปไหนให้ใครคะ

พ่อเอาหนังสือไปบ้านให้ลูกครับ

(คุณสวัสดิ์ส่งกระดาษไปสถานทูตให้คุณยัง, นะคะ)

คุณยังส่งใช่ไหมคะ

ไม่ใช่ครับ

ใครส่งคะ

คุณสวัสดิ์ครับ

ส่งดินสอใช่ไหมคะ

ไม่ใช่ครับ

ส่งอะไรคะ

กระดาษครับ

ส่งไปบ้านใช่ไหมคะ

ไม่ใช่ครับ

ส่งไปไหนคะ

ส่งไปสถานทูตครับ

ส่งไปให้คุณสวัสดิ์ใช่ไหมคะ

ไม่ใช่ครับ

ส่งไปให้ใครคะ

คุณยังครับ

ใครส่งอะไรไปไหนให้ใครคะ

คุณสวัสดิ์ส่งกระดาษไปสถานทูตให้คุณยังครับ

18.9 **Conversation.**

a. Answer with any of the four times of day not mentioned in the questions.

| | |
|---|---|
| khƗan tɔɔn thîaŋ rʉ́ plàaw khá. | **mây dây khƗan khráp. khƗan tɔɔn .....** |
| faŋ tɔɔn săay rʉ́ plàaw khá. | **mây dây faŋ khráp. faŋ tɔɔn .......... .** |
| phûut tɔɔn cháaw rʉ́ plàaw khá. | **mây dây phûut khráp. phûut tɔɔn .....** |
| ʔàan tɔɔn yen rʉ́ plàaw khá. | **mây dây ʔàan khráp. ʔàan tɔɔn .......** |

Etc.

**b. Questioning information,**

(phɔ̂ɔ ʔaw naŋsʉ̌ʉ pay bâan hây lûuk. ná khá.)

mɛ̂ɛ ʔaw pay chây máy khá.
　mây chây khráp.
khray ʔaw pay khá.
　phɔ̂ɔ khráp.
ʔaw kradàat pay chây máy khá.
　mây chây khráp.
ʔaw ʔaray pay khá.
　naŋsʉ̌ʉ khráp.
ʔaw pay ráan ʔaahǎan chây máy khá.
　mây chây khráp.
ʔaw pay nǎy khá.
　ʔaw pay bâan khráp.
ʔaw pay hây phîi chây máy khá.
　mây chây khráp.
ʔaw pay hây khray khá.
　hây lûuk khráp.
khray ʔaw ʔaray pay nǎy hây khray khá.
　phɔ̂ɔ ʔaw naŋsʉ̌ʉ pay bâan hây lûuk khráp.

(khun sawàt sòŋ kradàat pay sathǎanthûut hây khun yaŋ. ná khá.)

khun yaŋ sòŋ chây máy khá.
　mây chây khráp.
khray sòŋ khá.
　khun sawàt khráp.
sòŋ dinsɔ̌ɔ chây máy khá.
　mây chây khráp.
sòŋ ʔaray khá.
　kradàat khráp.
sòŋ pay bâan chây máy khá.
　mây chây khráp.
sòŋ pay nǎy khá.
　sòŋ pay sathǎanthûut khráp.
sòŋ pay hây khun sawàt chây máy khá.
　mây chây khráp.
sòŋ pay hây khray khá.
　khun yaŋ khráp.
khray sòŋ ʔaray pay nǎy hây khray khá.
　khun sawàt sòŋ kradàat pay sathǎanthûut hây khun yaŋ khráp.

### ๑๘.๑๐ การเขียน

ฝน ฉาย

| | | |
|---|---|---|
| ฝน | ชุย | ผัว |
| ฟน | ฉุย | ผลัว |
| ฟาน | ฉุน | ลัว |
| ฝาน | ฉัน | กลัว |
| ฝาย | ฝัน | กลวย |
| ฟาย | ฟัน | ขลวย |
| ฉาย | พัน | ลวย |
| ชาย | ผัน | ฉวย |

### 18.10 Writing.

| ฝน | ฉาย |
|---|---|
| fǒn | chǎay |
| Rain. | To shine. |

| | | | | | |
|---|---|---|---|---|---|
| ฝน | *fǒn | ชุย | chuy | ผัว | phǔa |
| ฟน | fon | ฉุย | chǔy | ผลัว | phlǔa |
| ฟาน | faan | ฉุน | chǔn | ลัว | lua |
| ฝาน | fǎan | ฉัน | chǎn | กลัว | klua |
| ฝาย | fǎay | ฝั่น | fǎn | กลวย | kluay |
| ฟาย | faay | ฟั่น | fan | ขลวย | khlǔay |
| ฉาย | *chǎay | พัน | *phan | ลวย | luay |
| ชาย | *chaay | ผัน | phǎn | ฉวย | chǔay |

### 18.10 Writing.

| ฝน | ฉาย |
|---|---|
| fǒn | chǎay |
| Rain. | To shine. |

| | | | | | |
|---|---|---|---|---|---|
| ฝน | *fǒn | ชุย | chuy | ผัว | phǔa |
| ฟน | fon | ฉุย | chǔy | ผลัว | phlǔa |
| ฟาน | faan | ฉุน | chǔn | ลัว | lua |
| ฝาน | fǎan | ฉัน | chǎn | กลัว | klua |
| ฝาย | fǎay | ฝั่น | fǎn | กลวย | kluay |
| ฟาย | faay | ฟั่น | fan | ขลวย | khlǔay |
| ฉาย | *chǎay | พัน | *phan | ลวย | luay |
| ชาย | *chaay | ผัน | phǎn | ฉวย | chǔay |

# LESSON 19

**19.1 Vocabulary and expansions.**

| | |
|---|---|
| kaan | |
| tɔ̂ŋkaan | To want, need. *yàak* refers more to internal motivation; *tɔ̂ŋkaan* to external inducements (not really as strong as *need*, though). |
| tɔ̂ŋkaan naŋsʉ̌ʉ | To want a book. |
| tɔ̂ŋkaan ʔàan naŋsʉ̌ʉ | To want to read a book. |
| pìt | To close, turn off. |
| pìt fay | To turn off the light. |
| ná | The response to *sí* is an action; the response to *ná* is a *khráp* (*khâ, câ*). This is the natural particle for delayed commands like 'Turn right at the next corner (but let me know right now whether you understand)'. |
| ʔɔ̃ɔ | Oh, I see. Interjections take intonations, not tones. The symbol used in place of a tone symbol simply means 'Notice and remember what this sounds like'. |
| kham | Word. |
| diaw | Single, only one, one and the same. |
| lɛ́ʔ | And. |
| láan | A million. |

**19.2 Patterns.**

| | |
|---|---|
| pìt fay dây lɛ́ɛw ná. | You can turn the light off now. |
| líaw khwǎa thîi siiyɛ̂ɛk ná. | Turn right at the intersection. |
| mây tɔ̂ŋ sʉ́ʉ mǔu ná. | You won't have to buy any pork. |
| ʔaw burìi pay dûay ná. | (Make sure you) take cigarets with you. |
| kham diaw | A single word. |
| khon diaw | A single person. |
| bàat diaw | Only one baht. |
| cháy kham diaw kan. | They use the same word. |
| yùu bâan diaw kan. | They live in the same house. |
| yùu sɔɔy diaw kan. | They live on the same Soi. |

**๑๘.๓ บทสนทนา**

ก. ฉันถามอะไรหน่อยได้ไหม

ข. เชิญ

ก. ถ้าฉันอยากจะอ่านหนังสือ แต่ห้องมืดไป
ต้องบอกคนใช้ว่ายังไง

ข. คนใช้ชื่ออะไร

ก. ชื่อต้อย

ข. บอกว่าเปิดไฟซิต้อย

ก. แล้วถ้าไม่ต้องการไฟล่ะ, บอกว่ายังไง

ข. บอกว่าปิดไฟได้แล้วนะต้อย

ก. อ๋อ, ใช้คำเดียวกับเปิดและปิดประตูใช่ไหม

ข. ใช่

**๑๘.๔ แบบฝึกหัดการฟังและการออกเสียงสูงต่ำ**

ก. หมอน

เตียง

ตู้

เสื่อ

พื้น

โต๊ะ

มุ้ง

เก้าอี้

วันอาทิตย์

วันอังคาร

วันพฤหัส

## 19.3 Dialog.

| | | |
|---|---|---|
| A. | chán thǎam ʔaray nɔ̀y dây máy. | May I ask you something? |
| B. | chɔɔn. | Go ahead. |
| A. | thâa chán yàak ca ʔàan naŋsʉ̌ʉ,<br>tɛ̀ɛ hɔ̂ŋ mʉ̂ʉt pay,<br>tɔ̂ŋ bɔ̀ɔk khon cháay wâa yaŋŋay. | If I want to read a book,<br>but the room is too dark,<br>what should I tell the servant? |
| B. | khon cháay chʉ̂ʉ ʔaray. | What's your servant's name? |
| A. | chʉ̂ʉ tɔ̂y. | Her name is Toy. |
| B. | bɔ̀ɔk wâa pɔ̀ɔt fay sí tɔ̂y. | Tell her, 'Turn on the light, Toy'. |
| A. | lɛ́ɛw thâa mây tɔ̂ŋkaan fay lâ,<br>bɔ̀ɔk wâa yaŋŋay. | And when I don't need the light anymore,<br>what do I say? |
| B. | bɔ̀ɔk wâa pìt fay dây lɛ́ɛw ná, tɔ̂y. | Tell her, 'You can turn the light off now, Toy. |
| A. | ʔɔ̂ɔ cháy kham diaw kàp pɔ̀ɔt<br>lɛ́ʔ pìt pratuu, chây máy. | Oh, you use the same words as for<br>opening and closing the door. Right? |
| B. | chây. | That's right. |

## 19.4 Tone identification and production.

**a.** Identify the tones and record the number of repetitions required.

| | | | | | |
|---|---|---|---|---|---|
| Pillow. | *mɔɔn | ........... | Mosquito net. | *muŋ | ........... |
| Bed. | *tiaŋ | ........... | Chair. | kâw*ʔii | ........... |
| Cupboard. | *tuu | ........... | Sunday. | wan ʔaa*thit | ........... |
| Mat. | *sʉa | ........... | Tuesday. | wan ʔaŋ*khaan | ........... |
| Floor. | *phʉʉn | ........... | Thursday. | wan phárʉ*hat | ........... |
| Table. | *toʔ | ........... | | | |

ข.

ใครกิน
ลุงกิน
ลุงกินอะไร
ลุงกินปลา
ลุงกินปลาอะไร
ลุงกินปลาทู

ลุงกินปลาทูที่ไหน
ลุงกินปลาทูที่ครัว
ลุงกินปลาทูที่ครัววันไหน
ลุงกินปลาทูที่ครัววันจันทร์
ลุงกินปลาทูที่ครัววันจันทร์ตอนไหน
ลุงกินปลาทูที่ครัววันจันทร์ตอนเย็น

---

ใครสั่ง
ปู่สั่ง
ปู่สั่งอะไร
ปู่สั่งไก่
ปู่สั่งไก่อะไร
ปู่สั่งไก่อบ

ปู่สั่งไก่อบที่ไหน
ปู่สั่งไก่อบที่ตลาด
ปู่สั่งไก่อบที่ตลาดวันไหน
ปู่สั่งไก่อบที่ตลาดวันศุกร์
ปู่สั่งไก่อบที่ตลาดวันศุกร์ตอนไหน
ปู่สั่งไก่อบที่ตลาดวันศุกร์ตอนบ่าย

---

ใครซื้อ
น้องซื้อ
น้องซื้ออะไร
น้องซื้อเนื้อ
น้องซื้อเนื้ออะไร
น้องซื้อเนื้อแพะ

น้องซื้อเนื้อแพะที่ไหน
น้องซื้อเนื้อแพะที่ร้าน
น้องซื้อเนื้อแพะที่ร้านวันไหน
น้องซื้อเนื้อแพะที่ร้านวันพุธ
น้องซื้อเนื้อแพะที่ร้านวันพุธตอนไหน
น้องซื้อเนื้อแพะที่ร้านวันพุธตอนเช้า

---

ใครขาย
หลานขาย
หลานขายอะไร
หลานขายหมู
หลานขายหมูอะไร
หลานขายหมูหวาน

หลานขายหมูหวานที่ไหน
หลานขายหมูหวานที่ถนน
หลานขายหมูหวานที่ถนนวันไหน
หลานขายหมูหวานที่ถนนวันเสาร์
หลานขายหมูหวานที่ถนนวันเสาร์ตอนไหน
หลานขายหมูหวานที่ถนนวันเสาร์ตอนสาย

---

ใครทอด
พี่ทอด
พี่ทอดอะไร
พี่ทอดกุ้ง
พี่ทอดกุ้งอะไร
พี่ทอดกุ้งแห้ง

พี่ทอดกุ้งแห้งที่ไหน
พี่ทอดกุ้งแห้งที่บ้าน
พี่ทอดกุ้งแห้งที่บ้านวันไหน
พี่ทอดกุ้งแห้งที่บ้านวันแม่
พี่ทอดกุ้งแห้งที่บ้านวันแม่ตอนไหน
พี่ทอดกุ้งแห้งที่บ้านวันแม่ตอนเที่ยง

**b. Response drill.**

Here, finally, is the complete game that the 4b sections have been leading to ever since lesson 7. It should be played, now, without books. The point is to give accurate answers as fast as possible. The questioner can either go straight through a dialog or ask corresponding questions (the last one, for example) from different dialogs. The student has no doubt noticed that. even though its declared purpose is tone practice, this game gives more systematic practice on sentence structure than any drill in the book. (Each item has twelve lines: 6–6.)

khray kin.
  luŋ kin.
luŋ kin ʔaray.
  luŋ kin plaa.
luŋ kin plaa ʔaray.
  luŋ kin plaa thuu.
luŋ kin plaa thuu thîi nǎy.
  luŋ kin plaa thuu thîi khrua.
luŋ kin plaa thuu thîi khrua wan nǎy.
  luŋ kin plaa thuu thîi khrua wan can.
luŋ kin plaa thuu thîi khrua wan can tɔɔn nǎy.
  luŋ kin plaa thuu thîi khrua wan can tɔɔn yen.

---

khray sàŋ.
  pùu sàŋ.
pùu sàŋ ʔaray.
  pùu sàŋ kày.
pùu sàŋ kày ʔaray.
  pùu sàŋ kày ʔòp.
pùu sàŋ kày ʔòp thîi nǎy.
  pùu sàŋ kày ʔòp thîi talàat.
pùu sàŋ kày ʔòp thîi talàat wan nǎy.
  pùu sàŋ kày ʔòp thîi talàat wan sùk.
pùu sàŋ kày ʔòp thîi talàat wan sùk tɔɔn nǎy.
  pùu sàŋ kày ʔòp thîi talàat wan sùk tɔɔn bàay.

---

khray sʉ́ʉ.
  nɔ́ɔŋ sʉ́ʉ.
nɔ́ɔŋ sʉ́ʉ ʔaray.
  nɔ́ɔŋ sʉ́ʉ nʉ́a.
nɔ́ɔŋ sʉ́ʉ nʉ́a ʔaray.
  nɔ́ɔŋ sʉ́ʉ nʉ́a phɛ́ʔ.
nɔ́ɔŋ sʉ́ʉ nʉ́a phɛ́ʔ thîi nǎy.
  nɔ́ɔŋ sʉ́ʉ nʉ́a phɛ́ʔ thîi ráan.
nɔ́ɔŋ sʉ́ʉ nʉ́a phɛ́ʔ thîi ráan wan nǎy.
  nɔ́ɔŋ sʉ́ʉ nʉ́a phɛ́ʔ thîi ráan wan phút.
nɔ́ɔŋ sʉ́ʉ nʉ́a phɛ́ʔ thîi ráan wan phút tɔɔn nǎy.
  nɔ́ɔŋ sʉ́ʉ nʉ́a phɛ́ʔ thîi ráan wan phút tɔɔn cháaw.

---

khray khǎay.
  lǎan khǎay.
lǎan khǎay ʔaray.
  lǎan khǎay mǔu.
lǎan khǎay mǔu ʔaray.
  lǎan khǎay mǔu wǎan.
lǎan khǎay mǔu wǎan thîi nǎy.
  lǎan khǎay mǔu wǎan thîi thanǒn.
lǎan khǎay mǔu wǎan thîi thanǒn wan nǎy.
  lǎan khǎay mǔu wǎan thîi thanǒn wan sǎw.
lǎan khǎay mǔu wǎan thîi thanǒn wan sǎw tɔɔn nǎy.
  lǎan khǎay mǔu wǎan thîi thanǒn wan sǎw tɔɔn sǎay.

---

khray thɔ̂ɔt.
  phîi thɔ̂ɔt.
phîi thɔ̂ɔt ʔaray.
  phîi thɔ̂ɔt kûŋ.
phîi thɔ̂ɔt kûŋ ʔaray.
  phîi thɔ̂ɔt kûŋ hɛ̂ɛŋ.
phîi thɔ̂ɔt kûŋ hɛ̂ɛŋ thîi nǎy.
  phîi thɔ̂ɔt kûŋ hɛ̂ɛŋ thîi bâan.
phîi thɔ̂ɔt kûŋ hɛ̂ɛŋ thîi bâan wan nǎy.
  phîi thɔ̂ɔt kûŋ hɛ̂ɛŋ thîi bâan wan mɛ̂ɛ.
phîi thɔ̂ɔt kûŋ hɛ̂ɛŋ thîi bâan wan mɛ̂ɛ tɔɔn nǎy.
  phîi thɔ̂ɔt kûŋ hɛ̂ɛŋ thîi bâan wan mɛ̂ɛ tɔɔn thîaŋ.

๑๕.๕ แบบฝึกหัดการสลับเสียงสูงต่ำ

ก.

เขียนตอนสาย
และอ่านตอนบ่าย
เขียนตอนบ่าย
และอ่านตอนสาย

ฟังตอนบ่าย
และพูดตอนเที่ยง
ฟังตอนเที่ยง
และพูดตอนบ่าย

ทอดตอนเย็น
และกินตอนเช้า
ทอดตอนเช้า
และกินตอนเย็น

ขายตอนเช้า
และซื้อตอนเย็น
ขายตอนเย็น
และซื้อตอนเช้า

ซื้อตอนเที่ยง
และขายตอนบ่าย
ซื้อตอนบ่าย
และขายตอนเที่ยง

ทอดตอนสาย
และกินตอนเย็น
ทอดตอนเย็น
และกินตอนสาย

อ่านตอนสาย
และเขียนตอนเช้า
อ่านตอนเช้า
และเขียนตอนสาย

เขียนตอนเที่ยง
และอ่านตอนเช้า
เขียนตอนเช้า
และอ่านตอนเที่ยง

๑๕.๖ แบบฝึกหัดการออกเสียงสระและพยัญชนะ

ก.

ใครยืมปืน
ปืดยืมปืน
ปืดยืมปืนใคร
ปืดยืมปืนชื่น

ปืดยืมปืนชื่น
ชื่นก็ยืมปืนปืด
ชื่นยืมปืนปืด
ปืดก็ยืมปืนชื่น

## 19.5 Tone manipulation.

### a. Transformation drill.

| | |
|---|---|
| khǐan tɔɔn sǎay, | Write in the late morning, |
| lɛ́ʔ ʔàan tɔɔn bàay. | and read in the afternoon. |
| khǐan tɔɔn bàay, | Write in the afternoon, |
| lɛ́ʔ ʔàan tɔɔn sǎay. | and read in the late morning. |
| thɔ̂ɔt tɔɔn yen, | Fry it in the evening, |
| lɛ́ʔ kin tɔɔn cháaw. | and eat it in the early morning, |
| thɔ̂ɔt tɔɔn cháaw, | Fry it in the early morning, |
| lɛ́ʔ kin tɔɔn yen. | and eat it in the evening. |
| sʉ́ʉ tɔɔn thîaŋ, | Buy at noon, |
| lɛ́ʔ khǎay tɔɔn bàay. | and sell in the afternoon. |
| sʉ́ʉ tɔɔn bàay, | Buy in the afternoon, |
| lɛ́ʔ khǎay tɔɔn thîaŋ. | and sell at noon. |
| ʔàan tɔɔn sǎay, | Read in the late morning, |
| lɛ́ʔ khǐan tɔɔn cháaw. | and write in the early morning. |
| ʔàan tɔɔn cháaw, | Read in the early morning, |
| lɛ́ʔ khǐan tɔɔn sǎay. | and write in the late morning. |
| faŋ tɔɔn bàay, | Listen in the afternoon, |
| lɛ́ʔ phûut tɔɔn thîaŋ. | and talk at noon. |
| faŋ tɔɔn thîaŋ, | Listen at noon, |
| lɛ́ʔ phûut tɔɔn bàay. | and talk in the afternoon. |
| khǎay tɔɔn cháaw, | Sell in the early morning, |
| lɛ́ʔ sʉ́ʉ tɔɔn yen. | and buy in the evening. |
| khǎay tɔɔn yen, | Sell in the evening, |
| lɛ́ʔ sʉ́ʉ tɔɔn cháaw. | and buy in the early morning. |
| thɔ̂ɔt tɔɔn sǎay, | Fry it in the late morning, |
| lɛ́ʔ kin tɔɔn yen. | and eat it in the evening. |
| thɔ̂ɔt tɔɔn yen, | Fry it in the evening, |
| lɛ́ʔ kin tɔɔn sǎay. | and eat it in the late morning. |
| khǐan tɔɔn thîaŋ, | Write at noon, |
| lɛ́ʔ ʔàan tɔɔn cháaw. | and read in the early morning. |
| khǐan tɔɔn cháaw, | Write in the early morning, |
| lɛ́ʔ ʔàan tɔɔn thîaŋ. | and read at noon. |

## 19.6 Vowel and consonant drills.

### a. Response drill. (ʉʉ).

| | |
|---|---|
| khray yʉʉm pʉʉn. | Who borrowed the gun? |
| pʉ́ʉt yʉʉm pʉʉn. | Puet borrowed the gun. |
| pʉ́ʉt yʉʉm pʉʉn khray. | Whose gun did Puet borrow? |
| pʉ́ʉt yʉʉm pʉʉn chʉ̂ʉn. | Puet borrowed Chuen's gun. |
| pʉ́ʉt yʉʉm pʉʉn chʉ̂ʉn. | Puet borrowed Chuen's gun. |
| chʉ̂ʉn kɔ̂ yʉʉm pʉʉn pʉ́ʉt. | Chuen borrowed Puet's gun, too. |
| chʉ̂ʉn yʉʉm pʉʉn pʉ́ʉt. | Chuen borrowed Puet's gun. |
| pʉ́ʉt kɔ̂ yʉʉm pʉʉn chʉ̂ʉn. | Puet borrowed Chuen's gun, too. |

ข.

เกียร ติกินแกงโก
    โกก็กินแกงเกียรติ

แขกข่วนแขนเข็ม
    เข็มก็ข่วนแขนแขก

หงวนง่วงนอน (เหงี่ยม)
    เหงี่ยมก็ง่วงนอน

โกกินแกงเกียรติ
    เกียรติก็กินแกงโก

เข็มข่วนแขนแขก
    แขกก็ข่วนแขนเข็ม

เหงี่ยมง่วงนอน (หงวน)
    หงวนก็ง่วงนอน

## ๑๘.๗ แบบฝึกหัดไวยากรณ์

ก.

ปิดไฟได้แล้วนะ, ต้อย (เปิด)
เปิดไฟได้แล้วนะ, ต้อย (หน้าต่าง)
เปิดหน้าต่างได้แล้วนะ, ต้อย (ปิด)
ปิดหน้าต่างได้แล้วนะ, ต้อย (ประตู)
ปิดประตูได้แล้วนะ, ต้อย (เปิด)
เปิดประตูได้แล้วนะ, ต้อย (พัดลม)
เปิดพัดลมได้แล้วนะ, ต้อย (ปิด)
ปิดพัดลมได้แล้วนะ, ต้อย

ข.

เอาหนังสือมานี่หน่อย (โน่น)
เอาหนังสือไปโน่นหน่อย (กระดาษ)
เอากระดาษไปโน่นหน่อย (นี่)
เอากระดาษมานี่หน่อย (ดินสอ)
เอาดินสอมานี่หน่อย (โน่น)
เอาดินสอไปโน่นหน่อย (บุหรี่)
เอาบุหรี่ไปโน่นหน่อย (นี่)
เอาบุหรี่มานี่หน่อย

**b. Response drill.** (k, kh, and ŋ).

kiat kin kɛɛŋ koo.
koo kɔ̂ kin kɛɛŋ kiat.

Kiat ate Ko's curry.
Ko ate Kiat's curry, too.

khɛ̀ɛk khùan khɛ̌ɛn khěm.
khěm kɔ̂ khùan khɛ̌ɛn khɛ̀ɛk.

Kaek scratched Kem's arm.
Kem scratched Kaek's arm, too.

ŋǔan ŋûaŋ nɔɔn. (ŋìam)
ŋìam kɔ̂ ŋûaŋ nɔɔn.

Nguan is sleepy. (Ngiam)
Ngiam is sleepy, too.

koo kin kɛɛŋ kìat.
kìat kɔ̂ kin kɛɛŋ koo.

Ko ate Kiat's curry.
Kiat ate Ko's curry, too.

khěm khùan khɛ̌ɛn khɛ̀ɛk.
khɛ̀ɛk kɔ̂ khùan khɛ̌ɛn khěm.

Kem scratched Kaek's arm.
Kaek scratched Kem's arm, too.

ŋiam ŋûaŋ nɔɔn. (ŋǔan)
ŋǔan kɔ̂ ŋûaŋ nɔɔn.

Ngiam is sleepy. (Nguan)
Nguan is sleepy, too.

**19.7 Grammar drills.**

**a. Substitution drill.**

pìt fay dây lɛ́ɛw ná, tɔ̂y.
(pə̀ət)

You can turn the light off now, Toy.
(turn on)

pə̀ət fay dây lɛ́ɛw ná, tɔ̂y.
(nâatàaŋ)

You can turn the light on now, Toy.
(windows)

pə̀ət nâatàaŋ dây lɛ́ɛw ná, tɔ̂y.
(pìt)

You can open the windows now, Toy.
(close)

pìt nâatàaŋ dây lɛ́ɛw ná, tɔ̂y.
(pratuu)

You can close the windows now, Toy.
(door)

pìt pratuu dây lɛ́ɛw ná, tɔ̂y.
(pə̀ət)

You can close the door now, Toy.
(open)

pə̀ət pratuu dây lɛ́ɛw ná, tɔ̂y.
(phátlom)

You can open the door now, Toy.
(fan)

pə̀ət phátlom dây lɛ́ɛw ná, tɔ̂y.
(pìt)

You can turn the fan on now, Toy.
(turn off)

pìt phátlom dây lɛ́ɛw ná, tɔ̂y.

You can turn the fan off now, Toy.

**b. Substitution drill.**

ʔaw naŋsɯ̌ɯ maa nîi nɔ̀y. (nôon)
ʔaw naŋsɯ̌ɯ pay nôon nɔ̀y. (kradàat)
ʔaw kradàat pay nôon nɔ̀y. (nîi)
ʔaw kradàat maa nîi nɔ̀y. (dinsɔ̌ɔ)
ʔaw dinsɔ̌ɔ maa nîi nɔ̀y. (nôon)
ʔaw dinsɔ̌ɔ pay nôon nɔ̀y. (burìi)
ʔaw burìi pay nôon nɔ̀y. (nîi)
ʔaw burìi maa nîi nɔ̀y.

Please bring the book here. (there)
Please take the book there. (paper)
Please take the paper there. (here)
Please bring the paper here. (pencil)
Please bring the pencil here. (there)
Please take the pencil there. (cigarets)
Please take the cigarets there. (here)
Please bring the cigarets here.

ค.

ต้องเลี้ยวที่โน่น
เลี้ยวที่นี่ไม่ได้หรือ

ต้องถามที่โน่น
ถามที่นี่ไม่ได้หรือ

ต้องทำงานที่โน่น
ทำที่นี่ไม่ได้หรือ

ต้องซื้อปลาที่โน่น
ซื้อที่นี่ไม่ได้หรือ

ต้องสั่งอาหารที่โน่น
สั่งที่นี่ไม่ได้หรือ

ต้องทอดกุ้งที่โน่น
ทอดที่นี่ไม่ได้หรือ

ง.

คุณพูดภาษาจีนได้ไหม
ไม่ได้

คุณพูดภาษาจีนได้หรือ
เปล่า, พูดไม่ได้

ต้องปิดประตูไหม
ไม่ต้อง

ต้องปิดประตูหรือ
เปล่า, ไม่ต้องปิด

ไปไหม
ไม่ไป

จะไปหรือ
เปล่า, ไม่ไป

**๑๙.๘ เลข**

๑,๐๐๐,๐๐๐ บาท ล้านบาท

๗,๒๖๙,๔๕๑ คน เจ็ดล้านสองแสนหกหมื่นเก้าพันสี่ร้อยห้าสิบเอ็ดคน

| | | |
|---|---|---|
| ๒ บาท | ๓ บาท | ๔ บาท |
| ๙๒ บาท | ๘๓ บาท | ๗๔ บาท |
| ๔๙๒ บาท | ๕๘๓ บาท | ๖๗๔ บาท |
| ๓,๔๙๒ บาท | ๔,๕๘๓ บาท | ๒,๖๗๔ บาท |
| ๘๓,๔๙๒ บาท | ๗๔,๕๘๓ บาท | ๙๒,๖๗๔ บาท |
| ๕๘๓,๔๙๒ บาท | ๖๗๔,๕๘๓ บาท | ๔๙๒,๖๗๔ บาท |
| ๖,๕๘๓,๔๙๒ บาท | ๒,๖๗๔,๕๘๓ บาท | ๘,๔๙๒,๖๗๔ บาท |
| ๒,๔๖๘,๙๗๕ บาท | ๑,๔๗๘,๕๒๙ บาท | ๙,๘๗๕,๓๐๑ บาท |

**c. Response drill.**

| | |
|---|---|
| tɔ̂ŋ líaw thîi nôon.<br>líaw thîi nîi mây dây lɔ̌ɔ. | You have to turn over there.<br>Can't I turn here? |
| tɔ̂ŋ thǎam thîi nôon.<br>thǎam thîi nîi mây dây lɔ̌ɔ. | You have to ask over there.<br>Can't I ask here? |
| tɔ̂ŋ tham ŋaan thîi nôon.<br>tham thîi nîi mây dây lɔ̌ɔ. | You have to work over there.<br>Can't I work here? |
| tɔ̂ŋ sʉ́ʉ plaa thîi nôon.<br>sʉ́ʉ thîi nîi mây dây lɔ̌ɔ. | You have to buy fish over there.<br>Can't I buy it here? |
| tɔ̂ŋ sàŋ ʔaahǎan thîi nôon.<br>sàŋ thîi nîi mây dây lɔ̌ɔ. | You have to order the food over there.<br>Can't I order it here? |
| tɔ̂ŋ thɔ̂ɔt kûŋ thîi nôon.<br>thɔ̂ɔt thîi nîi mây dây lɔ̌ɔ. | You have to fry the shrimps over there.<br>Can't I fry them here? |

**d. Response drill.**

| | |
|---|---|
| khun phûut phasǎa ciin dây máy.<br>mây dây. | Can you speak Chinese?<br>No. |
| khun phûut phasǎa ciin dây lɔ̌ɔ.<br>plàaw. phûut mây dây. | You can speak Chinese?<br>No. I can't speak it. |
| tɔ̂ŋ pìt pratuu máy.<br>mây tɔ̂ŋ. | Do I have to close the door?<br>No. |
| tɔ̂ŋ pìt pratuu lɔ̌ɔ.<br>plàaw. mây tɔ̂ŋ pìt. | I have to close the door, huh?<br>No. You don't have to close it. |
| pay máy.<br>mây pay. | Do you want to go?<br>No. |
| ca pay lɔ̌ɔ.<br>plàaw. mây pay. | You're going?<br>No. I'm not going. |

**19.8 Numbers.**

| | |
|---|---|
| 1,000,000 baht | láan bàat |
| 7,269,451 people | cèt láan sɔ̌ɔŋ sɛ̌ɛn hòk mʉ̀ʉn kâaw phan sìi rɔ́ɔy hâa sìp ʔèt khon |

Practice reading the following amounts of money. Try to get the time under 1 minute and 40 seconds.

| | | |
|---:|---:|---:|
| 2 bàat | 3 bàat | 4 bàat |
| 92 bàat | 83 bàat | 74 bàat |
| 492 baat | 583 bàat | 674 bàat |
| 3,492 bàat | 4,583 bàat | 2,674 bàat |
| 83,492 bàat | 74.583 bàat | 92,674 bàat |
| 583,492 bàat | 674,583 bàat | 492,674 bàat |
| 6,583,492 bàat | 2,674,583 bàat | 8,492,674 bàat |
| 2,468,975 bàat | 1,478,529 bàat | 9,875,301 bàat |

## ๑๕.๕ การสนทนาโต้ตอบ

ก.

ไปตอนเช้าและกลับตอนเย็น, ใช่ไหมคะ
ไม่ใช่ครับ, ไปตอนเย็นและกลับตอนเช้า
เปิดตอนสายและปิดตอนบ่าย, ใช่ไหมคะ
ไม่ใช่ครับ, เปิดตอนบ่ายและปิดตอนสาย

ทอดตอนเย็นและกินตอนเที่ยง, ใช่ไหมคะ
ไม่ใช่ครับ, ทอดตอนเที่ยงและกินตอนเย็น

ข.

(คุณยังให้คนใช้เอาหนังสือไปโรงเรียนให้ลูกชายเขาวันพุธตอนบ่าย, นะคะ)

ใครเอาไปคะ
คนใช้ครับ

เอาอะไรไปคะ
หนังสือครับ

เอาไปไหนคะ
เอาไปโรงเรียนครับ

เอาไปให้ใครคะ
ให้ลูกคุณยังครับ

เอาไปวันไหนคะ
วันพุธครับ

วันพุธตอนไหนคะ
ตอนบ่ายครับ

ใครให้เอาไปคะ
คุณยังครับ

เขาให้ลูกสาวเอาไป, ใช่ไหมคะ
ไม่ใช่ครับ

ให้ใครเอาไปคะ
คนใช้ครับ

เอาวิทยุไป, ใช่ไหมคะ
ไม่ใช่ครับ

เอาอะไรไปคะ
หนังสือครับ

เอาไปโรงแรม, ใช่ไหมคะ
ไม่ใช่ครับ

เอาไปไหนคะ
เอาไปโรงเรียนครับ

เอาไปให้พี่ชาย, ใช่ไหมคะ
ไม่ใช่ครับ

เอาไปให้ใครคะ
ให้ลูกครับ

ลูกสาว, ใช่ไหมคะ
ไม่ใช่ครับ

ลูกชาย, ใช่ไหมคะ
ใช่ครับ

ลูกคุณประสงค์, ใช่ไหมคะ
ไม่ใช่ครับ

ลูกใครคะ
ลูกคุณยังครับ

เอาไปวันจันทร์, ใช่ไหมคะ
ไม่ใช่ครับ

เอาไปวันไหนคะ
วันพุธครับ

ตอนเช้า, ใช่ไหมคะ
ไม่ใช่ครับ

ตอนไหนคะ
ตอนบ่ายครับ

ใครให้ใครเอาอะไรไปไหนให้ใครคะ
คุณยังให้คนใช้เอาหนังสือไปโรงเรียนให้ลูกครับ

วันไหนตอนไหนคะ
วันพุธตอนบ่ายครับ

**19.9 Conversation.**

**a.** Answer each question with the opposite pairings of actions and times.

pay tɔɔn cháaw lɛ́ʔ klàp tɔɔn yen, chây máy khá.
  mây chây khráp. pay tɔɔn yen lɛ́ʔ klàp tɔɔn cháaw.

pɔ̀ət tɔɔn sǎay lɛ́ʔ pìt tɔɔn bàay, chây máy khá.
  mây chây khráp. pɔ̀ət tɔɔn bàay lɛ́ʔ pìt tɔɔn sǎay.

thɔ̂ɔt tɔɔn yen lɛ́ʔ kin tɔɔn thîaŋ. chây máy khá.
  mây chây khráp. thɔ̂ɔt tɔɔn thîaŋ lɛ́ʔ kin tɔɔn yen.

Etc. (See 19.5 for additional items.)

**b. Questioning information.**

(khun yaŋ hây khon cháay ʔaw naŋsʉ̌ʉ pay rooŋrian hây lûuk chaay kháw wan phút tɔɔn bàay. ná khá.)

khray ʔaw pay khá.
  khon cháay khráp.

ʔaw ʔaray pay khá.
  naŋsʉ̌ʉ khráp.

ʔaw pay nǎy khá.
  ʔaw pay rooŋrian khráp.

ʔaw pay hây khray khá.
  hây lûuk khun yaŋ khráp.

ʔaw pay wan nǎy khá.
  wan phút khráp.

wan phút tɔɔn nǎy khá.
  tɔɔn bàay khráp.

khray hây ʔaw pay khá.
  khun yaŋ khráp.

kháw hây lûuk sǎaw ʔaw pay, chây máy khá.
  mây chây khráp.

hây khray ʔaw pay khá.
  khon cháay khráp.

ʔaw wítthayúʔ pay, chây máy khá.
  mây chây khráp.

ʔaw ʔaray pay khá.
  naŋsʉ̌ʉ khráp.

ʔaw pay rooŋrɛɛm, chây máy khá.
  mây chây khráp.

ʔaw pay nǎy khá.
  ʔaw pay róoŋrian khráp.

ʔaw pay hây phîi chaay, chây máy khá.
  mây chây khráp.

ʔaw pay hây khray khá.
  hây lûuk khráp.

lûuk sǎaw, chây máy khá.
  mây chây khráp.

lûuk chaay, chây máy khá.
  chây khráp.

lûuk khun prasɔ̌ŋ, chây máy khá.
  mây chây khráp.

lûuk khray khá.
  lûuk khun yaŋ khráp.

ʔaw pay wan can, chây máy khá.
  mây chây khráp.

ʔaw pay wan nǎy khá.
  wan phút khráp.

tɔɔn cháaw, chây máy khá.
  mây chây khráp.

tɔɔn nǎy khá.
  tɔɔn bàay khráp.

khray hây khray ʔaw ʔaray pay nǎy hây khray khá.
  khun yaŋ hây khon cháay ʔaw naŋsʉ̌ʉ pay rooŋrian hây lûuk khráp.

wan nǎy tɔɔn nǎy khá.
  wan phút tɔɔn bàay khráp.

๑๕.๑๐ **การเขียน**

โฮเต็น หา ไหน หมู หลัง หวาน

| | | | |
|---|---|---|---|
| แคน | แขน | เก | เก๋ |
| ชุน | ฉุน | จี | จี๋ |
| ทิง | ถึง | ดู | ดู๋ |
| พอม | ผอม | ตัว | ตั๋ว |
| ฟน | ฝน | โบ | โบ๋ |
| ซาว | สาว | ปา | ป๋า |
| เฮ็น | เห็น | โอย | โอ๋ย |
| ยิม | หยิม | แง | แหง |
| รู | หรู | ใน | ไหน |
| ลัง | หลัง | มู | หมู |
| วาน | หวาน | | |

**19.10 Writing.**

The three ways of writing rising tones shown below ('high' consonants with no tonal marker, 'mid' consonants with the marker + , and 'low' consonants with *hɔ̌ɔ*) separate the Thai consonants into three classes. All vowels and consonants introduced in Book 1 are included here.

| โฮเต็น | หา | ไหน | หมู | หลัง | หวาน |
|---|---|---|---|---|---|
| hooten | hǎa | nǎy | mǔu | lǎŋ | wǎan |
| Hotel. | To look for. | Where. | Pork. | Back. | Sweet. |

| **Low Consonants** | | **High Consonants** | | **Mid Consonants** | | **Mids with +** | |
|---|---|---|---|---|---|---|---|
| แคน | khɛɛn | แขน | *khɛ̌ɛn | เก | kee | เก๋ | kěe |
| ชุน | chun | ฉุน | chǔn | จี | cii | จี๋ | cǐi |
| ทึง | thɯŋ | ถึง | *thɯ̌ŋ | ดู | duu | ดู๋ | dǔu |
| พอม | phɔɔm | ผอม | *phɔ̌ɔm | ตัว | tua | ตั๋ว | tǔa |
| ฟน | fon | ฝน | *fǒn | โบ | boo | โบ๋ | bǒo |
| ซาว | saaw | สาว | *sǎaw | ปา | paa | ป๋า | *pǎa |
| เฮ็น | hen | เห็น | *hěn | โอย | ʔooy | โอ๋ย | ʔǒoy |

| **Low Consonants** | | **Lows with hɔ̌ɔ** | | **Low Consonants** | | **Lows with hɔ̌ɔ.** | |
|---|---|---|---|---|---|---|---|
| ยิม | yim | หยิม | yǐm | แง | ŋɛɛ | แหง | ŋɛ̌ɛ |
| รู | ruu | หรู | rǔu | ไน | nay | ไหน | *nǎy |
| ลัง | laŋ | หลัง | *lǎŋ | มู | muu | หมู | *mǔu |
| วาน | waan | หวาน | *wǎan | | | | |

# บทที่ ๒๐

**ข.**

พ่อแม่นั่งอยู่ที่โต๊ะที่นี่ ลูกชายกับลูกสาวนั่งอยู่ที่โต๊ะที่โน่น พ่อมีไม้ขีด แม่มีหนังสือ ลูกชายมีดินสอ และลูกสาวมีกระดาษ ลูกชายเป็นพี่ ลูกสาวเป็นน้อง พ่อเรียกแม่ว่าน้อง และแม่เรียกพ่อว่าพี่

ถ้าลูกชายอยากได้หนังสือ เขาต้องไปพูดกับแม่ว่า "ขอหนังสือหน่อยแม่" หรือพูดกับน้องว่า "ช่วยไปเอาหนังสือที่แม่มาให้พี่หน่อยน้อง"

ถ้าลูกชายอยากได้กระดาษเขาต้องพูดกับน้องว่า "ช่วยส่งกระดาษให้พี่หน่อยน้อง"

ถ้าแม่อยากได้ดินสอ เขาต้องพูดกับลูกชายว่า "ช่วยเอาดินสอมาให้แม่หน่อยลูก"

ถ้าพ่ออยากได้หนังสือ เขาต้องพูดกับแม่ว่า "ช่วยส่งหนังสือให้พี่หน่อยน้อง"

ถ้าลูกสาวอยากจะให้กระดาษพ่อ เขาต้องถามว่า "เอากระดาษไหมพ่อ" และถ้าพ่อบอกว่า "เอา" ลูกสาวต้องเอาไปให้เขา

ถ้าลูกสาวอยากจะให้กระดาษพี่ เขาต้องถามว่า "เอากระดาษไหมพี่" และถ้าพี่บอกว่า "เอา" เขาต้องส่งให้

ถ้าพ่ออยากจะให้ไม้ขีดลูกชาย เขาต้องถามว่า "เอาไม้ขีดไหมลูก" และถ้าลูกบอกว่า "เอา" ลูกต้องไปเอาที่พ่อ

ถ้าแม่อยากจะให้หนังสือพ่อ เขาต้องถามว่า "เอาหนังสือไหมพี่" และถ้าพ่อบอกว่า "เอา" แม่ต้องส่งให้

ถ้าลูกชายอยากจะให้ดินสอแม่ เขาต้องถามว่า "เอาดินสอไหมแม่" และถ้าแม่บอกว่า "เอา" ลูกชายต้องเอาไปให้เขา หรือลูกชายต้องส่งดินสอให้น้อง และบอกว่า "ช่วยเอาดินสอไปให้แม่หน่อยน้อง"

# LESSON 20
## (Review)

**a. Review sections 3, 5, 7, and 9 of lessons 16 - 19.**

**b. Narrative.** (For comprehension only.)

phɔ̂ɔ mɛ̂ɛ nâŋ (sit) yùu thîi tóʔ (table) thîi nîi. lûuk chaay kàp lûuk sǎaw nâŋ yùu thîi tóʔ thîi nôon. phɔ̂ɔ mii máykhìit, mɛ̂ɛ mii naŋsʉ̌ʉ, lûuk chaay mii dinsɔ̌ɔ, lɛ́ʔ lûuk sǎaw mii kradàat. lûuk chaay pen phîi, lûuk sǎaw pen nɔ́ɔŋ. phɔ̂ɔ rîak mɛ̂ɛ wâa nɔ́ɔŋ, lɛ́ʔ mɛ̂ɛ rîak phɔ̂ɔ wâa phîi.

thâa lûuk chaay yàak dây naŋsʉ̌ʉ, kháw tɔ̂ŋ pay phûut kàp mɛ̂ɛ wâa "khɔ̌ɔ naŋsʉ̌ʉ nɔ̀y, mɛ̂ɛ" rʉ̌ʉ phûut kàp nɔ́ɔŋ wâa "chûay pay ʔaw naŋsʉ̌ʉ thîi mɛ̂ɛ maa hây phîi nɔ̀y, nɔ́ɔŋ".

thâa lûuk chaay yàak dây kradàat, kháw tɔ̂ŋ phûut kàp nɔ́ɔŋ wâa "chûay sòŋ kradàat hây phîi nɔ̀y, nɔ́ɔŋ".

thâa mɛ̂ɛ yàak dây dinsɔ̌ɔ, kháw tɔ̂ŋ phûut kàp lûuk chaay wâa "chûay ʔaw dinsɔ̌ɔ maa hây mɛ̂ɛ nɔ̀y, lûuk".

thâa phɔ̂ɔ yàak dây naŋsʉ̌ʉ, kháw tɔ̂ŋ phûut kàp mɛ̂ɛ wâa "chûay sòŋ naŋsʉ̌ʉ hây phîi nɔ̀y, nɔ́ɔŋ".

thâa lûuk sǎaw yàak ca hây kradàat phɔ̂ɔ, kháw tɔ̂ŋ thǎam wâa "ʔaw kradàat máy, phɔ̂ɔ", lɛ́ʔ thâa phɔ̂ɔ bɔ̀ɔk wâa "ʔaw", lûuk sǎaw tɔ̂ŋ ʔaw pay hây kháw.

thâa lûuk sǎaw yàak ca hây kradàat phîi, kháw tɔ̂ŋ thǎam wâa "ʔaw kradàat máy, phîi", lɛ́ʔ thâa phîi bɔ̀ɔk wâa "ʔaw", kháw tɔ̂ŋ sòŋ hây.

thâa phɔ̂ɔ yàak ca hây máykhìit lûuk chaay, kháw tɔ̂ŋ thǎam wâa "ʔaw máykhìit máy, lûuk", lɛ́ʔ thâa lûuk bɔ̀ɔk wâa "ʔaw", lûuk tɔ̂ŋ pay ʔaw thîi phɔ̂ɔ.

thâa mɛ̂ɛ yàak ca hây naŋsʉ̌ʉ phɔ̂ɔ, kháw tɔ̂ŋ thǎam wâa "ʔaw naŋsʉ̌ʉ máy, phîi", lɛ́ʔ thâa phɔ̂ɔ bɔ̀ɔk wâa "ʔaw". mɛ̂ɛ tɔ̂ŋ sòŋ hây.

thâa lûuk chaay yàak ca hây dinsɔ̌ɔ mɛ̂ɛ, kháw tɔ̂ŋ thǎam wâa "ʔaw dinsɔ̌ɔ máy, mɛ̂ɛ", lɛ́ʔ thâa mɛ̂ɛ bɔ̀ɔk wâa "ʔaw", lûuk chaay tɔ̂ŋ ʔaw pay hây kháw. rʉ̌ʉ lûuk chaay tɔ̂ŋ sòŋ dinsɔ̌ɔ hây nɔ́ɔŋ lɛ́ʔ bɔ̀ɔk wâa "chûay ʔaw dinsɔ̌ɔ pay hây mɛ̂ɛ nɔ̀y, nɔ́ɔŋ".

Read the following questions and answers for comprehension. Then listen for comprehension while looking at the picture - not the sentences. Next, while looking at the following frames and the picture

thâa ........... yàak dây ..........., kháw tɔ̂ŋ tham yaŋŋay.
thâa ........... yàak ca hây ......... .......... kháw tɔ̂ŋ tham yaŋŋay.

ถ้าลูกสาวอยากได้ไม้ขีด, เขาต้องทำยังไง
เขาต้องไปพูดกับพ่อว่า "ขอไม้ขีดหน่อยพ่อ"

ถ้าลูกสาวอยากได้ดินสอ เขาต้องทำยังไง
เขาต้องพูดกับพี่ว่า "ช่วยส่งดินสอให้น้องหน่อยพี่"

ถ้าพ่ออยากได้กระดาษเขาต้องทำยังไง
เขาต้องพูดกับลูกสาวว่า "ช่วยเอากระดาษมาให้พ่อหน่อยลูก"

ถ้าแม่อยากได้ไม้ขีดเขาต้องทำยังไง
เขาต้องพูดกับพ่อว่า "ช่วยส่งไม้ขีดให้น้องหน่อยพี่"

ถ้าลูกชายอยากจะให้ดินสอพ่อ เขาต้องทำยังไง
เขาต้องถามพ่อว่า "เอาดินสอไหมพ่อ" และถ้าพ่อบอกว่า "เอา"
เขาต้องเอาไปให้ หรือส่งให้น้องและบอกว่า "ช่วยเอาดินสอไปให้พ่อหน่อยน้อง"

ถ้าลูกชายอยากจะให้ดินสอน้อง เขาต้องทำยังไง
เขาต้องถามน้องว่า "เอาดินสอไหมน้อง" และถ้าน้องบอกว่า "เอา"
เขาต้องส่งให้

ถ้าแม่อยากจะให้หนังสือลูกสาว เขาต้องทำยังไง
เขาต้องถามว่า "เอาหนังสือไหมลูก" และถ้าลูกบอกว่า "เอา"
ลูกต้องไปเอาที่แม่

ถ้าพ่ออยากจะให้ไม้ขีดแม่ เขาต้องทำยังไง
เขาต้องถามว่า "เอาไม้ขีดไหมน้อง" และถ้าแม่บอกว่า "เอา"
พ่อต้องส่งให้

ask the teacher several of the 24 possible questions to get practice keeping up with the answers (slightly faster now). Finally, ask several questions while looking at the picture only. Race the answers with your mind. If you fall behind, the teacher should reduce the speed a little. (It is not intended that the student should be able to answer questions from the teacher.)

thâa lûuk sǎaw yàak dây máykhìit, kháw tôŋ tham yaŋŋay.
  kháw tôŋ pay phûut kàp phɔ̂ɔ wâa "khɔ̌ɔ máykhìit nɔ̀y, phɔ̂ɔ".

thâa lûuk sǎaw yàak dây dinsɔ̌ɔ, kháw tôŋ tham yaŋŋay.
  kháw tôŋ phûut kàp phîi wâa "chûay sòŋ dinsɔ̌ɔ hây nɔ́ɔŋ nɔ̀y, phîi".

thâa phɔ̂ɔ yàak dây kradàat, kháw tôŋ tham yaŋŋay.
  kháw tôŋ phûut kàp lûuk sǎaw wâa "chûay ʔaw kradàat maa hây phɔ̂ɔ nɔ̀y, lûuk".

thâa mɛ̂ɛ yàak dây máykhìit, kháw tôŋ tham yaŋŋay.
  kháw tôŋ phûut kàp phɔ̂ɔ wâa "chûay sòŋ máykhìit hây nɔ́ɔŋ nɔ̀y, phîi".

thâa lûuk chaay yàak ca hây dinsɔ̌ɔ phɔ̂ɔ, kháw tôŋ tham yaŋŋay.
  kháw tôŋ thǎam phɔ̂ɔ wâa "ʔaw dinsɔ̌ɔ máy, phɔ̂ɔ", lɛ́ʔ thâa phɔ̂ɔ bɔ̀ɔk wâa "ʔaw",
  kháw tôŋ ʔaw pay hây, rʉ̌ʉ sòŋ hây nɔ́ɔŋ lɛ́ʔ bɔ̀ɔk wâa "chûay ʔaw dinsɔ̌ɔ pay hây phɔ̂ɔ
  nɔ̀y, nɔ́ɔŋ".

thâa lûuk chaay yàak ca hây dinsɔ̌ɔ nɔ́ɔŋ, kháw tôŋ tham yaŋŋay.
  kháw tôŋ thǎam nɔ́ɔŋ wâa "ʔaw dinsɔ̌ɔ máy, nɔ́ɔŋ", lɛ́ʔ thâa nɔ́ɔŋ bɔ̀ɔk wâa "ʔaw".
  kháw tôŋ sòŋ hây.

thâa mɛ̂ɛ yàak ca hây naŋsʉ̌ʉ lûuk sǎaw, kháw tôŋ tham yaŋŋay.
  kháw tôŋ thǎam wâa "ʔaw naŋsʉ̌ʉ máy, lûuk", lɛ́ʔ thâa lûuk bɔ̀ɔk wâa "ʔaw",
  lûuk tôŋ pay ʔaw thîi mɛ̂ɛ.

thâa phɔ̂ɔ yàak ca hây máykhìit mɛ̂ɛ, kháw tôŋ tham yaŋŋay.
  kháw tôŋ thǎam wâa "ʔaw máykhìit máy, nɔ́ɔŋ", lɛ́ʔ thâa mɛ̂ɛ bɔ̀ɔk wâa "ʔaw",
  phɔ̂ɔ tôŋ sòŋ hây.

ค.

| | |
|---|---|
| พ่อ: | พ่อยากจะเขียนอะไรหน่อย<br>น้องมีดินสอกับกระดาษไหม |
| แม่: | ไม่มี<br>(พูดกับลูก) ลูกมีดินสอกับกระดาษไหม |
| ลูกชาย: | มีครับ |
| แม่: | ช่วยเอามาให้พ่อหน่อย |
| ลูกชาย: | (พูดกับน้อง) นี่, เอาดินสอกับกระดาษไปให้พ่อ<br>แล้วถามเขาด้วยว่ามีไม้ขีดไหม พี่อยากได้ |
| ลูกสาว: | นี่ค่ะ, พ่อ ดินสอกับกระดาษ<br>พ่อมีไม้ขีดไหม พี่เขาอยากได้ |
| พ่อ: | มี, นี่ เอาไปให้เขา |
| แม่: | นี่ลูก, หนังสือดี อยากจะอ่านไหม |
| ลูกสาว: | อ่านไม่ได้, แม่ ลูกต้องทำงาน |
| แม่: | ถ้ายังงั้นเอาไปให้พี่ เขาอยากจะอ่าน |

c. **Dialog.**

| | |
|---|---|
| phɔ̂ɔ: | phîi yàak ca khǐan ʔaray (something) nɔ̀y.<br>nɔ́ɔŋ mii dinsɔ̌ɔ ka kradàat máy. |
| mɛ̂ɛ: | mây mii.<br>(phûut kàp lûuk) lûuk mii dinsɔ̌ɔ ka kradàat máy. |
| lûuk chaay: | mii khráp. |
| mɛ̂ɛ: | chûay ʔaw maa hây phɔ̂ɔ nɔ̀y. |
| lûuk chaay: | (phûut kàp nɔ́ɔŋ) nîi. ʔaw dinsɔ̌ɔ ka kradàat pay hây phɔ̂ɔ.<br>lɛ́ɛw thǎam kháw dûay wâa mii máykhìit máy. phîi yàak dây. |
| lûuk sǎaw: | nîi khâ, phɔ̂ɔ. dinsɔ̌ɔ ka kradàat.<br>phɔ̂ɔ mii máykhìit máy. phîi kháw yàak dây. |
| phɔ̂ɔ: | mii. nîi. ʔaw pay hây kháw. |
| mɛ̂ɛ: | nîi. lûuk. naŋsʉ̌ʉ dii. yàak ca ʔàan máy. |
| lûuk sǎaw: | ʔàan mây dây, mɛ̂ɛ. lûuk tɔ̂ŋ tham ŋaan. |
| mɛ̂ɛ: | thâa yaŋŋán (if it's like that, in that case) ʔaw pay hây phîi.<br>kháw yàak ca ʔàan. |

# GLOSSARY

The following alphabetical order is followed in the glossary: ʔ a b c d e ə ɛ f h i k l m n ŋ o ɔ p r s t u ʉ w y. The number immediately following each entry refers to the section where it is first used.

**ʔaahǎan** 3.3 Food.
**ʔàan** 13.5 To read.
**ʔaathít** 19.4 Week.
  **phráʔ ʔaathít** Sun.
  **wan ʔaathít** Sunday.
**ʔameerikaa** 17.2 America.
**ʔameerikan** 9.3 American.
**ʔaŋkrit** 9.2 England, English.
**ʔaŋkhaan** 19.4
  **daaw ʔaŋkhaan** Mars.
  **wan ʔaŋkhaan** Tuesday.
**ʔaray** 6.5 What? Something.
**ʔaw** 17.3 To take, to accept.
**ʔeerawan** 6.3 Erawan.
**ʔee yuu ʔee** 11.7 AUA. American University Alumni Association.
**ʔèt** 4.8 One (used in combinations like 21. 31).
**ʔiik** 8.3 Another. one more, more.
  **ʔiik thii** Again, another time.
**ʔòp** 8.4 To roast or bake.
**ʔɔ̂ɔ** 19.3 Oh, I see.
**ʔûan** 1.5 To be fat.
**bàʉ** 2.6 Shoulder.
**bâan** 10. House, home.
**bâaŋ** 17.3 Some.
**bàat** 7.8 Baht, ticals.
**bàay** 14.4 Afternoon.
**bay** 1.6 Leaf.
**bəə** 13.3 Number. (See 13.1)
**biip** 9.6 To squeeze.
**bon** 8.3 On, the upper part of.
  **khâŋbon** Upstairs.
**bɔ̀ɔk** 18.3 To tell.
**burii** 14.7 Cigaret.
**càʔ, ca** 11.3 Will.
**câ** 1.2 Polite particle, confirmative. (See 1.1 and 3.1)
**cá** 4.2 Polite particle. (See 1.1)
**caan** 12.6 A plate.
**can** 17.4
  **phrácan** The moon.
  **wan can** Monday.
**càp** 12.6 To catch, grab.
**ceen** 12.7 Jane.
**cèt** 3.8 Seven.
**cháa** 14.3 To be slow.
**cháaw** 14.4 Morning.
**chaay** 7.3 Male (people only).
**chǎay** 18.10 To shine a light.
**chây** 9.3 To be the one meant, to be so, to be a fact. That's right.
**cháy** 13.5 To use.
**chét** 12.6 To wipe.
**chəən** 11.3 To invite. Go ahead. Please do.
**chɔ́ɔn** 12.6 A spoon.
**chɔ̂ɔp** 7.4 To like.
**chûay** 17.3 To help. (See 17.1)
**chʉ̂ʉ** 18.3 Name, to be named.
**ciin** 14.2 Chinese.
**cɔɔn** 12.7 John.
**daaw** Star.
**dâay** 11.6 Thread.
**dam** 16.6 Black.
**dây** 8.3 Can, to be able.
**dây** 18.1 To get, receive.
**deewít** 12.7 David.
**dèk** 7.1 Child (the age term: boy or girl).
**dəən** 6.3 To walk.
**dɛɛŋ** 14.4 Red.
**dɛ̀ɛt** 17.4 Sunlight.
**diaw** 19.3 Single. only one, one and the same.
**dichán** 8.2 I (woman speaking). (See 8.1)
**dii** 1.5 To be good.
**dinsɔ̌ɔ** 16.3 Pencil.

**dûay** 17.3 Also, too. (see 17.1)
**duŋ** 11.6 To pull.
**fáa** 14.4 Sky. Light blue.
**faŋ** 18.5 To listen to.
**fay** 16.3 Fire, light, electricity.
**fǒn** 18.10 Rain.
**hâa** 1.8 Five.
**hǎa** 13.3 To look for.
**hây** 17.3 To give. (see 17.1)
**hěn** 7.4 To see.
**hɛ̂ɛŋ** 8.4 To be dry.
**hǐn** 18.4 Rock.
**hm̂m** 3.5 A confirmative. (see 3.1)
**hòk** 2.8 Six.
**hɔ̂ŋ** 3.2 Room.
  **hɔ̂ŋ náam** 7.3 Bathroom.
**hɔ̂ŋkoŋ** 15. Hong Kong.
**hǔa** 16.4 Head.
**hǔu** 16.4 Ear.
**kâaw** 3.8 Nine.
**kâaw** 14.6 A step, to step.
**kan** 6.5 The other, each other, mutually.
**kàp, ka** 6.9 With, and.
**kàt** 9.6 To bite.
**kâwʔîi** 19.4 Chair.
**kày** 7.4 Chicken.
**kèŋ** 15. To be skillful or good at something.
**kə̀ət** 9.6 To be born.
**kɛ̂ɛm** 16.4 Cheeks.
**kɛɛŋ** 13.6 Curry.
**kɛ̂ɛw** 13.6 Glass. A glass.
**khâ** 1.3 Polite particle, confirmative. (See 1.1 and 3.1)
**khá** 2.3 Polite particle. (See 1.1)
**khǎa** 16.4 Legs.
**khâaŋ** 4.1 A side.
**khǎaw** 14.4 White.
**khǎay** 11.4 To sell.
**kham** 19.3 Word.
**kháw** 1.9 He, she, they (people only).
**khâwcay** 8.3 To understand.
**khɛ̌ɛn** 13.6 Arm.
**khìa** 17.3 To remove or dislodge something with light stroking movements of the finger or some instrument.
**khian** 13.5 To write.
**khǐaw** 14.4 Green.
**khon** 2.9 Person, people.
**khɔ̌ɔ** 2.3, 20. To ask for.
  **khɔ̌ɔ thôot** Excuse me, I'm sorry.
**khɔ̀ɔpkhun** 3.3 Thanks.
**khɔɔ sɔ̌ɔ** 14.8 The Christian era.
**khráp** 1.3 Polite particle, confirmative (see 1.1 and 3.1)
**khray** 7.5 Who?
**khrua** 13.4 Kitchen.
**khùan** 13.6 To scratch (painfully).
**khun** 4.3 A respectful title, you. (See 4.1 and 6.1)
**khwǎa** 4.2 Right side.
**khwaay** 6.5 Water buffalo.
**kii** 14.6 How many?
**kin** 11.4 To eat.
**klàp** 12.3 To return.
**klây** 11.3 To be near.
**kɔ̂** 14.6 Also, too.
**kɔ̀ɔn** 11.3 Before, first.
**kradàat** 16.3 Paper.
**kûŋ** 7.4 Shrimp.
**kwàa** 6.5 More (than), -er (than).
**lâ** 4.3 A question particle. (See 4.1)
**láan** 19.8 A million.
**lǎan** 11.4 Nephew, niece, grandchild.
**lâaŋ** 8.3 Lower.
  **khâŋ lâaŋ** Downstairs.
**lǎŋ** 4.2 The back.
  **khâŋ lǎŋ** In back of.
**lêek** 12.3 Number. (See 13.1)
  **lêek thîi** 12.3 A number used as a designation. (See 13.1)
**lèk** 18.4 Iron.
**lék** 2.5 To be little.
**lə̌ə** 2.3 A question particle. (See 2.1)
**ləəy** 4.5
  **mây ... ləəy** Not ... at all.
**lɛ́ʔ** 15, 19.3 And.
**lɛ́ɛw** 4.3 And then, subsequently.
**lɛ́ɛw** 8.3 Already. (See 8.1)
**líaw** 6.3 To turn.

**lom** 16.3 Wind, air (in motion or under pressure).

**lòm** 2.4 A muddy place.

**lóm** 2.4 To fall over.

**luŋ** 11.4 Older brother of father or mother, uncle.

**lûuk** 7.5 Child (the relationship term: son or daughter).

**lûuk chaay** 15. Son.

**lûuk sǎaw** 15. Daughter.

**lǔaŋ** 14.4 Yellow.

**luum** 17.3 To forget.

**maa** 8.1 To come.

**mâak** 3.3 Very, a lot.

**máay** 17.3 Wood, a stick.

**máykhìit** Matches.

**mày** 11.3 To be new, anew.

**mây** 1.5 Not.

**mây dây** ... 13.5 Didn't. (See 13.1)

**mây** 3.4 To burn.

**máy** 1.5 A question particle. (See 1.1)

**mǎy** 3.4 Silk.

**máykhìit** (See *máay*)

**mêek** 17.4 Clouds.

**mɛ̂ɛ** 17.4 Mother.

**mɛɛríi** 12.7 Mary.

**mii** 7.4 To have, there is.

**mɔ̌ɔn** 19.4 Pillow.

**mûaŋ** 14.4 Purple.

**múŋ** 19.4 Mosquito net.

**mǔu** 7.4 Pig, pork.

**muu** 16.4 Hands.

**mùun** 16.8 Ten thousand.

**mûut** 18.3 To be dark.

**ná** 7.9 14.3 A question particle. (See 7.1, 14.1, and 19.1)

**naa** 1.4 Rice field.

**nâa** 1.4 Face.

**khâŋ nâa** 4.2 In front of.

**náa** 4.4 Mother's younger brother or sister (aunt, uncle).

**nǎa** 1.4 To be thick.

**naalikaa** 11.8 Watch, clock, o'clock (in the 24 hour system).

**náam** 7.3 Water, liquid, juice, fluid.

**nâatàaŋ** 16.3 Window (the opening and shutters–not the glass).

**naathii** 11.8 Minute.

**nǎaw** 17.4 Cold (weather).

**námŋən** 16.6 Blue.

**nân** 6.2 There, that, the one mentioned

**nán** 2.9 That, the one mentioned (adjective).

**nâŋ** 20. To sit.

**naŋsǔu** 14.3 Book.

**nǎy** 3.3 Where? Which?

**nîi** 3.2 Here, this.

**níi** 6.3 This (adjective).

**nítnɔ̀y** 14.3 A little bit.

**níw** 16.4 Fingers, toes.

**nôon** 3.3 Over there, that.

**nóon** 6.2 That (farther away than *nán*).

**nɔɔn** 7.1 To lie down.

**nɔ́ɔŋ** 11.4 Younger brother or sister, younger sibling.

**nɔ̀y** 14.3 A little. (See 14.1)

**nǔu** 4.2 Mouse. (See 4.1, 6.1, and 8.1)

**núa** 7.4 Meat, beef.

**nùŋ** 2.8 One.

**ŋaan** 9.3 Work, party, ceremony.

**ŋən** 18.4 Silver, money.

**ŋûaŋ nɔɔn** 8.6 To be sleepy.

**pàa** 2.6 Jungle.

**pǎa** 9.6 Father, Papa (used mainly with foreigners).

**pàak** 16.4 Mouth.

**pàt** 17.6 To brush or dust off.

**pàw** 9.6 To blow (with the mouth).

**pay** 6.3 To go.

**pen** 2.3, 10. To be someone or something.

**pə̀ət** 17.6 To open, turn on.

**pɛ̀ɛt** 3.8 Eight.

**phàa** 2.6 To split.

**phâa** 9.6 Cloth.

**phahǒnyoothin** 17.8 Paholyothin.

**phàk kàat** 9.6 Lettuce.

**phamâa** 14.2 Burmese.

**phan** 13.8 A thousand.

**pháruhàt** 19.4

**daaw pháruhàt** Jupiter.

**wan pháruhàt** Thursday.

**phasǎa** 14.3 Language.
**phát** 16.3 To blow (as the wind).
**phátlom** 16.3 Electric fan.
**phôŋ (phûŋ)** 18.6 Just now, just a minute ago.
**phɛ́ʔ** 8.4 A goat.
**phîi** 9.6 Older brother or sister, older sibling.
**phləəncit** 9.2 Ploenchit.
**phǒm (phóm)** 8.2 I (man speaking). (See 8.1)
**phǒm** 3.2 Hair (head only).
**phóp** 11.3 To see, meet, find.
**phɔɔ** 17.4 Enough.
**phɔ̂ɔ** 7.5 Father.
**phɔ̌ɔm** 1.5 To be thin.
**phɔɔ sɔ̌ɔ** 14.8 The Buddhist era.
**phút** 17.4
**daaw phút** Mercury.
**wan phút** Wednesday.
**phûu** 7.3 Person (rarely used alone).
**phûu chaay** Boy, man.
**phûu yǐŋ** Girl, woman.
**phûut** 8.3 To speak.
**phúun** 19.4 Floor.
**pìi** 9.6 A wind instrument, horn.
**pìt** 19.3 To close, turn off.
**plaa** 7.4 Fish.
**plàaw** 11.3 Empty. No. Used to reject a wrong assumption.
**pratuu** 16.3 Door.
**pùu** 9.6 Father's father, grandfather.
**puun** 19.6 Gun.
**ráan** 3.3 Shop, store.
**râatdamrìʔ** 11.2 Rajdamri.
**râatprasǒŋ** 11.3 Rajprasong.
**ray** 2.3 Short form of *ʔaray*.
**rɛɛm** 4.3, 11.2 To spend the night.
**rîak** 14.3 To call.
**rian** 11.3 To study.
**rooŋ rian** 11.3 School.
**rooŋrɛɛm** 4.3 Hotel.
**rɔ́ɔn** 2.5 To be hot.
**rɔ́ɔy** 12.8 A hundred.
**rúu** 13.3 To know (a subject). (See 13.1)
**rúucàk** 6.3 To know a person, place, or thing. To be acquainted with. (See 13.1)
**rɨ́, rɨ̌ɨ** 7.9 Or.
**sǎaladɛɛŋ** 11.2 Saladaeng.
**sǎam** 1.8 Three.
**sâap** 13.3 To know (information). (See 13.1)
**sǎaw** 15. Young woman, unmarried woman.
**sáay** 4.3 Left side.
**sǎay** 14.4 Late morning.
**sabaay** 2.3 To be comfortable, feel nice.
**sân** 3.5 To be short (in length).
**sanǎam** 17.4 Yard, field court.
**sàŋ** 11.4 To order.
**sathǎanthûut** 9.3 Embassy.
**sǎw** 17.4
**daaw sǎw** Saturn.
**wan sǎw** Saturday.
**sawàt** 4.7 Well being, good fortune. A man's name.
**sawàtdii** 1.3 A greeting used for either meeting or parting. Greetings. Hello. Goodbye. Aloha.
**sày** 7.4 To put in or on.
**sɛ̌ɛn** 18.8 A hundred thousand.
**sɛ̀ɛt** 14.4 Orange (the color).
**sí** 18.3 A particle used to request an action. (See 18.1)
**sìi** 2.8 Four.
**sìiyɛ̂ɛk** 6.3 Intersection (four forks).
**sǐi** 14.4 Color.
**sìp** 3.8 Ten.
**sòŋ** 17.3 To send. (See 17.1)
**sɔ̌ɔŋ** 1.8 Two.
**sɔɔy** 12.3 Soi, lane.
**sûam** 7.1 Toilet.
**sùk** 17.4
**daaw sùk** Venus.
**wan sùk** Friday.
**sùkhǎa** 7.1 Toilet (formal).
**sùkhǔmwít** 12.3 Sukhumvit.
**sǔun** 12.3 Zero.
**sǔuŋ** 2.5 To be tall.
**sùa** 19.4 Mat.
**sɨ́ɨ** 7.4 To buy.
**taa** 11.6 Eyes.
**talàat** 4.3 Market.
**tàt** 3.2 To cut.
**tɛ̀ɛ** 15. But.

**thâa** 18.3 If.

**thăam** 18.3 To ask.

**thaaŋ** 4.3 Way, path.

**tháaw** 16.4 Feet.

**tham** 9.3 To do, make.

**tham ŋaan** 9.3 To work.

**thanǒn** 9.3 Street, road.

**tháp** 12.3 To superimpose, lay on top of, run over.

**thâwnán** 15. Only.

**thâwrày** 12.3 How much? How many?

**thay** 14.2 Thai.

**thəəm** 2.6 Term.

**thîaŋ** 14.4 Noon.

**thii** 8.3 A time.

**thîi** 3.3 At.

**thîi** 17.3 A place.

**thîi khìa burìi** 17.3 Ash tray.

**thîi** 12.3 Precedes cardinal numbers to form ordinals, -th.

**thíŋ** 11.6 To throw away.

**thoorasàp** 13.3 Telephone.

**thôot** 2.3 Punishment.

**thɔɔŋ** 18.4 Gold.

**thɔ̂ɔt** 11.4 To fry (in large pieces).

**thǔŋ** 1.6 Sack.

**thuu, plaa thuu** 8.4 A fish resembling a herring or a mackerel.

**thùuk** 16.3 To be correct. (See 16.2)

**thǔŋ** 6.3 To arrive at, reach.

**tîa** 2.5 To be short (in height).

**tiaŋ** 19.4 Bed.

**tii** 1.6 To hit.

**tóʔ** 20. Table.

**tɔ̂ŋ** 18.3 To have to, must.

**tɔ̂ŋkaan** 19.3 To want, need. (See 19.1)

**tɔɔn** 14.4 A section or period.

**tɔɔn yen** 14.4 Evening.

**tɔ̀y** 11.6 To hit with the fist.

**troŋ** 4.3 To be straight.

**tûu** 19.4 Cupboard, closet

**wâa** 14.3 A quotation signal. (See 14.1)

**wăan** 8.4 To be sweet.

**wan** 16.4 Day (either daylight period or 24 hour period).

**wiatnaam** 14.2 Vietnamese.

**wítthayú** 9.3 Radio, wireless.

**woŋwian** 11.2 A traffic circle.

**wua** 6.5 Cattle, cow, bull.

**yàak** 18.3 To want.

**yàaŋ** 18.3 Kind, sort, variety.

**yàaŋray (yaŋray, yaŋŋay, ŋay)** 18.3 In what way? How?

**yaaw** 3.5 To be long.

**yaŋ** 4.7 The English name 'Young'.

**yaŋŋay** (See *yàaŋray*)

**yày** 2.5 To be big.

**yen** 2.5 To be cold (of things), cool (of weather).

**yɛ̂ɛk** 6.3 To fork, separate.

**yîi** 6.8 Two (used only for the twenties).

**yiŋ** 7.3 Female (people only).

**yùu** 3.3 To be some place.

**yɯɯm** 19.6 To borrow, lend.

## SOUTHEAST ASIA PROGRAM PUBLICATIONS

Cornell University

### Language Texts

INDONESIAN

*Beginning Indonesian through Self-Instruction,* John U. Wolff, Dédé Oetomo, Daniel Fietkiewicz. 3rd revised edition 1992. Reprinted 2004. Vol. 1. 115 pp. ISBN 0-87727-529-7. Vol. 2. 434 pp. ISBN 0-87727-530-0. Vol. 3. 473 pp. ISBN 0-87727-531-9.

(See below for information on ordering audiotapes for these books.)

*Indonesian Readings,* John U. Wolff. 1978. 4th printing 1992. 480 pp. ISBN 0-87727-517-3

*Indonesian Conversations,* John U. Wolff. 1978. 3rd printing 1991. 297 pp. ISBN 0-87727-516-5

(See below for information on ordering audiotapes for this book.)

*Formal Indonesian,* John U. Wolff. 2nd revised edition 1986. 446 pp. ISBN 0-87727-515-7

TAGALOG

*Pilipino through Self-Instruction,* John U. Wolff, Maria Theresa C. Centeno, Der-Hwa V. Rau. 1991. Vol. 1. 342 pp. ISBN 0-87727—525-4. Vol. 2. 378 pp. ISBN 0-87727-526-2. Vol 3. 431 pp. ISBN 0-87727-527-0. Vol. 4. 306 pp. ISBN 0-87727-528-9.

THAI

*A. U. A. Language Center Thai Course,* J. Marvin Brown. Originally published by the American University Alumni Association Language Center, 1974. Reissued by Cornell Southeast Asia Program 1991, 1995, 1998, 2000, and 2004. Book 1. 267 pp. ISBN 0-87727-506-8. Book 2. 288 pp. ISBN 0-87727-507-6. Book 3. 247 pp. ISBN 0-87727-508-4.

(See below for information on ordering audiotapes for these books.)

*A. U. A. Language Center Thai Course, Reading and Writing Text (mostly reading),* 1979. Reissued 1997. 164 pp. ISBN 0-87727-511-4.

*A. U. A. Language Center Thai Course, Reading and Writing Workbook (mostly writing),* 1979. Reissued 1997. 99 pp. ISBN 0-87727-512-2.

KHMER

*Cambodian System of Writing and Beginning Reader,* Franklin E. Huffman. Originally published by Yale University Press, 1970. Reissued by Cornell Southeast Asia Program, 4th printing 2002. 365 pp. ISBN 0-300-01314-0.

*Modern Spoken Cambodian,* Franklin E. Huffman, assist. Charan Promchan, Chhom-Rak Thong Lambert. Originally published by Yale University Press, 1970. Reissued by Cornell Southeast Asia Program, 3rd printing 1991. 451 pp. ISBN 0-300-01316-7.

(See below for information on ordering audiotapes for this book.)

*Intermediate Cambodian Reader,* ed. Franklin E. Huffman, assist. Im Proum. Originally published by Yale University Press, 1972. Reissued by Cornell Southeast Asia Program, 1988. 499 pp. ISBN 0-300-01552-6.

(See below for information on ordering audiotapes for this book.)

*Cambodian Literary Reader and Glossary,* Franklin E. Huffman, Im Proum. Originally published by Yale University Press, 1977. Reissued by Cornell Southeast Asia Program, 1988. 494 pp. ISBN 0-300-02069-4.

HMONG

*White Hmong-English Dictionary,* Ernest E. Heimbach. 1969. 8th printing, 2002. 523 pp. ISBN 0-87727-075-9.

VIETNAMESE

*Intermediate Spoken Vietnamese,* Franklin E. Huffman, Tran Trong Hai. 1980. 3rd printing 1994. ISBN 0-87727-500-9.

***

**To order, please contact:**

Cornell University
Southeast Asia Program Publications
95 Brown Road
Box 1004
Ithaca NY 14850

Online: http://www.einaudi.cornell.edu/southeastasia/publications/
**Tel: 1-877-865-2432 (Toll free – U.S.)**
Fax: (607) 255-7534

E-mail: SEAP-Pubs@cornell.edu
Orders must be prepaid by check or credit card (VISA, MasterCard, Discover).

Audiotapes to accompany SEAP language texts can be ordered separately from:

The Language Resource Center
Tape Sales
Room G11, Noyes Lodge
Cornell University
Ithaca, NY 14853-4701
Tel: (607) 255-8793
Fax: (607) 255-6882
http://lrc.cornell.edu

Milton Keynes UK
Ingram Content Group UK Ltd.
UKHW030131020824
446387UK00009B/391

9 780877 275060